Lady Pr

D1489770

Can a submissive
wife and mother
be an ordained
minister?

by Rev. Helen Elliott Correll

RHYMEO
INK

I S B N 0-9636177-8-8

*I dedicate this book
to my blessed Lord and Saviour
Jesus Christ*

*and my beloved husband
of 66 years
Sidney North Correll.
(1907-1991)*

This book was written by my mother, Helen Correll.
Before she died in 2004, at age 96, she asked that
we "give a copy to anyone it would be a blessing to".
Contact me if you need more copies.
Rebecca Correll Cauble
704/376-6817 or beckycc@yahoo.com

Acknowledgements

Rev. Helen Correll gratefully acknowledges the following friends who helped in the editing and preparing of this manuscript.

Dr. Dan Davidson
Angie Cundiff
Diane Gills
Julie Booth
Peggy Obenchain
Debbie Janney
Orion Parrott
Jackie Green
Larry Janney
Alan Frost
Michael Correll
Karen Correll
Roanoke City Public Library

Contents

Chapter 1

Introduction

May I answer the question given on the title of this book? **Can** a submissive wife and mother be an ordained minister? The answer is yes; I know because I am one!

Let me say at the beginning, I do not presume to speak for all women. Also, I am not a professional writer. Nor is this book designed like any other. But I would like to tell you the story of my life. At this writing, I am 86 years old. Please don't be nervous, for though I believe I am in my right mind, I am not depending on my memory to tell the story. The facts in this book are authenticated by diaries, letters, publications and many other sources.

Without a doubt, I know where I have been and I know where I am going, though I do not know the amount of time in between here and there.

Before I tell my life story I will answer the question of many organizations and individuals: Should a woman preach the Gospel? I have never been afraid of God's Word on the subject.

Then I want to tell of my childhood. I want to include the story of my youth, my call to preach, and my romance (which you are going to love) all the way to wedding bells and my life as a wife.

I will talk about my life as a mother of six children of my own and one adopted son, and as a grandmother of twenty-two grandchildren, thirty great grandchildren, and one great, great grandson.

I will tell you about my life as an ordained minister. This will include over 66 years of ministry with my beloved husband.

Then there is the chapter about the homegoing of my companion, Sidney North Correll, entitled "The Old Warrior Goes Home."

This journey through my life will take us up high mountain peaks and down into many valleys. I hope you will laugh with me, and I believe you will cry a bit, too. There will be many stories I will tell which I think will interest every member of the family. It is not just routine information.

Believe it or not, I have a word processor and I have sat for hours at a time, getting every page of the story in script. Then I have had wonderful help in getting it in manuscript form and to the printer.

We have promised this book for a long time, and it seems like a dream that has finally come true.

1

After the close, I will share with you a legacy to my grandchildren and great grandchildren, which means a lot to me.

God bless you! Happy reading!

Chapter 2

What About The Scriptures?

I have never been afraid to stand on the Word of God! Let us start with the scripture that is usually used. I Corinthians 14:33-34: *God is not the author of confusion, but of peace as in all the churches of the saints.* (Verse 34) *Let your women keep silent in the church.* For it is *not permitted unto them to speak* (it didn't say preach), *and if they will learn anything let them ask their husbands at home, for it is a shame for a woman to speak* (talk) *in church.*

I have been utterly amazed at how lovely, intelligent men can make a case out of this about women preaching.

Let us just take a look at where this took place. It was to the Corinthians in that Grecian city where the men were educated and the women were left in ignorance. Even in their place of worship, the men sat on one side and the women on the other. I have seen this still a custom in many places today. They did it in Romania and they do it in India to an extent. These were the first Gentiles to receive the preaching of the Words of God. I can also recall a number of places I have been and preached, where the people, as they came in, could not get it into their heads that they had **just as much right** to talk out loud as the person up front. I know what the confusion is. The women were **talking** while Paul was **preaching**; if they didn't understand what he was saying, they would yell across the aisle to their husbands, "What does he mean?" Paul was very upset, and had taken just about as much as he could take, when he said, "Will someone please tell those women to be quiet? We are in church. If they want to learn anything, let them ask their husbands at home."

Isn't that what it says? Paul was not talking about preaching. I challenge anyone to find a place where a woman is forbidden to preach! In I Timothy 2:12, it does say, *"But I suffer not a woman to teach nor to usurp authority over the man, but be in silence."*

Let me say right here, **I am not a feminist** or a **woman's libber**. I do not think that women are the same as men. I believe men **are the head of the house**, and I am glad of it. God made women to have babies. Try as they might, the men will never do that. I also believe that if every man had followed the call of God as he should have, they might not have needed women to preach. But the message must get out! So let's telephone, telegraph, or tell a woman - any way to spread the Word!

3

(Just a little jest!) Paul was also saying in this chapter that women had not been good examples of Christian women and had gone overboard, doing some things that were not becoming to women professing godliness.

Ladies, I think there is a middle of the road in our personal appearance that will bring glory to God.

Paul said, **teach**, not preach! What if there were no teachers in our Sunday Schools or ladies Bible classes? If the men had to do it all, what would become of the churches?

Let us go back now to our Lord. What was His attitude? Someone said to me one time, "God wants only men to preach and I can prove it!" I said, "Okay, how can you prove it?" His reply was, "Well, the Lord chose twelve disciples and they were all men." That doesn't prove a thing, and I will give you two examples to the contrary.

In John 20:17, it was resurrection day. Jesus appeared unto a **woman,** Mary Magdeline, **first**. He said to her, "*Go, tell my disciples that I am risen from the dead.*" Where were the men? Jesus had told them again and again that He would rise. No doubt they were sleeping. But there it is; the first resurrection message was given by **a woman**. "Go tell, go tell." Isn't that what preaching is all about?

Let's look at John 4, and the woman at the well. You know this beautiful story, about how Christ led her step by step in spiritual understanding until He made the divine revelation, "*I that speak to thee am He!*" I am the Savior you have been looking for. In that moment she believed. She was filled with the urge to go and tell others this good news. She even forgot her water pot in the excitement and ran to the city to spread the Word. "*Come see a Man that has told me everything I ever did. Is not this the Christ?*" What was the result? Because of the woman going and telling, the whole city came out to see Jesus. John 4:39 says, "*Many of the Samaritans of that city believed on Him for the saying of the woman.*"

What a wonderful revelation the Lord made to the woman at the well when He told her about the Living Water that could really quench her thirst. She wanted it so very much. Have you ever been thirsty? I mean really thirsty? Maybe you came to an old pump well that could bring up real fresh cold water. Did you look to see if it was served in a **porcelain cup**, and did you refuse it if there was only a **tin dipper**? Why do we put so much importance on the vessel and not the water? Souls are being lost for lack of the Water of Life. Will we let a lost world die because the bearer of Good News does not have certain credentials?

I remember someone else who said they were sure the Lord didn't want women to minister, because no woman preached on the day of Pentecost. Isn't that just as ridiculous? There were one hundred and twenty in the upper room that day, and the only one who preached was Peter. The women, including Mary, the Mother of Jesus, were in the prayer room when the Holy Spirit fell. Let me remind you what happened after Pentecost. In fact, it was in Peter's sermon he preached in Acts 2:17-18: *"And it shall come to pass in the last days that I will pour out My Spirit upon all flesh. Your sons and **your daughters** shall prophesy. On My servants and **handmaidens** I will pour out My Spirit and they shall **prophesy**."* What is prophecy? I Corinthians 14:3: *"But he that prophesieth speaketh unto men to edification, exhortation and comfort."* Can you think of a better definition for preaching? Oh, by the way, I heard a new answer I had never heard before. A pastor who was very much against women preachers had a call-in radio program. A caller said, "Why can't women preach and teach?" The preacher answered, "That ministry is for men only and I can give you a very good reason: God made roosters to crow and hens to lay eggs!" Now that is logic, wouldn't you say?

Paul believed in women preachers. I Corinthians 11:5: He told them how they should be attired when they preached or prayed. She had to cover her head. So, someone says, "Well, do you cover your head?" No, but does your pastor wear long robes when he preaches? He might, but most of them don't. Why? Those were the customs of the times.

In Romans 16:1, Paul said, *"I commend unto you Phebe our sister, which is a servant in the church, assist her in any way she has need of you."* Phebe is said to have been **pastor** of the church at Cenchrea. That doesn't sound like keeping your women silent in the church, does it? Verse three mentions both **Priscilla** and Aquilla as both being ministers of the gospel. He goes on to say *"likewise greet the church that is in thy house."*

Romans 16:7 lists a woman called Junia among the apostles.

Women are mentioned again in Philippians 4:3, where it says, *"And I intreat thee also true yoke fellow, help **those women** which **labored with me** in the gospel."*

One more thing and I believe that should be enough. If Paul had been against women, he surely would have been in trouble when they got the Macedonian call. Do you remember when Paul and Silas started on one of their missionary journeys? They were in the region of Galatia and wanted to go on to Asia. But the Holy Spirit said, "No," they were not to go that way. A vision was sent with a message: Go west, young man, go west. Well, it wasn't exactly in those words. But they saw the vision and a man pleading with them to **come over into Macedonia and help us**. Being obedient to the call, they started out with, I am sure, great expectations. When they arrived, the only place they were having a service was by the river. Lo and behold, it was a **women's prayer group**. They could have said, "All that vision and special instructions and we end up in a women's prayer group." But Paul and Silas sat down and spoke to the women. Among them was a very influential woman named Lydia. She was very touched by the message and opened her heart to the Lord. The very first Macedonian convert was a woman. She and her whole household were baptized. They had a very precious time. Lydia was so moved that she offered her house for these preachers to come and stay. Paul and Silas felt the Lord was in it, so they went to her home.

Can I share something with you that touched my heart in this story? I am not saying Lydia was a preacher, but she wasn't the type Paul would tell to hush up in the church. I am sure God sent them there to receive **a blessing** and **strength** to help them face some things they were about to endure. If you read the rest of the chapter, you will see that as they were preaching, it turned out to be trouble, not the citywide revival they expected. There was a raging mob. Paul and Silas were seized, their clothes were ripped off, they were beaten and bruised and they landed in jail. I am sure they said, "Lord, why didn't You want us to go to Asia? It surely couldn't have been as bad as this." But God had not forsaken them, and you remember how they sang and praised God until an earthquake came and liberated them. The result was **revival at the jail house**. But who knows the blessing and preparedness they had because a group of **women were praying for them**? Thank God for all the praying women down through the years. Every pastor should have a group. Even two or three women could move God in prayer.

We could go on to tell of Phillip who had **four daughters** and they were **all preachers**. This is in Acts 21.

There are other scriptures, but let me close with this. Galatians 3:28 says, *"There is neither Jew nor Greek, there is neither bond nor free, there is neither **male nor female**, for you are all one in Christ."*

6

If God had not wanted women - or me - to preach , then why did I so powerfully feel His hand on my life at age 13, and why has He kept His anointing on me for 74 years? **I am still preaching.**

> "Out where the fields are whiter,
> Out where the reapers are few,
> I am willing to go
> Where He wants me to go,
> To be what He wants me to be.
> Yes, I'm willing to go
> Where He wants me to go,
> To do what He wants me to do."

Reverend Helen Correll was a member of the first graduating class of the International Institute of Foursquare Evangelism.

Chapter 3

From Childhood To Bible School

Let us go back, as the psychologists say, to what happened in my childhood.

My father, Edwin Austin Elliott was married to my mother, Maybelle Dennison. A first son was born named Leverette Vere Elliott. Five years later another son was born, but he died ten days later. The whole family was saddened by this event, but my father was devastated. He wanted a little girl. So, being a very devout man, he prayed, "Lord, give me a baby girl and I will give her to you for a missionary to India." (I don't know why he chose India.) God answered that prayer by sending him a little girl seven years younger than their oldest son. They named her Helen Elliott. I never had a middle name, for he wanted Elliott to be my middle name. This little girl was almost a Christmas present, as I was born December 21, 1907. My father saw so many promises for the future.

Alas, a dark cloud was to cover that home. As happens in so many homes, when I was three years old, another man came into my mother's life and swept her out of our lives. I was only to see her a few times in the future, as our paths were far apart. When I was six years old, my brother and I were awarded by the court to my father and grandmother Elliott. I loved my father and he adored me. My grandmother (who was 60 years old when I was given into her care) loved me very much too, for she said I was the only daughter she ever had. (She had three sons.)

As the years have gone by, I can appreciate what it must have meant for her to take on that responsibility at her age. In spite of the generation gap, I remember mostly happy times as a child. But there were a few tears shed when I saw other little girls with black patent leather slippers and half socks while I was wearing long stockings and high-buttoned shoes. "Why couldn't I have a young mother and do lots of things my friends do?" However, a great heritage was mine because I grew up in a godly home where Christ was honored. I shall always be grateful for the Bible background my father gave me. He taught me the books of the Bible, so that I could find where the scripture references were without using the index in the front of the Bible. Later, my father sent off for a chord stick with many colors and designs on it, to teach me

9

how to play chords on the old pump organ or piano. In this way, I was able to play in church at a very early age.

I was born in Silverton, Colorado. It was known as the highest incorporated city in the United States. My father worked at the mines, assaying the different ores that were mined. I was too young to remember anything there, but when I was around nine or ten we were living in a mining town named Vanadium. There, Vanadium was the ore. I remember them saying that once Madam Currie visited there, to check the ore for some project she was working on.

If you had time to listen, I could tell you a number of things which occurred there that are etched in my memory. There was the winter I rode my sled down a very long hill to the town below. When I got to the street that ran in front of **the only store**, a team of horses pulling a large wagon came roaring past. I was never sure whether I went under them or in front of them, but I had the scare of my young life. I must get on with my story.

My father, a very religious man as I have indicated, heard that God's special blessing and power was moving in churches in California. He felt this was what he had been looking for, so we moved to Southern California.

We found some very alive churches that seemed to have more than we had been used to. Oh, the fervor and inspiration as they worshiped the Lord. Even as a young girl, I loved it.

My father was also a carpenter, and we moved several times because of his work. We would always take time to find a church with revival fire.

One place we were was in San Pedro, California. There are several things I remember about this place. For instance, I got the mumps there - on both sides.

Also, I remember my grandmother and I going out to the long breakwater there. We would take a crowbar and pry abalone shells off of the huge rocks that made up the breakwater. One day, we were near the end of it where the lighthouse stood. I had wondered what the lighthouse was like inside. On foggy days, we could hear the old fog horn sound out its booming blast. Then on this special day, we looked up to see the lighthouse keeper coming toward us. He said he had watched us as we were getting our shells. My grandmother was also taking pictures. He said, "I know with the war going on (World War I) I am not supposed to let anyone into the lighthouse, but I have made a beautiful piece of furniture in my spare time, and I wondered if you could take a picture of it for me?" Of course, my grandmother did.

The man showed us the inside of the lighthouse, and how the light worked, and the fog horn, and everything. He explained how important it was to keep the reflector behind the light spotlessly clean, so that nothing would hinder the light going out for miles to warn ships of their location and of rocks, etc. I was fascinated. Little did I know then that I would someday be a lighthouse keeper of the Light of the world, even Jesus. I remembered one of the verses I had learned was to "*let your light so shine before men that they may see your good works and glorify your Father which is in heaven.*"

We moved to Redman Street in Highland Park, near Los Angeles, when I was thirteen. I recall that, because I had a touch of the flu and was in bed on my birthday. (Influenza took many lives during that epidemic.) While I was ill, I memorized the 91st Psalm. It has been very close to me ever since.

I remember many things that happened when we lived there, but what I want to relate is something that had a very important bearing on my future life. This was some time after my illness.

My father and I had been attending some very special meetings. My heart was so touched by the Lord. One day, while at home, I was washing the windows of our house. Suddenly a scripture thundered almost like an audible voice, *"Freely ye have received, freely give."* Matthew 10:8. I was so moved by it that I got down from the ladder I was on and went into the shed where I kept the rabbits that I raised and sold.

My heart was so full with the challenge of this scripture I had just heard, that I fell to my knees and started to pray for a lost and dying world. I was praising the Lord because He loved them enough to die for them. I don't know how long I was on my knees in prayer and thanksgiving, but heaven came down and overflowed my heart and God filled me with His blessed Holy Spirit. I knew in that hour that God had called me to preach!

This experience was so real. It has been like an anchor which has kept me secure when the waves of opposition and controversy have tried to swamp my boat. That was over seventy years ago. I have had the same burden that Paul had when he said, "Woe is me if I preach not the gospel." Through the years, I have met with the declaration that women have no right to preach, but must keep silent in the churches. I cannot remember **once** when I ever doubted my call to preach.

11

Teenage Testing

It is true that the next couple of years I became discouraged and, being a teenager, the devil tried very hard to sidetrack me through a girlfriend who was a little older than I was, who came to visit us. She did not have the same goals or desire for church that I had, so she was trying to wean me away from church. She did succeed in taking me to a movie (which my family never attended), and to other worldly amusements. I remember one night when she had gotten a couple of boys to accompany us. Her first goal was to get me to smoke a cigarette. I took it, but never smoked it. Then one of the boys attempted to show me how to kiss. This brought me back to my senses and my guardian angel opened my eyes to what was happening. Needless to say, this girlfriend soon left town.

As I look back over those days, I am amazed. Why was I spared the heartache and years in the world, as so many people go through, before going on with my dedication to the Lord? It had to be God Who protected me for His purpose.

The Beautiful Angeles Temple

It was shortly after my 15th birthday that my father began to talk with real enthusiasm about a unique building that was being built in Los Angeles, and was to have its grand opening on January 1, 1923. It was the beautiful Angeles Temple. It was unique because it had a great dome on the top, the largest of its kind. Angels were frescoed on the walls under the dome, and reached completely around the whole auditorium.

The day the Angeles Temple opened, my father and I were seated in the third balcony. There were 5,300 people that filled the auditorium, and there were hundreds on the outside that could not get in.

A lady preacher, Aimee Semple McPherson, was not only the speaker of the day, she was the pastor. As she came down the long ramp leading to the platform, she was dressed in a simple white uniform with a long blue cape. In her arms was a bouquet of red roses. She had a glorious smile on her face as she praised the Lord. A singer stood in front of that congregation and sang, "Open the Gates of the Temple," and I thought my heart would burst. It was like hearing music from heaven. What joy and enthusiasm when every one sang together!

When Mrs. McPherson opened her Bible and began to speak, she talked of Christ in such a way that you felt He was right there. When the invitation was given at the close of the message, she simply held out her hands and said, "Come to Jesus." The aisles filled with those coming to give their hearts to the Lord. The altar filled, and tears were flowing as men, women and children came.

Update

I was in that same Angeles Temple on January 2, 1993, for its 70th anniversary. The work still goes on.

Enter Bible School

The opening of the Angeles Temple began a new era in my life. My father and I returned again and again. I not only rededicated my life to the Lord, I sang in the choir and was eager to have a share in any way I could.

What a day, when the evangelist announced that they were going to open a Bible Institute the next month! I was overwhelmed with a desire to attend. When I approached my father about it, he was afraid that at my age (15), I would never get permission to enter, but he was overjoyed that I had the desire to do so. Didn't we believe that all things are possible with God? My dad said that the Lord would have to work on both the school board of my high school in Pasadena, and the new Bible Institute to see that they would take someone this young. It wasn't easy, but when opening day came in February of 1923, I was there with permission from my high school and with the invitation to join LIFE Bible Institute. What a glorious feeling!

There wasn't a school building at that time, but classes were held in a large room in the new church which they called the 500 room (because it held 500 people). How I loved every moment of it.

We had the most terrific teachers. Among them was Dr. Frank C. Thompson, author of the Thompson Chain Reference Bible. Then there was Dr. A.E. Mitchell. He was not only an artist, but a deep Bible scholar. He taught a series on the cross that was classic. Then there was Dr. Farr, also a very famous Bible scholar, and Dr. William Black. One of our favorites was Mrs. McPherson. She taught Evangelism, among other things. Many of the lessons we learned from her have stayed with us a lifetime.

We had a well-rounded curriculum, both in study and in practical activities. If you wonder what they taught in the LIFE Bible College, here it is.

The Curriculum

These are the courses that were offered: Bible Atlas, Bible Introduction, Bible Analysis, the Pentateuch, Prophetical books, Doctrinal Treatise I and II, The Cross, Art, H istorical Books, Poetical Books, Gospel of John, Revelation, The Pauline and General Epistles, Foursquare Treatise, the Synoptic Gospels, Acts of the Apostles, Homiletics, Church History, The Life Of Christ: Exposition and Interpretation of Great Bible Themes, Dispensational Truths, Topology, Sunday School Organization, Field Work, Evangelism, Physical Education, Music, Missions, Expression, Practical English, and Class Criticism. Some of the above were elective, but strongly recommended.

This was quite a bit to store into a teenager's mind, but I loved every minute of it. Much of it may be forgotten, but the concern for a lost and dying world is ever with you.

What a privilege it was to have missionaries and special men and women of God to visit the school and share their burdens. We also held street meetings, shop meetings, jail services and Senior Citizen services. We not only learned scriptures, we put them into practice, along with the message of faith.

I don't think I have told this story before, but one day a group of students was in my Model T Ford truck and we were going to one of the big factories for a noon meeting. We had to be there right at lunch time. All of a sudden, as we were racing to get there, we heard a **loud bang**. We had a flat tire. Yes, you really heard a blowout in those days. We got out, dismayed. There was no spare. What would we do? We dared not be late. When all else fails, **pray**! We laid hands on the car, and I mean we prayed the prayer of faith. You can believe it or not, but after we prayed, that tire was ready to roll. We climbed in and got to our meeting on time. All things are possible with God!

First Graduating Class

When the school first opened, it was a two-year course. So two years of devoted study, and constant and enthusiastic application to Christian work were brought to a successful conclusion on the evening of

April 17, 1925. There were now hundreds of students in full uniform who marched into the great Temple Auditorium. Thousands came to the Temple to do honor to **the first graduating class**, called "The Pioneers". There were **16 of us** that had completed that first class. It was a beautiful service. At the close of the ceremonies, Sister McPherson gave to each graduate a Morocco Bagster Bible.

At the close of the service, hundreds of young people pressed to the front and dedicated their lives to the service of Christ. In these last 70 years I suppose thousands have graduated, but as of **1994, I am the last living member of that first class of 16 graduates** of LIFE Bible College. Because it had been a new school, many came in late for the very first class. Several months later, there was another, much larger class that graduated, which was really a continuation of the first class. But for the record, as I write this in 1994, I am the last living member of that first class of 16 graduates in 1925.

Helen and the goats

Grandmother

Helen, Father and brother Vere

Chapter 4

The Young Man Sidney Correll

We leave the story of my graduation to tell you of the man that I will marry.

Sidney North Correll was born in Fullerton, Nebraska, on May 12, 1907. His father was Ralph Herbert Correll, and his mother was Stella Alice Gentry Correll.

The Correll family moved from Nebraska, and homesteaded in Eastern Colorado, near the little town of Proctor. This meant starting from scratch. They built a house very much like a log cabin.

Sidney remembered his mother warning him as a little boy to watch out for snakes. Incidentally, this part of Colorado was noted for rattlesnake dens. The Corrells had many battles with snakes. Once, as they were about to eat, they looked up to see a snake hanging from the ceiling over their table.

But they weathered all the hardships, as did the other pioneers of that country. They developed a farm, and had several good horses. One of them was called "Frosty" because the frost had frozen one of his ears off. Sidney often rode him to school. I have heard my husband tell the kids, "I was a **real cowboy**, not the drugstore variety."

Sidney was surrounded by many uncles and aunts from both sides of the family. When he was growing up, the recreation of the week was the old barn dance. Sidney had a good life, but **no Bible** and **no church** background.

As Sidney grew older, his father had one thing in mind, and that was to make money. Dad Correll had become involved in real estate, but that is a different story. Suffice it to say, the crash came. The bottom dropped out of everything. Ralph Correll's partner went to the barn and hung himself. But Sidney's father, with his optimistic outlook, said, "We will go to California and make a million dollars."

California Bound

The Correll family moved to California in the 1920's. Jobs were not easy to come by there, either. However, Ralph was never one to just sit down and give up, so while looking for work, he observed the great need for cleaning the weeds off of the city's empty lots, the owners of which could not be contacted. To clean these lots off with only hand

17

tools was an endless job, so he became very inventive. He put together steel rails in a triangle three feet on each side. The blades were very sharp on the bottom. Then this was hooked by chain to a harness, and the whole device was pulled by a mule. It cleared the weeds from the lot like magic. Instead of cleaning only one lot a day, he could do many, and the money begin to come in. The Correll family lived in a fine house in Huntington Beach.

Sidney went to high school there and became very popular. He was held in such high regard by the teachers and officials that, through their congressman, Sidney was offered a scholarship to Annapolis. He felt very honored.

About that time, one of Sidney's many uncles came to California. He came to visit Sidney's home and he said to Sidney's father and mother, "You can't guess what I did this week. I went to hear a **woman preacher**! Her name was Aimee Semple McPherson, and you should have heard her. She changed my life. I even threw away my old plug of tobacco I was always chewing. Why don't you go with me next Sunday?" The Corrells had never heard of such a thing. **A woman preacher?** They agreed to go. The next Sunday, Mom and Dad asked Sidney if he would like to go, and he decided to join them. What a new experience!

At the close of the message came the appealing invitation to come to Jesus. Though Sidney had never heard such an invitation before, his hand was the first to go up, and he was the first one to head for the altar to receive Christ into his heart. His face was tearstained as he met his mother and father afterward. His first words were, "Mom and Dad, why didn't you come to Jesus tonight too?" His mother replied, "Son, we were right beside you. Dad was on one side, and I was on the other. You were so involved, you didn't even see us." It was a happy threesome that went back home that night.

A New Life . . . A New Beginning

Many times did I hear dear Sidney say how much he loved Christ from that very night. When Dad Correll was cleaning lots, Sidney would drive one of the teams. When they took the animals back, they drove wagons. Sidney was so in love with Jesus that he would move over in the wagon seat and say, "Jesus, sit beside me and hold my hand." Then as they drove home, he would talk to the Lord.

When the season of lot cleaning was over, the very first thing that Sidney wanted to do with his new found faith was to get a Bible. He returned to the Angeles Temple and bought his very first Bible, a Thompson Chain Reference Bible. How he cherished it! It was all so new and wonderful. He wanted to give his life in service to the Lord.

Sidney heard about LIFE Bible Institute at Angeles Temple, and a consuming desire burned in his heart to enter this school in September. His teachers tried to persuade him that he would be making a mistake. They kept asking him, "What about Annapolis?" He questioned himself about other **plans** and **goals** he had made, such as to go to **Stanford University**, and to **someday become governor of the state of California**. Also, he wasn't especially good at sports, but he loved them, and the LIFE Bible Institute did not offer a sports program. But somehow, all of these things faded away with his overwhelming urge to study the Word of God.

Sidney enrolled in Bible College. Everything was so fresh and amazing. Early in that first school year, they had a visiting speaker from Addis Abba, Africa. He was a tall black man who wore flowing robes. He spoke with fire, concern, compassion, urgency and challenge! He poured out his heart for the need of his country. "Come over to our country and help us!" It was truly a Macedonian cry. Sidney, with tears streaming down his face, made a commitment to the Lord that never left him in his long life, a burden that was to make him the **missionary statesman** that he would become.

Love

I had already been attending the LIFE Bible Institute for a year when Sidney came. There were so many students that had enrolled that term, that I was not especially aware of him until the day that all of the new students were giving their testimonies.

When this tall, handsome, dark-eyed, enthusiastic young man walked across the platform and spoke with a burning heart of what God meant to him, I was smitten right there on the spot. My heart just screamed, "That's the man for you!" Perhaps a week or so later, I was sitting at the piano playing for devotions. I noticed him look my way, and I smiled. At that moment, **he discovered me**. He thought he had seen me first, but I knew he had to be God's gift to me. We would talk at school about things of general interest. Then he said, "I don't live very far from here, and my folks want very much to meet you. Would you

19

come for dinner?" His father loved making Irish stew, which was a big hit with me, so we were off to a good start.

I was still living in Pasadena with my father and grandmother. It was fifteen miles or more away, so our dates consisted of him driving me home after church in his Model T Ford. I found him to be one of the **most unusual men** I had ever met.

He was so vibrant, so refreshing, such a man of goals. He talked of his life in Colorado, his dreams for the future, the kind of home he wanted, and his dream girl. He wanted a happy home, and a love that was **special**. He said he had seen lots of quarreling in his family, between the aunts and uncles. None of them had grown up in Christian homes. He talked of seeing young folks dating and the things they did. **He promised himself he would have a home where there was love and peace**. The amazing thing was, he had all of these **goals before he ever met Christ**.

Then he said something that blew my mind. He said **one of his goals was to never kiss a girl until he found the one he would marry**. Wow! Even in my day, that was unusual. My father and grandmother had been very strict. My grandmother would say to me, "When you go out with a young man, remember, no hands below the neck!" But Sidney had said he was not even going to **kiss** a girl! Even though I was young, I knew this man was different.

When we went out, we talked of many things. He was so much fun to be with. But at the end of our dates, when he took me home, he would walk me to the door, and after few minutes he would take off his hat, (they wore hats in those days) bow very deeply, say how nice it was to be together, and then he would leave for his car, almost falling over his feet on the way. With a wave of his hand, he was gone. My heart was full to bursting. I would say to myself, **"What a man!"**

San Diego In The Moonlight

In January of 1925, my father and a friend of his were going to San Diego. He had already asked my grandmother to go along, and he decided to also invite Sidney and myself. We all went.

It was a wonderful day. We went over the border of Mexico and had our pictures taken. In one photo, Sidney stood on the Mexico side of the border and I stood on the U.S. side. We held hands while grandmother took the picture. We laughed, and acted silly throughout the day. We had an enjoyable picnic lunch. To say the least, we had a good time.

By the time we were ready to head home, it was almost dark. We were on the highway headed back toward Los Angeles, and in those days the road ran along the shore line, close to the beach. You could hear the giant waves of the Pacific Ocean dashing up onto the shore. The light of a full moon glistened and sent beams of light across the waters. Talk about romantic! All that was lacking was for a cassette player to be softly playing <u>Moon River</u>. My father and his friend were in the front seat involved in conversation. I was in the middle of the back seat. Sidney was on one side of me, and Grammie was on the other side. We were just drinking in the beauty along the coast as daddy drove.

Conversation had ceased and **I think** Grammie was asleep. Sidney's arm was over the back of the seat. I realized my head had sunk back and I was resting on Sidney's shoulder. It felt so right and comforting. Then an amazing thing happened. Sidney reached down and kissed me on the lips. Wow, and hallelujah! Not a word was spoken, but my mind was racing. What could this mean? Am I engaged? Was that a proposal? Does that mean he knows for sure that I am his dream girl? He held me tight all the way back. He said many times after that how astounded he was to find that God had created a man's shoulder for a woman's head.

Because it was late when we arrived at our home in Pasadena, my father suggested that Sidney stay overnight instead of driving back to Los Angeles. I don't think I slept a wink that night. Those same thoughts were still going through my head. I was still awake the next morning. Before anyone else woke up, I had an inspiration. Putting on my robe, I peeked in and saw Sidney was asleep. I tiptoed in, kissed him on the cheek, and made my exit. Sidney woke up just as my robe was going out the door. In this present day that doesn't sound very exciting, but so much was tied up in those quiet actions.

I drove my car and he drove his back to school the next day, but during recess, we met to talk. Sidney said, "Can we take a little walk before it's time to go in?" We did, and he said, "When I kissed you last night, did you know what that meant?" I replied, "You were asking me to marry you?" He said, "That's right." Then I said, "And when I kissed you this morning, I was saying yes."

Lord, We Want You To Be First

Later, as we talked about the future and about our plans for marriage, I opened my heart to him and said that even though I never knew anyone I would rather marry than him, I would feel better if we could really talk to the Lord about it. We each had made our consecrations to the Lord. We wanted to be sure it was His will for us to be married. We had a beautiful time of prayer, and we promised the Lord that if He saw fit for us to be married, **Christ would always be first in our lives**.

I believe I can say we kept that promise, and always reminded people that that was the secret of the most exciting and wonderful life we lived together.

Fullerton Meetings Begin

Early that spring, the Bible graduates chose new areas in which to set up the tents for ministering. Five of my classmates and I went to Fullerton, California. Our evangelistic team consisted of one couple and three singles. The interest that was stirred up in Fullerton was quite remarkable. The crowds came. We had children's meetings, and they were a real success. This interested the adults, and we had a very rewarding time. Many people gave their hearts to the Lord, and felt that they had found a reason for living.

I did not see very much of Sidney those days. The school officials thought it would not **look good** for Sidney to be there with me, as people might be critical, knowing we were so very much in love. I had moved from Pasadena to Fullerton because it was too far to go back and forth. After the Sunday night services, I would drive to Los Angeles to Sidney's folks' home. Sidney and I would have Monday to talk and plan.

The tent was only supposed to be in Fullerton for several months, but when we talked of bringing the meetings to a close, the people of Fullerton wouldn't hear of it. They said, "You can't leave. What will our children do? Or our young folk? Some of us have just begun to live. We want you all to stay and start a church."

What could we do? The couple in our group said "We have already made promises. We can't stay." One young lady, Mae Wildman, said "My folks have bought me a tent and I am scheduled to leave." I can't remember what the other teammate said. But it turned out that I was the **only one available**.

The people of Fullerton still insisted that I stay. That was a big order for a new graduate. What a responsibility! Sidney and I had not planned to be married until December, when I would be 18. I will tell you more on this later. But our supervisor at the school called Sidney in one day (Sidney was still in school) and said, "Sidney, do you really love Helen?" Sidney replied, "Why, I certainly do." The supervisor asked, "Do you plan to get married?" Sidney told them our plans were to be married in December. Then the supervisor asked him, "Why don't you get married **now**, so that you and Helen can take over the church in Fullerton? They are ready to get you a building when summer is over." The office did not know how much we wanted to get married, but there were problems.

Decisions, Decisions, Decisions

I think you've gathered that my father was a wonderful man, and had truly brought me up in the nurture and admonition of the Lord. He was always encouraging me in all my spiritual growth, and was very positive about my going to Bible College. He felt that that was preparing me for the reason I was born, which was to fulfill the promise my father had made to the Lord about his daughter being a missionary to India. This had been **his** highest goal.

My father liked Sidney very much, and he didn't mind my having friends, but when he was faced with the fact I wanted to get married, he was devastated. That would spoil my chance for being my very best for the Lord. I was to be pure, and if I married, my attention would be given to my husband and not to God. My father had also gotten into a cult that was putting down marriage, and focusing on the "bliss" of single life. You could say I was between the devil and the deep blue sea. I remember hearing someone say, "If you want to stay in the middle of the road, just get hit on both sides with opposition."

I loved the Lord, I loved my father, and I loved Sidney. We needed to get married in order to take over the work in Fullerton . It couldn't wait until December. We had hoped for a June wedding after our advisors had asked us to get married, but my father would not give his permission. The Lord being first in our life, we left it to Him.

The other side of the problem was what I would face in a **critical world** about the question, **should a woman preach the gospel**? Or was

23

it more important that she be a very docile, submissive wife and have no part in active ministry?

Ephesians 5:21-23 is such wonderful scripture - but read all twelve verses. We were very much aware of these scriptures, and the part about the woman being submissive, but that was not the problem. I am very much for this in its proper context. I will admit, it might depend on the man. But let's look at the **whole text**.

God is the head of man.

Man is the head of woman. Let us talk abut the head, the one in charge, the leader. Everyone knows that, to have order in anything, there has to be someone in authority. There is the Commander in Chief of the Military. There are superintendents in school systems, principals in schools, and teachers in classes. There is a main boss in any company. The problem in our country today is, **who is in authority**? No matter whether it is a nation or a home, there must be someone in authority.

I am not a feminist in any way. In fact, I feel sorry for them. I have been so grateful for a man who had a strong head that I could rely on; someone who could make decisions; someone to bear the brunt of things, and to be the final word. And I've been grateful to have a shoulder to cry on when I've thought things are just too much. Sidney was all of this and more.

The real secret of this scripture is love. **If a man really loves a woman**, and **tells her so**, and **shows her so**, then **there will be no problem with submission and respect**. His wife will be putty in this man's hand. People have used this scripture as a weapon, never seeming to dwell on the beautiful 25th verse about husbands loving their wives as Christ loved the church.

As far as **my husband being the head** of the home or of me, there was **never any question**. He loved and adored me until the day he died.

So you see, I had two different questions to face. Should I give all my life and ministry to the Lord and have no husband? Or should I give all my attention to my husband and have no ministry?

I am glad I had both.

But in the meantime, we had much to do before we got married. The days were full of wonder. Sidney was never a conformist, so you could always expect the unexpected. He continued to go to school in the mornings, and worked in the afternoons at the Broadway department store. When we could, we went to the Angeles Temple together at night. We usually sat on the front seats and held hands (which we did for a

24

lifetime). On one of these evenings, the Reverend Paul Rader was holding a revival meeting. He was preaching on love. He shouted, "Love is a feeling! I said, love is a feeling! I said, love is a feeling, isn't it?" And he pointed to us on the front seat.

Another night while in church, Sidney put his hand into his pocket and took out a ring. He had finally gotten enough money to buy it. (It cost $16.) He slipped it on my finger, sitting right there in church. He couldn't do it later because my father was taking me home after church. Daddy drove going home, but I held my hand so that the lights would hit the ring and make it sparkle.

Now, it was just a matter of waiting.

Carroll, Maxine, Sidney

Mom & Dad Correll

Tall, dark and handsome   *Sidney's dream girl*

In Love

Chapter 5

Wedding Bells

My dream of a June wedding came true on Friday, June 19, 1925. The wedding was held in the beautiful Angeles Temple. Bible students decorated the platform with flowers and vines. The auditorium was full. We had six brides maids, six male orderlies, a flower girl and a ring bearer. The minister was Aimee Semple McPherson.

As I walked down the long aisle to the platform, my heart was thrilled as I looked toward the stage and saw my groom waiting for me. My father was not there to give me support as I walked down the aisle. As I was going up the steps, I toppled a bit, and Sidney thought I was going to fall. It was not because I had a long flowing wedding gown on. How I wish I had. But money was very scarce. My dress came just a bit below my knees. It was white, and it had a number of pleats in the front. I think it cost me $20. I know the ring cost Sidney $16, but it was worth its weight in gold to me.

It was a beautiful ceremony. Our vows were very real and important to us. As I looked into his wonderful, big brown eyes and said I do, it was **for life**. I cherished the words, **"I now pronounce you husband and wife, in the name of the Father and of the Son and of the Holy Ghost. Amen."**

The Reception

The wedding reception took place a few blocks away from the church, in the Correll's home. My grandmother had come all the way from Pasadena on a trolley car. She carried with her a bouquet of flowers she had gathered from her own yard. We had a very enjoyable time with Bible students, friends and family. There were enough gifts to help us get started in housekeeping.

The Honeymoon

Sidney and I stayed at the Correll home on our wedding night. Early the next morning, we loaded up the family pickup truck. Sidney and I sat in the back, and Mom and Dad drove. We went from Los Angeles, out past Pasadena, along the foothills, and on until the road led toward the famous resort, Lake Arrowhead. It is a lovely place with a beautiful dining room, spacious bedrooms and lovely recreation areas. But we did not stop there. We drove five miles past the resort, to a camping area beside a lovely stream. We unloaded our camping supplies, and then prepared a cookout dinner on a stone grill beside the stream. Mom and Dad ate with us, then got into the truck and took off back home, leaving us like babes in the woods. We really were, in a way, for I was 17 and a half, and Sidney was 18 years old.

My husband had planned and dreamed of this honeymoon, and as a submissive wife, it delighted me. We found a spot where a tree and some bushes formed a little hideaway. We gathered ferns and soft vines to form a comfortable mattress. Then we put the bedding on top of it, and there was our bridal suite.

There was just one problem. One night, a thunder and lightning storm with pouring rain moved in. We didn't have much protection. Sidney always loved a good storm, but I am afraid I didn't. My only consolation was being able to bury my head in his shoulder, which was a real comfort. Sidney didn't object to that in the least.

During the day, we traveled up and down the stream, and we both loved to fish. Sidney liked to fly-fish, or cast, as it was called. I really preferred to find a nice deep pool, sit on a grassy slope, and drop my baited hook in the water. I would watch the fish as they would swim around looking, sometimes biting. We did catch enough to have a fish dinner every night.

We would also walk through the mountains arm in arm, or sit on a big flat rock, and talk and talk. (This was before television, when couples talked together.) I was so glad I wasn't a woman's libber or feminist. I wonder if they know how much they really miss. I like God's idea of a husband and wife. I enjoyed having a man to lean on, not always having to make the big decisions myself.

Many times in the year that followed, my husband would say to me, "Honey, I am sorry that on our honeymoon I didn't take you to a nice hotel, and do something more glamorous and exciting." I would reply, "Sweetheart, anyone can go to a hotel and be like everyone else, but we did something different!" And I loved it. Anyway, we didn't have that kind of money, but we did have each other. What more could we want?

Church Welcome

The day came when the folks returned to pick us up and take us back to the realities of life, and to our waiting congregation. The news spread fast that the newlyweds, who were the new pastors of the church, would be having their first service Sunday night. We sang, and Sidney gave his testimony, but I preached the sermon, "Behold the Bridegroom Cometh." Of course, I was talking about our wonderful Lord, the heavenly Bridegroom. (Revelations 21)

The Bride

Little lady at the altar,
Vowing by God's book and psalter
To be faithful, fond and true
Unto him who stands by you.
Think not that romance is ended
That youth's curtain has descended,
And love's pretty play is done
For it's only just begun.

Marriage, blushing little lady,
Is love's sunny path and shady,
Over which two hearts should wander,
Of each other growing fonder.
Sharing joy and sharing sorrow
As you stroll to each tomorrow,
And a faithful man and wife
Read the troubled book of life.

Bitter cares will some day find you,
Closer, closer they will bind you,
If together you will bear them,
Cares grow sweet when lovers share them.
Love unites two happy mortals
Brings them here to wedlock's portals
Arm in arm, through weal or woe.

Little lady, just remember,
Every year has its December,
Every rising sun its setting,
Every life its time of fretting.
And the honeymoon's sweet beauty
Finds too soon the clouds of duty,

But keep faith, when trouble-tried,
And in joy you shall abide.

Never let your courage falter,
Keep your pledge, made at the altar,
Never stoop to unbelieving,
Even when your heart is grieving.
To what comes of wintry weather
Or disaster, stand together,
Through life's fearful hours of night
Love shall bring you to the light.

Anonymous

*Our wedding day June 19, 1925 at the Angeles Temple Los Angeles,
ceremony performed by Aimee Semple McPherson. Attendants from left to
right were Jack Cowie, Ernest Hardwick, Carl Smith, Roy Gray, Forrest
Correll, Rhoderick Morrision, Vera Overgard, Teddy Correll, Clella Prough
and Viola Morrison. The ring bearer was Gerald Wallick.*

Chapter 6

My Life As A Wife

"Can a teenage marriage last?" Or let me put it this way, "**How** did a teenage marriage last?" Sidney was just 18 and I was 17 and a half years old.

The ceremony is over and the honeymoon has been a special time, but now a young man and woman stand at the threshold of the rest of their life. What's ahead?

Back To The Garden

Let's go back to the very beginning and see what God has to say about a wedding. Genesis 1:27: *"So God created man in His own image. In the image of God created He Him."* Then God goes on to say, *"male and female created He them."*

But before Eve came on the scene, there was just Adam. God gave him the task of naming all the animals. Wasn't that exciting? It must not have been enough, for God looked at him and said, "Adam is lonely . . . I will make a help meet for him." So He put Adam to sleep and performed an operation. God took a rib from Adam and formed a beautiful woman. He did not take her from man's foot, lest he walk on her. Nor did He take her from his head, lest she lord it over him. But He took from the closest thing to Adam's heart, so he could love her.

Then God brought her to the man, and performed the ceremony **that made them one** (Genesis 2:23). Here is a part that amazes me. In Genesis 2:24, why did God say, *"Therefore shall a man leave his father and mother, and shall cleave unto his wife: and they shall be one flesh,"*? Adam and Eve had no mother or father. They were the only ones! I believe it was such an important rule that God gave it before there was an occasion to put it to use.

God wanted to be a part of their lives and, though it doesn't say it in so many words, I believe God walked with them in the cool of the day (Genesis 3:8) and found sweet fellowship in those evening hours.

I love the words from the Oratorio - Regem Adorate:

> "And they walked and they talked
> 'til the setting sun
> made crimson and gold the encircling hills.
> And in that sacred trusting place,
> God and man talked face to face."

Why do I think this is so? It is because God came at the end of the day, and Adam wasn't there. Sin had broken the nearness to God. He called to him, "Adam, where are you?" What a dark day. But Christ made it possible that we could know **that fellowship** once again. That is why I share this challenge with everyone: "To have a happy marriage, **put Christ first in your life.**"

Light The Candle

It is such a lovely custom in a wedding ceremony, when the bride and groom each take a candle that has been lit by their mothers. Then they light the one candle that reminds them they are no longer two individual persons, but miraculously they now become one flesh. It is a mystery, but a beautiful one. They are a team, two individuals with a single purpose, but with respect and love. I appreciate Ephesians 5:21-31 (notice verse 31 is the same as Gen. 2:24). I was glad to have my husband as the head of our home. I honored and respected him. He in turn gave me a lifetime of love. What more could one want!

Our First Home

I still remember our first little home in Fullerton, California. There was one small bedroom, one bath, a small kitchen and a not so large living room. We received many lovely gifts from our friends and wonderful school classmates. It made the house sparkle with a feeling of home sweet home. Then our congregation filled the cupboards until there was nothing lacking.

In those days, we would get up early and go play tennis. Whoever lost bought the other one a coke. For months, people called us the honeymoon couple. However, it wasn't all moonlight and roses. As I look back on it now, perhaps in some ways, **that first year was the**

most difficult. We had come from different backgrounds. Our personalities needed to be adjusted to each other.

Even though Sidney did not come from a Christian home, his people were a very loving and emotional, "touching" family. All the aunts and uncles were very demonstrative. The door was always open to strangers who were greeted like long lost friends. Though Sidney had put limits as far as girlfriends were concerned, he had such a heart filled with love.

Maybe it was that love that the Lord saw, and knew that Sidney would share that love compassionately with a lost world, and to people everywhere.

My life was much different. I am so grateful that I grew up knowing the Word of God. But, I fear there was a stiffness, a rigidity, or an attitude of "just don't get too close" that took me years to overcome, and find a healthy freedom. Sidney was so wonderful in helping me to do this.

Does this sound like a contradiction? My father was a wonderful man, and had a great sense of humor. I have always been very quick to catch a joke. He loved to make me laugh. Yet, I can't remember him putting his arms around me and giving me a hug and kiss like Sidney had always done with our daughters. It was never my father's nature to be intimate or tender, even with his own mother (my grandmother). I have wondered many times through the years, if my father could have been a little more affectionate, loving and caring with my mother, might she have been more apt to stay instead of stray? Let me hasten to say, I do believe my father loved my mother, but he never knew how to show it.

We didn't have counselors or psychologists to go to in those years. But, because Christ was first in our lives, and He was Head of our home and our great Teacher, we did have a very happy home. We must have learned well, because I don't know anyone who had a more wonderful life than Sidney Correll and I had for over **sixty-six years**.

Perhaps another secret was learning to please each other, rather than ourselves. We also made it a rule to never say anything, even in jest, to each other that later might be **misconstrued** and cause a question. What we say to each other is so important. Words! Words!

Sidney was a master at wonderful things to say. I can't remember a day we were together that he did not say to me, "Honey, I love you. You are beautiful." Many times he would say it with tears in his voice. I knew he really meant it. When Sidney and I first met, I had freckles. I had hated them since I was a little girl, because I was teased about them. When I mentioned it to Sidney, he said, "I love freckles. They are beautiful on you and I could kiss every one of them." I never worried about them again. I don't even remember when they went away.

It may seem that I am stressing this too much, but what the whole world needs is **love sweet love**. Let us remember that, in I John 4:16, the apostle John said, *"God is love."*

Sidney showed his love in other ways too. When he would travel, he would always bring something back for me. For years he bought all of my negligees, robes, blouses, and even a black gown. Relating these acts of caring are what **some folk pay** a psychologist money for. (Smile) This is not a book telling you how to do it, but **how we did it**.

I hear some women say, "Wow, I wouldn't want my husband buying my things!" But, you never had my husband, thank goodness. The truth is, he knew more about what I wanted than I did myself. Was this because I was a submissive wife? (Smile)

I was never as good at saying nice things. But I could write a love note, or I could show my love by baking a lemon pie or meat loaf (which were his favorites). I could also **give myself** as a love gift.

While we are talking about giving, let me tell you a story about when my husband was in his seventies. He had gone on an around the world trip, and he wanted me to meet him in Hawaii on his return. Because of his many missionary tours, he always had a free room in hotels where he had stayed. He arrived in Hawaii ahead of me and was walking down the street window shopping when he saw it . . . the perfect suit for me. So he went into the store and explained to the clerk that his wife was coming into the city soon, and he wanted to have this suit to present to her. The lady said to him, "What size does she wear?" When he said, "size 18," the clerk looked at him very coldly and said, "We don't sell those sizes here." She turned and stormed off. He was crushed.

When I arrived, he told me about the episode and said, "What can I buy you, some jewelry?" That sounded good, so we walked down the streets of Waikiki arm in arm. We came to a jewelry store and I found a pair of simple earrings that I liked. **I still wear them often in memory of him.**

We Were Pals

We have been talking about my life as a wife. What can I share that will shed a little light on "the secret of happiness"? Let me say, we were pals. Pals love being together. We enjoyed each other's company. We did so many things together. "Let me count the ways." We prayed together. Of course we prayed separately, also. They say that the family that prays together, stays together. It is so special when husbands and wives can come into God's presence together, and take one of His promises and believe it together. We always prayed together before separating for a journey (of which there were many).

You often hear leaders speaking of the importance of communication. I remember times when one of us had been on a trip. When we would get together again, and maybe have to drive a distance to get home, we would be so engrossed in conversation that we would pass right by our turn-off without even realizing it!

Oh, I am not saying there were never times we had misunderstandings, and found communication cut off, but the secret was to never go to sleep without coming to a sweet understanding. Ephesians 4:26 says "Let not the sun go down on your wrath."

I told you how we loved to fish together on our honeymoon. We also loved to swim together. I'm thinking of times we were at a large lake in Wisconsin. We would go out in the rowboat. One would row while the other swam, sometimes for miles.

I am not suggesting others do it this way; I am just talking about us.

Flying Together

There was one thing we did that was a bit unusual. We flew together.

We were living in Dayton, Ohio. It was the home of the Wright Brothers. Our radio program was Wings Over Dayton. Our associate pastor flew a plane. Lt. Col. Richard Headrick, who was an ace flyer in World War II, was at Wright Field, and when the war was over, Dick came to assist us in the church (I tell more of this later). The Col. said to my husband, "Sidney, why don't you learn to fly? It just fits in with this air city, and then you can fly to many of your meetings and save lots of time." It didn't take much to persuade Sidney, and very soon he was taking flying lessons. This was very exciting, but I said, "Well, if I am the Lady Sky Pilot, I surely ought to be able to fly also." They agreed that I should, but there was just one hitch. I was six months pregnant with my sixth child, so my training was put off until the following year.

I Get My Wings

When our son Michael was about six months old, I took my flying lessons and passed the test! I will never forget my solo flight. It was pretty scary up there by myself, wondering if I could see the different check points and recognize the airports where I was supposed to land and take off again. But I did it. I got my license and my wings! I was a pilot! I never flew as much as Sidney did, as he flew across America to many of his meetings. In fact, he flew to 90 of his 103 speaking engagements in the next year or two.

California Bound

Speaking of flying together, we had gone on different trips to other states, but let me tell you of our trip to California. Actually, we started by car. Before we had even gotten far from home, the generator burned out in our Studebaker and we couldn't go any further. Someone said, "Well, why don't you fly?" To shorten the story, Mr. Fred Gray took care of our car. We got our baggage and someone took us to the hanger where our plane was. We made out our flight plan, said our good-byes, and we were off to California.

What a wonderful time we had. Sidney was a much better navigator than I, so I was the pilot and he navigated. In fact, he could tell which direction we were going even without a compass. I would be lost without one. It was so much fun seeing America from a ringside seat in the sky, just floating through the air, in our Aronca Chief.

We left from Ohio, of course, and flew west over the states of Indiana, Missouri, Oklahoma, Texas and New Mexico. We would fly low over the countryside, watch the cattle grazing in the fields and see the great expanse of alfalfa, looking so green and lush. We could even see the farm women hanging up their washing on the lines. Then we would watch the cars lined up bumper to bumper for miles. It would feel good just sailing right on past them. Weren't we fortunate to be up there and not bucking all that traffic?

Then on to those glorious Rocky Mountains. I remembered that I was born up there among them, in a city called Silverton, Colorado.

36

But we had to go much farther south to get over them with our small plane. I think we had to climb about nine thousand feet to get over the pass and down into the salt flats. "The Chief" had a cruising speed I believe of 110 miles an hour. But as we were flying, the wind was getting stronger, with a head wind of about 70 to 80 miles an hour. We just couldn't seem to get altitude. It seemed like we were almost standing still. It looked like the ground was coming right up to meet us. As we looked down, we saw a funny sight. **A coyote was running along the ground faster than we were flying**. Sidney said, "Honey, this is a "front" coming through, we have got to get out of here. I think we just past a weather station a little way back." So he grabbed the wheel and turned us around 180 degrees to head for the weather station. Sure enough, there it was. He didn't wait to make a pattern but headed for the only landing strip. We came in for a wheel landing on full power. We saw men running out of the building, coming to meet us. As we taxied in, they held onto each side of the plane until we could come to a stop, then quickly tied the plane securely. We all ran for the building and just as they shut the door, the front moved through. Wow! What gusts of wind that shook the whole place. Then the rain, thunder and lightening stormed through, and we were thanking the dear Lord for the shelter He had led us to. It was a shelter in the time of storm.

Through The Desert

We went from the mountains to the desert. In those days, when you went through the desert, most of the way there were no check points such as highways, rivers, small towns, or towers to check on your air map. It would be quite easy to get lost. We had no radio. We had a new navigational aid, called "flying the beam". You would check your compass for a distant city that sent the beam, then head toward it. As you would listen on this device, you could hear a dit dit - dit dit on the right side. If you turned a bit to the left you heard a da da - da da. You had to stay between those sounds and hear a solid daaaaaaaaaaaaaaa. You would know you were "on the beam".

Needless to say, as great as our trip had been, it was good to land at the airport in Los Angeles, and our friend Colonel Headrick was there to meet us.

Well, this was another story of a life together. Perhaps the most important thing was, we were a **couple with a mission**.

Before I leave this narrative of my life as a wife, I want to mention something that I feel is very important.

In the 1940's, or over forty years before my husband died, he had his first heart problem. He was traveling at the time. I, of course, went to be with him. He began to talk very seriously. He, as the head of the house, had taken care of most of the finances, handling the checkbook and most of the business, including insurance, investments of the future, etc., which I was very happy for him to do. He took my hand and said, "Honey, I want to prepare you to be a good widow." I gulped and thought, wow, is it that bad? What was that supposed to mean? Then he went on, "You know how many times in our ministry I have had to assist women of our congregation whose husbands have died, and they didn't even know how to write a check. They were almost helpless. They didn't know where to begin, which left them vulnerable to the sharks and shysters who prey upon women like that with unscrupulous deals. I don't want you to ever be in that position."

From that day on, even though **I did know how to write a check**, and in my position, I don't think I was naive, but he insisted I take over the checkbook, pay the bills, and be aware of how to handle situations. He was always pointing out things I should watch for, such as salesmen that come by or call on the phone. I did appreciate his attitude and it was very good for, with him traveling like he did, it was important for me to know the ropes. Though he did handle many of the things, he made me aware of them.

Needless to say, he did recover very well (though he did have two massive heart attacks in the 1970's), but for over those many years, it was sort of a private joke that he was teaching me to be a good widow. I am glad I was 83 before this happened. But it did make me glad that I had a husband **who cared enough to think of my future**. (Would that all husbands did.)

We did have a life of joys and sorrows, as I will relate as we go on to "My Life As A Mother".

Chapter 7

My Life As A Mother

Sidney came from a large family, and at first he felt that we, too, should have a large family. Then, for different reasons, he said, "Maybe it would be better for us to just give ourselves to the Lord as a couple and not have a family just now." But as the months went by, something began to happen. I had a yen to hold a little baby in my arms. If I looked at a magazine that had pictures of babies in it, I would look at them and weep. I would see a baby on a billboard and sigh. It was an overwhelming desire. All this time Sidney had thought we ought to wait, but talk about planned parenthood - I planned. We both planned. What a thrill to get the assurance that a baby was on the way. We were both so happy about the coming event. The months ahead brought many moods and apprehensions. I had reached the days of morning sickness. I had "As the World Turns" daily in my stomach. My head, and indeed, my world was turning. In fact it almost crashed when Sidney got a telegram which read, "Aunt Cecil died today. Can you come?" What a blow! This was one of Sidney's favorite aunts. What a conflict of emotions. He had not been back to Colorado since his conversion, but how he had prayed for those relatives. He had always hoped for this opportunity, but this was so sudden. He held the telegram in his hand. This was one of the first tests of consecration. Sidney didn't want to leave me or the church at this time, **yet he knew he had to go.** This is what he had prayed for - to give his relatives the gospel, as most of them did not know Christ. Sidney said it should not be any problem at home or the church, for his wife was a minister and could take care of things.

So we said our good-byes with kisses salted with tears. He flew to Sterling, Colorado, and then proceeded to Proctor down by the Platte River. The village consisted of a granary, a mill, and one general store. (The general store was the mall of its day.) He arrived at the old farmhouse, and there were uncles, aunts, and relatives all over the place. It brought back memories of his childhood. Then Sidney witnessed grief as he had never seen it before when his uncle Homer, so distressed at his great loss, would run into the yard, throw himself down and literally grind his face into the frozen gravel, beating his hands on the ground. Sidney prayed, "Oh God, help me to show to my uncle and those loved ones the God of all comfort. I believe, Lord, that you sent me here for this hour. I throw myself on you. Please help."

That evening as they sat in the living room, many sat on the floor. They asked Sidney to sing. (He had brought his banjo along.) He sang a few songs for them. Then someone suggested, "Say, Sidney, we hear you are a preacher now. Why don't you show us how you do it? Some of us haven't been to church since way back when." Sidney didn't need a second invitation. To them it was curiosity, but this was the very goal he had in mind. So he moved the old phonograph in front of him for a pulpit. He got out his Thompson Chain Reference Bible, chose a text, breathed a prayer for divine guidance, and preached his heart out. He told how Christ was not only a Savior, but also the One who could comfort in a time of sorrow, and He would guide us along life's pathway. He went on to say Christ was right there, just waiting to come into their hearts. Then came the moment he had waited and prayed for. As Sidney finished his message he said, "How many of you would like to receive this wonderful Lord as your own personal Savior? Would you lift your hands, and I will pray for you?" He said, "I couldn't believe my eyes. Every hand in the living room went up. I thought they had misunderstood me, so I said, 'If you really mean it, and you want to become converted and give your life to Christ, stand up.' They *all* stood. I prayed the sinner's prayer, and they repeated it after me." Sidney said it was the first and only time in his ministry that the whole congregation responded to an altar call.

After the funeral, Uncle Fred said, "Sidney, doesn't the Bible say after you repent you ought to be baptized?" "Yes it does, Uncle Fred." "Well, I have repented, hadn't I ought to be baptized?" "Yes, I think you should, Uncle Fred. When you get back to Nebraska, find a church where they have a baptistery and be baptized." He said, "But Sidney, I might not live that long. Can't I be baptized right here? It doesn't have to be any special place, does it?" "No." "Well, what's the matter with the stock tank? That's big enough." (For all you non-farmers, this is a water trough the cattle drink from, maybe two feet high and six or eight feet long.) "But Uncle Fred, doesn't that have ice on it?" "Sure, but we can fork it off." Have you ever been in Colorado in February? Do you know how cold the water can be when you fork off two inches of ice? Have you ever felt the chill of that wind that blows across the prairie? If you have, then you know what these uncles were asking for. By now there were two, as Uncle Todd sauntered in and said, "Count me in too, Sid." The Holy Spirit whispered, "Isn't this what you have been praying for?" So I said, "Okay Uncle Fred, that is just fine." While somebody cleared the ice off the water trough, the two farmers prepared for the baptismal service. They all wore heavy coats as they braved the cold. As they prepared, Sidney said he was willing to get into the tank, too, but there wasn't room. He also said, "I'll promise you one thing. It won't be a long, drawn out ceremony." One at a time, they were put under that cold water, in the name of the Father, and of the Son and of the Holy Ghost, amen. They shot out of the water like bullets, grabbed their coats, and ran for the house. The congregation watched from the kitchen windows.

Isn't this an exciting story? After this, the opportunity came to hold a two-week meeting in the schoolhouse there. I won't take time to tell you about that, but one month had passed before Sidney boarded the train to come home.

In the meantime, what was happening to **the lady preacher**? I was having a "pity party". I just didn't think it was fair for him to be away from me at this time. After all, I needed him. Suddenly, I was aware that I had developed a bitterness and a selfishness in my heart. As I tried to pray, the Lord revealed to me just how selfish I was. Sidney was giving these relatives what they had never had before. This was harvest time, and I was complaining. The Lord seemed to say to me, "You are carrying the baby you so wanted to have. Do you want your bitterness and selfishness to affect the little one?" That brought me to repentance, and I begged the Lord to give me an unselfish child. Thank God he answered that prayer. As every mother knows, those nine months can seem forever, especially when delivery time is in the hot summer months. The long days not only came, but seemed to never end. Now it was overtime. I began to have other fears. The enemy of my soul would bring to my remembrance some of the **prophesies or predictions** my father had made. I had not gone to India as a missionary, and now I was having a baby, which he inferred might be a judgment for having married instead of remaining single and pure for the Lord.

August 15, 1926, I began to go into labor. My grandmother (who was living with us at this time) did not agree with my father's ideas, but she began to relate just **what it was like** to have a baby. Have you ever heard of old wives' tales? Some of the descriptions were gruesome. I have never been prone to fear, but now fear was running the gamut of my imagination and anxiety. As the pains became greater and closer, I could see and feel a very dark valley. Then I saw the Lord draw near, and I was at peace. He was walking through the valley with me.

I was having the baby at home, which many did in those days. The doctor had been there for some time. In fact, he was taking a nap in the living room until it was time. But my dear husband was right there with me, and though they didn't have the Lamaze method in those days, Sidney was holding my hand and saying sweet, comforting things to me. Finally, as he took a look, he shouted, "Doctor, it's coming!" What a hurry and scurry there was. Everyone was on the move, including me, and with one last great effort, our first son was born. I just must tell you this. When he was wrapped in a blanket and laid in my arms, oh, the thrill, the joy, the peace, the relief. He was not only here, he was perfect. The devil is a liar. All those things he had been telling me were not true. Then the scripture came to me from Isaiah 53:11, *"He shall see the travail of his soul and shall be satisfied."* At that moment I had a new revelation of what that scripture meant. I had been through some very rough days. I had traveled a deep valley. I had known pain, suffering and travail, but now it was over, and how quickly it was forgotten. Just to look down into that sweet face and know he was mine made me forget the valley, and I had an overwhelming ecstasy that is out of this world. At that moment, I caught a glimpse of what it meant when my Lord went through such suffering in His life: Gethsemane, the whipping post, the crown of thorns, so much pain, the long walk to Golgotha with the cross on His back, the excruciating ordeal of the crucifixion, and His death. But, Hallelujah! There was resurrection! Lost sinners could now know a new birth and be born into the kingdom of God. Then I realized just what it must have meant after Calvary when a sinner receives Christ. He is a babe in Jesus' arms, and all the pain He went through was worth it. Christ not only rejoices, but He asks the angels to rejoice with Him. Say the verse again with me. *"He shall see the travail of his soul and shall be satisfied."* You know, I saw something else that day, too. When a new baby is born, the greatest joy is not to the baby but to the mother who bore it. Did you get it? When a person is born again, they think of their own joy, but **think** of the joy the Lord receives.

In the years to come, I would walk through this valley five more times. They were not all planned, but they were all welcomed, and they were all loved. Later we added number seven to our list when our dear nephew, Kenneth Richard Correll, came to us at age eleven to be our son. He just fit, for he was just two years younger than Michael, our youngest son.

Our daily routine was a family altar of prayer and scripture verses, giving God a place in our everyday life. It was a part of growing up to be enjoyed, not a burden to be endured.

It is not only true that "The family that prays together stays together," but because of our many activities, we tried also to feel that "The family that plays together stays together." As the children grew, we all learned to skate, not only on the roller rink but also on the ice.

We all loved to swim. Everyone learned to swim at an early age. Each summer they went to the swimming pool, and we all went, as a family, to summer camps. The summer camps offered not only swimming, but also many other sports.

Every member of the family learned to play ping pong. The children and their father became quite expert. In fact, a couple of the children won tournaments. That might have been because at our house on Belmont Park, we had a large porch, and on it was a ping pong table. It was a fun place, not only for the family but for our guests, too.

When it came to work, the children were expected to have some part. They were all part of the team.

Because we were the pastors, I suppose, we knew it was important for parents to keep an eye on their children in church, so ours were required to sit on the front seats. I don't think they especially enjoyed it, and there were times we had to check up on a "missing person," but our goal was to get the other young folk to sit down front also. The youth were always very special, and we tried to pay extra attention to them. For the most part, it did become a habit. It was while we were in Dayton, Ohio, pastoring the Christian Tabernacle, that our two youngest children were born. Helen Rowena (who came to be known as Penny) was born in 1940. Roger was ten years old when "Little Helen" was born. That is what we called her when she would sing on our regular radio program called Wings Over Dayton. She was a star as her daddy would put her through a "spelling lesson." She was only two or three years old. I wasn't getting any younger, but I said I wanted one more child, as I didn't want to raise one alone. Over five years later (I was 39), our youngest son, Michael Richard Todd Correll, came to us. He was twenty years younger than his older brother, Sidney Robert.

We are talking in this chapter about life as a mother. I could write chapters and chapters. But when Michael was eleven months old, my husband said "Honey, would you mind if we moved to a farm?" Sidney had been brought up on one, as I have mentioned before, but I never had. Our home in Dayton was a very lovely place, but as pastor of a large church (as many pastors can verify), it is almost impossible to sit down to a meal without the doorbell or the phone ringing. It wasn't that we minded company, as our house was always full and we loved it, but this would give Sidney a chance to get out and milk a cow or ride a horse or plant some corn. It would be relaxing and an opportunity to meditate.

Sidney Robert

Chapter 8

The Farm - Sky Ranch

So we bought the farm. 103 acres on Seybold Road, outside of Dayton, just north of Trotwood, Ohio. What a lovely spot. There were woods, and a stream, and a huge new barn, plus other smaller sheds or buildings. There was a place for everything we would want to do.

I had never thought of doing any thing like this, but I was soon convinced it was a wonderful idea. I only wish we had done it when the two older children were small. But now Robert was a graduate from Wheaton College. He had married Betty Oaks, one of the girls from our church who had loved Robert ever since he was eleven years old. Then later he went to Harvard, and eventually Harvard Medical School, and became a doctor. Rebecca, after one year of college in Wheaton, met Robert Cauble, son of one of the pastors affiliated with us. This is a lovely story of love at first sight. So she decided she would much rather get married and have a family than continue college. They were now living in Louisville, KY. (She had her family of six children. They also adopted one.)

So there was Roselyn, who was in her last year of high school. She transferred to Trotwood Madison High School. Those next couple of years she had a ball, using the family Jeep as her transportation, and the farm became the center of fun for all her school chums. Roger also transferred to Trotwood Madison High. He did graduate from there, but I will tell you about that later.

Thirteen Years

We had thirteen wonderful years on the farm and right now, I just feel like talking, so would you like to come on in to my kitchen and "sit a spell" while I tell you some things about "home on the farm"? Don't you love my big kitchen? There's so much room, and here in the corner is our kitchen table. It is like a big booth in a restaurant, with seats long enough to accommodate four or five on each side, and a high back with the table to match. It sure beat a lot of chairs always in the way. It was against a big window looking out into the yard with a big pear tree just outside.

How many people have sat at this table and just talked? Oh, we did have a big dining room with a big table, which was full almost every

45

Sunday, of not only our family but guests. But the kitchen, that's where a lot of great conversations and just plain living took place.

Now that both Sidney and I had our "wings" and flew our own plane, it was only right that we put an air strip to the north going toward the railroad. And we named the farm Sky Ranch.

Michael was just eleven months old when we moved here. We had a dear colored lady from the south. (That is what they called the black Americans in those days.) She did not read or write but could she cook! Most important, she loved Michael. As long as she was with us, she would always say, "That's my boy," and in turn, Mike loved her. It was no small job, watching after a one year old, or a two year old, and on up. What experiences we had.

Those Terrific Twos

In as much as we have been talking about my life as a mother, let me tell you what I know about a two year old. We had thought that the farm would be such a safe place to raise a baby, and to get away from the dangers of the city streets. No one had warned us of the big milk trucks that drove up into your yard to pick up big milk cans, etc. So, will I ever forget the day we forgot to watch for the truck? Michael loved roaming around our yard and there was no front fence to protect him, so someone would always be there to hold the baby when this huge monster arrived. Sidney Robert just happen to be home from Harvard for the summer, and he was in the main barn, helping to put up some bales of hay. He heard the big old truck come up the lane. The driver would always pull up toward the big tree and turn around before getting the milk cans from the cooler down below. In the meantime, Michael had waddled over and plopped down right behind the truck. (He wasn't walking too good yet.) Sidney Robert just felt an urge to go to the barn door and look out. He did just in time to see the red and blue jumper under the truck. He screamed and the driver slammed on his brakes. Yes! It was Mikie, and had he driven forward, those great rear dual wheels would have gone right over him. Surely the guardian angel was there.

Michael loved to go to the barn (to the lower level where all the cows were). We had a terrific herd of registered Brown Swiss cows. Incidentally, they were all given family names. The cows were gentle enough, but they were so big and Mike was so little. We had turned our back and were watching the cows coming out of the milking barn. We looked around just in time to see Michael sitting right in the path of these bovine elephants. Before we could get to him, 1500 pounds of beef had stepped right over him. On another occasion, one of the cows had nosed him over and was licking the top of his head with her big tongue.

There are other stories I remember of this two year old, but I want to tell the one that nearly did us in, and Mike, too. One noon, Sidney and I came home for lunch. We usually spent most of the day at the church office. Being nine miles from church, we didn't come home for lunch very often, but Dad and Mother Correll were staying with us at the time. Daddy had gone somewhere with his car. Mother had fed Mikie early, and he was playing out in the back yard. We had to get back for the two o'clock broadcast, but as I went out to the car, Mikie came running toward me with his arms out, crying and staggering as he ran. I went to him and picked him up. I smelled his breath and rushed into the house. I racked my brain, trying to think what he had drank. We all hunted all over the yard. I found an empty bottle, but what was it? There was no label on it. Then I remembered. I had put a brand new bottle of roost paint by the chicken pen. I had gotten it to kill the chicken lice. It had never been opened. How in the world had he gotten the top off? Now there was only one tiny drop left. Even the label had washed off.

We gave him cream to make him vomit, but as we held him over the bowl, he would just grow limp. Dr. Correll said, "Let's get him to the hospital quick." Shall I ever forget that ride? My husband drove and I held Michael. We took Free Pike at 80 miles an hour. It was a country road, not interstate. All the time, Mikie was throwing up all over me. I would say, "Daddy, slow down." He would, and Mike would pass out on me. I would yell, "Go faster!" We did this all the way in. Would we ever get there? Then we had to wait in the emergency room. There ought to be a law against the indifference one encounters at such a time. Does this ring a bell? Our doctor couldn't be reached at the moment. The interns were having lunch. In the meantime, we were answering all the stock questions while we paced the floor and said inside, "Why don't they do something?"

By this time, Mike was completely unconscious. I was a mess where he had thrown up on me, but who cared about that? Sidney called the church and let them know that we would not be there for the broadcast, and requested everyone to pray for our son. Not until an intern sauntered in and put the stethoscope to his heart did we get action. Quickly he gave Mikie some kind of a shot to revive him, and by this time, our doctor was reached - and believe me, we got some action! I will not go into detail about what it took to find out what was in the bottle, and what the anecdote was. In the meantime, Mikie's stomach was pumped, and a full dose of caster oil was put to work. The afternoon and evening wore away while our baby was motionless. Once or twice his eyes would open, but when we spoke to him, he didn't seem to see us. We were thinking that even if he did live, would he be blind? Would his bowels be paralyzed? How glad we were that we knew the Lord. We would just trust. About midnight, he opened his eyes and as I took his hand, he looked up at me and smiled and said, "Mama." As I leaned over the bed he put his arms around my neck. Hallelujah, what a glorious moment! Well, that is enough of the terrific twos.

As the years rolled on I remember both Michael and "Helen" Rowena (Penny) getting on the school bus, and seeing them coming home up the long lane from the road to the house. And there were the times Penny and her girl friend from across the road played croquet, or in the winter, had fun sliding down the hills on their sled. I remember Penny taking piano lessons, etc. And there's the time they had brought a little Texas Pony for Michael from the famous Rodeheaver ranch in Florida. We had visited there. (Homer Rodeheaver was the song leader and singer for the evangelist Billy Sunday.)

After grade school, Helen Rowena left for the Christian Academy in Florida, coming home during the summers.

Roselyn graduated from Trotwood Madison High School. That summer she worked for Dayton Power and Light and also played on the girls' softball team. She was third baseman, (in case anyone is interested). In the fall, she entered Bob Jones University in South Carolina. The next year she went to West Suburban Hospital near Wheaton and entered nurses training.

Roger, (who was just a year younger than Rose) applied himself to being a farmer. He helped "Murph" in the milking of the cows and working in the field. He also had a narrow escape one day as he was plowing. As he got to the end of a row, he is not sure what happened, but the plowshare must have hit a rock or something, and the plow flew up in the air, just missing his head by inches. Had it hit him, it would have killed him. He also remembers painting the barn, and that was a job.

He also went to Trotwood Madison High School, and played football. But everything just got to be a little to much for him, and like many a boy has done, he just took off. To make a long story short, he missed being at home, and like a prodigal he came back. He had some new ideas of what was important, so he went back to high school, even though he was two years behind and didn't have enough credits to count for the time he had been there. The "new Rog" did four years of high school in two years and graduated at age 19. How well I remember that graduating program when Roger was the soloist and sang the song of the famous Lawrence Tibbett, "The Glory Road." Roger sounded like Enrico Caruso. (Luciano Pavarotti wasn't singing yet.)

Well, here I have just rattled on, talking about my family. But let's walk around and let me show you the master bedroom that Sidney, with the help of a builder, had added to the farm house. Most of our bedrooms had been upstairs. They were almost always filled with guests. The new addition was almost as big in size as our whole house. Across the north end, there were two dressing rooms. One was Sidney's and one was mine. There was a bathroom in the center. It had a specially shaped bathtub. On Sidney's side, there was a shower stall. We both had a clothes closet. Underneath the entire floor, radiant heat had been put into the floor. (I don't know if they still have radiant heat or not.) The whole floor is heated, then completely covered with a rug.

This had sort of become our family room. Many times we would sit up in our king-sized bed, and the children and their friends would sit on the warm floor. We would sing and sing. Sidney would play his guitar. We not only sang gospel songs and Negro spirituals, but cowboy songs, and my husband would yodel. Or we would listen to classical music, or even opera on our beautiful Magnavox record player. Here was always laughter and fun.

Discipline

Life, however, is not always fun and games. To have a well ordered house, there must be rules. Some do's and don'ts are necessary. There needs to be a curfew. It is so important for fathers and mothers to be agreed on all of this, not pulling against each other as some parents do. We had a rule, "be home by 10 o'clock or call." Sometimes it was extended to 11:00pm.

During those years as a mother, I never went to bed until every "chick" was tucked in and accounted for. I always held my breath when our daughter, Roselyn, would take the Jeep filled with her school friends (more people than there should have been) and they would go off singing and laughing to their football games, or whatever. We always called

49

Roselyn our "giggling gal", for she laughed a lot. I am so glad I did not have to be concerned about dope and drink in those days. My main worry was the railroad track that ran along the back of our property, which she would have to cross when going in that direction. There was no gate, and not even a signal warning, and there were many trains that went by. I always prayed for the guardian angels to go with her.

One night she was very late. The strange thing was, I had perfect peace. I wasn't even worrying. However, Roselyn didn't know that. What had happened was, after she had let all of the other young people off, she headed home. The roads were very icy, and the Jeep slid off the road. She wasn't hurt, but she couldn't get the Jeep back onto the road. Going to a house nearby, she told her story to the people there. They told her to just leave the Jeep there until morning, and they would take her home. On the way home, she wanted to prepare them for the fact that her Mother might be very upset because she had not called. So she told them, "Don't worry about anything. My mother is just going through the 'change'," (which, by the way, I wasn't). When they arrived at the house, the couple proceeded to explain to me why Roselyn was late. There was no emotional scene, and our daughter couldn't understand why. Well, of course, this is only one of the many stories through the years.

The farmhouse

Chapter 9

My Life As A Hostess At Sky Ranch

As I look back over the wonderful life the Lord has allowed us to live down here, I am so glad He made us wealthy! Oh, not in money, but friends. I have heard a few folk in my life who have said, "I don't have a friend in the world." How sad. Proverbs 18:24 says, "A man that hath friends must show himself friendly." My husband, who was a super host, cherished his friends. He often said, "You have to cultivate friendship. You have to work at it."

Well, anyway, I want to tell you about some of the wonderful people that we entertained here at Sky Ranch. Remember I told you how much fun we had with the children in our master bedroom, which was sort of a family room because it was the largest. I remember entertaining several groups for a special dinner right in this unusual setting. Let me tell you about two of them. Several times during our children's school years, we made it a point to invite their teachers from school for a dinner. We did it in Dayton when the older children were with us. Now we wanted to repeat it here on the farm. We sent invitations to the teachers at Trotwood Elementary, as well as the high school, for a dinner on the farm.

We had a young lady named Fumio, from Japan, who had been a great help to my husband in showing him important places to photograph. Her dream had been to come to the States for a visit. So it was made possible. She loved fixing Japanese meals for us. So, on this special occasion, the teachers were surprised when they came to learn they would be sitting on pillows on the floor, with a low table in front of them. They were all good sports and had a hilarious time. This is something they had never done. Besides that, we received letters of thanks from the teachers, several of them saying that in all their years of teaching, this was the first time they had been invited into the home.

A short while ago as I was writing my book, I was visiting friends, John and Geneva Borgwardt in Florida. We got to talking about some of the wonderful times on the farm those years ago. I recalled about the teachers (which I have just related). Geneva said, "I remember Fumio, and we were there another time when she cooked a Japanese dinner. And we sat on the floor on pillows. I don't remember everything we had to eat, but I know there was a raw egg in a small cup which I think you were supposed to dip your food in. Well, I didn't touch that, but I remember there were apples for desert. I don't remember what other dignitaries there were that night, but I was sitting next to Dr. Bob Jones, Jr. from Bob Jones University. (He was in Dayton, speaking at our church.) Everyone was having a good time. I had peeled my apple and laid it on my plate. Dr. Bob reached over and took a piece and commented 'That's good.'"

The Palermos

How you have missed it if you never met the Palermo brothers, Phil and Louis, two Italian evangelists. Both of them married Swedish girls. We had the opportunity to meet them several places around the world. One time was in 1950, in Brussels Belgium. Over 500 people had come as delegates to attend the World Conference, sponsored by Youth For Christ. The crowds filled the place. There were over 2,000 in attendance. Bob Cook was the President of YFC then. But I must not get into that here. I want to tell you of one of the features of the meeting, which was the World Miler, Gil Dodds. The evening meetings were held in the Sports Palace. After a rousing song service, it had been announced that the famous Miler, Gil Dodds, would run. In the meantime, Gil had been warming up on the track. He put out a challenge to some of the Belgium Youth to come and race and give him some competition. Several lined up, but I don't think they were professionals. Among them was Louis Palermo. The race began and Gil had given them a hundred yard start. Louis made it around just once and then fell by the wayside while Phil counted him out. The audience was roaring with laughter. The other volunteers ran most of the time, but Gil Dodds, of course, passed them up like they were standing still. It was a great service, but I only gave you a peep. I was telling you about the Palermos. They both played guitars, and how they could sing.

Another time in 1950, we met the Palermos in Venice, Italy. Venice was beautiful. The streets were water. There are the famous "gondolas" in which we had a ride with, guess who? The Palermo brothers. We ran into them while walking down the Lido. They gave us a report of what they had been doing for the Lord. They are fearless, and usually stir things up. With their guitar and accordion, and knowing the language, they would hold street meetings, and thousands would attend.

But how the people loved them in Dayton. They were our guests a number of times. This one time, they were at the farm, and their specialty was to cook a spaghetti dinner. This time they were cooking for the church staff. There they were, in cook's hats and aprons, with a huge kettle of the real thing. Someone remembered that Phil said the blessing before and prayed, "Lord, bless this food we have repaired for them." There was never a dull moment.

Just the stories of our friends and those who were guests at Sky Ranch would fill a library. I don't even know how many missionary children stayed with us while their parents were traveling on itineration.

But then there were those who might have been notable in another way. We had those from the Dayton jails, and from the Penitentiary. We gave them a chance. Some succeeded, others failed. I don't know how long we had "Murph" with us. He had been in jail for writing bad checks, but he faithfully cared for our Brown Swiss cows. They were his whole life. You see, Murph was fine when he wasn't drinking. That is why the farm was a good place for men like him. He lived in the bunk house. He had all the money that he needed for his needs at the farm, but one night when some neighbor came by to visit, he brought his "bottle" with him. The next day, Murph was gone. Several days later, we discovered that he had **forged a check on us**. He spent the rest of his days in the Penitentiary. Out of shame, I don't think he wanted out, even though we offered. Did this discourage us? No. There were those who made good.

Another wonderful group that we hosted at the farm was the Claus Indian Family. When they first came to the church and the farm, it was in the 1940's. There was Mama Claus and Daddy Claus. He mostly looked after the family. Then there was Sonny Claus and his sister Shirley. Sonny (Tom) was quite young then. He sat right there at the kitchen table day after day and regaled us with laughter. What a terrific story teller he was. Mama Claus was the "spark plug", and really led them in a terrific singing group. I can still hear them singing, "I just got the heaven and I can't sit down." They were with us a number of times, and we helped in their support. Later, Shirley and her husband, Antone, were at the farm, and they had their first child, Kathy, with them. They stayed in our home and were so loved, especially by Mike. You see, when it was time to go to church, Sonny or Ken would put on their huge **feather headdress**. You can imagine what kind of stories there were at school, when Mike told them of the real Indians that stayed at his place. That was many years ago. The father passed on, then the mother did, and I just learned that Shirley passed away in the early 90's.

Do you see the excitement we had at our place? I could tell you so many stories. I must mention what a lively place Sky Ranch was on

Friday nights. It was youth night in the barn. We had a beautiful $25,000 barn. It was newer than the house. It had been built a little while before we came. The upper floor was where the hay and feed were kept, but it served as seats on youth night. Thank the Lord it wasn't for a barn dance, but an enthusiastic young people's meeting. They would sing until the rafters rang. They played Bible games. They had special musical guests, and dynamic speakers. Many a young person wept their way through to Christ. Many missionary calls were received. Eternity alone will tell the real results.

There were also real ol' country hay rides. It was super.

Chapter 10

The Farm

I guess I have just gotten carried away with reminiscing. And when I think of all the very dear individuals I could talk about, and there are so many, it would be unfair to even start to name all the dear friends who visited us on the farm for so many would be left out.

I am glad I have been able to show you a few places around the farm, but would you like to come with me as we walk through the meadow below and along the stream that we all loved? The sheep loved it along this path, also.

We are so proud to talk about our wonderful friends that we have known. But I would be amiss if I did not talk about the most Wonderful Friend of all. I am awed when I think that the Lord said, He was not just our Lord and Savior but our Friend.

Could we sit here on this log for just a few moments while I read the wonderful Scripture in John 15? He had been showing how close we could really be to Him when He said He was the Vine and we were the branches abiding in Him. One of the results would be full of joy that would always be there. But here, let me read from the 12th verse. *"This is My commandment that you should love one another, as I have loved you. Greater love hath no man than this that a man lay down his life for his friends. You are My friends if you do whatever I command you. No longer do I call you servants but I have called you friends."* Can you imagine not only knowing about the King of Kings, but He said if we know Him, He will be a real true Friend, even when everything and everyone else fails? How many times I have needed that Friend.

Come and walk with me along the stream toward the barn. The time I am thinking of now is just three months before I was to leave the farm to escort five missionary children to Africa. We had been on the farm thirteen wonderful years. Before we go back to the house, I want you to stand right here. This is the lane where the cows leave the stream and go up to the barn. This is one of the best views to look at and see our lovely barn. I have to smile when I think of some of the scenes that took place there. Most of the time we did have help, but there were times when both Sidney and I were on the job, pouring feed into the troughs, washing down the cows' udders, putting on the milkers, filling up the ten gallon cans with the milk, and lifting them into the coolers. It would have surprised many of the people in church on Sunday, who saw their pastor dressed so immaculately in his striped trousers and black coat, if they could have seen him a few hours earlier in his barn-wearing overalls and boots. And excuse me if I take time to smile about another funny sight. We enjoyed a line up of cats (that had rid the place of rats) as they vied for first chance at the milk. We had one big old cat that liked to have his share squirted right directly into his mouth from the cow. I just had to get that story in! I have another story to tell you, too.

The Burning Of The Barn

You would have thought we were running a children's home. First there were of course my own children, Michael and Kenny; then Rebecca and Bob's children, Pam, Pat, Kevin, Gary, and Kathy, who was a baby. (Number six had not been born to Rebecca and Bob yet.) Then there were Denise and Greg, children of Betty and Paul Schubert who were in France studying French before going to Africa as missionaries. Greg and Denise were staying with us for several months till we would leave for Africa on a freight ship to meet their parents in Dakar, Africa. This farm really was a great place for kids. How they loved the barn. They made tunnels in the hay and had forts, and all kinds of imaginative games. Do you get the picture?? I (one adult) was there with **nine kids**. My husband was in South America.

On this momentous day, November 12, 1959, I don't remember what I was doing at the time, but several of the older children were in the house and the rest were playing in the barn. As Denise came in to the dining room, she looked out of our picture window and shouted, "Auntie Helen, the barn is on fire!" I looked out to see flames leaping out both sides. Michael was just coming down the stairs and I shouted, "Go get all the children and bring them up to the house, while I call the Fire Department!" After making the call, I ran out and saw all the children running toward the house. We huddled close together before the big picture window and watched the barn burn. The heat was so intense, we could feel it inside of the house.

Fortunately, we had already sold all the cattle and horses. We stood there terrified. While we were watching there was a terrible explosion, which sounded like a bomb. The hay had acted like gasoline. The whole place was ablaze. Flames leaped higher and higher, then seemed to reach like fingers towards the house. The wind was blowing the flames in our direction. The children began to scream, "What if the house catches on fire?" "Auntie Helen, where can we go?" "Oh,

Grandma, I'm afraid." Amidst the din and outcries I shouted, "**Be quiet every one of you!** God is with us and He will not allow us to be harmed. We are going to pray." Did I say I was alone with nine children? I was not alone; God was there. My Friend was there. I gathered them all into a huddle. We put our arms around each other in a tight circle and we cried out for God's protection. Then something came over me and I commanded the flames to go in the other direction! A wonderful calm came over the children and as we looked out the window, we could actually see the flames turning to the opposite direction. It was amazing how quickly that beautiful barn became an ugly mess. Among the rubble that was in the barn was Rebecca and Bob's furniture they had stored there until they moved, as well as some of our machinery and equipment.

It seemed forever before the Fire Department got there from Trotwood. By this time, Seybold Road was filled with cars and people wanting to know where the fire was. This, of course, made it difficult for the fire trucks to get through. They couldn't do anything to save the barn, but they trained their hoses on the other surrounding buildings to spare them. The Fire Chief looked over the situation and said to me, "You can surely thank the good Lord that the wind was blowing in the opposite direction, or the house would have been in danger." I looked at him and said, "Sir, we do thank God because **He changed the winds** to another direction to save the house."

I imagine this is one time the children never forgot. The ironic thing about it was, Rebecca and Bob were on their way at that very moment to pick up their children, and the furniture, to move to their new home. On their way from Columbus they stopped to phone to say they were coming. Rebecca was six months pregnant and was driving their car. Bob was driving a U-Haul truck. I informed them that at that very moment the barn was on fire. Rebecca was near hysterics but I assured her the most important thing was that all the children were safe. What a shock it would have been had they not phoned, but heard about it on the evening news instead. The good part also was that Bob had the foresight to have had **all their belongings** covered with insurance from their old house to their new. So, they were awarded enough money to get a new stove, refrigerator and washer.

Imagine what a shock it was to Sidney in South America to get a wire saying, "Today the barn burned to the ground. Everyone safe." He had just come out of Wycliff Bible Translators camp to their headquarters in Lima, Peru. Fortunately, for me, it was the end of his mission session and he could fly home immediately.

That night, after everyone was tucked into bed, I sat alone in the living room, before the fireplace. It was always a great place to just sit and think. I looked out the window and saw the burning embers of our once proud barn. I could see the lights of the firemen passing by, just checking to see if there were any new fires. I sat and remembered the good times we had all had in the barn, and how the children had loved it.

Then I shuddered as I remembered how many tunnels they had made among the bales, and I realized that if some of the children had been in them, they would never have gotten out. I believe because of this fact, I was so thankful that not one child was hurt. I don't believe I ever grieved over the barn itself, even though we didn't have insurance to pay for it.

I believe after Sidney Robert died, the Holy Spirit impressed on my heart that **you don't hold things too tightly.** Your priorities change. I confess that I felt very lonely that night, and wished my husband was there so I could lay my head on his shoulder. But I was content knowing he was doing what God wanted him to do. And I had God's promise, *"Lo, I am with you always."* He was my ever present Friend!

The barn that burned

58

Chapter 11

Mother - Road Of Suffering And Death

Now that I have told you about the farm, let's get back to the business of being a mother.

Road To Suffering

Another view I want to share with you is the pathway of suffering. I cannot speak for you mothers who have gone through these many trials alone. God has spared me from having to raise my children without a father. I was so fortunate that we could walk this path together. Believe me, my heart does go out to you who have weathered this alone.

Many times, when situations seemed too much for me, I found strength in my husband, and a shoulder to weep on. But for those who don't have a husband, let me assure you there is a heavenly Father, and there are the promises in the Bible that *"He is a Father to the fatherless."*

When Sickness Comes

It is very good that we do not know the things we may have to face in the future. Remember your wedding day, when everything was so glorious and romantic. With your eyes full of stars, and overflowing with love, you repeated the vows:

> For better, for worse,
> for richer, for poorer,
> in sickness and in health,
> to love and to cherish,
> till death us do part.

Then the days come when you face some difficult realities!

Does this sound familiar? A man who had been married for some time came to the point where he decided that he had **had** it! He finally came to his pastor for some solutions or counseling. Things had gotten so bad that he just couldn't see any way out. Divorce had to be the answer. The pastor laid his hand on his shoulder and said, "But, John, don't you remember when you were married and took the vows, you said 'I take this woman for better or worse'?" The man sighed and said, "Yes, pastor, I know, but she is worse than I took her for."

There is a song I learned when I was young that has stayed with me through the years. It goes like this:

> If all were easy, if all were bright,
> Where would the cross be? Where would the fight?
> But in **the hardness**, God gives to you
> Chances for proving what He can do.
>
> (Chorus)
> Keep on believing, Jesus is near.
> Keep on believing, there is nothing to fear.
> Keep on believing, this is the way;
> **Songs in the night** as well as the day.

Isaiah 43:2 says *"When you pass through the waters, I will be with you; and through the rivers, they shall not overflow you; when you walk through the fire, you shall not be burned; nor shall the flame scorch you, for I am the Lord your God!"*

So my life as a mother was to know dark hours of suffering through sickness. Not so my sickness, but that of my children. It started out early, with our youngest son, Sidney Robert. I so wanted to nurse him, but as the days went by, he seemed to be losing weight, and not gaining as he should. I would not believe him when the doctor said he was not getting any nourishment from breast-feeding. By this time, he couldn't keep anything down. By the time he was six months old, he cried all the time, and was getting thinner. The handwriting was on the wall. We might not have him for long. We had dedicated him to the Lord when he was two weeks old, so he did belong to the Lord, but that didn't ease the pain.

My husband and I were visiting a church that Sunday. The preacher spoke about Abraham putting Isaac on the altar. God was making this demand. It was as though the Lord was requiring this of us. We went forward and knelt in submission to the Lord's will. We both wept and cried out, "Lord, we already gave him to You at his dedication, but it is so hard to actually give him up and let You take him now. But he is Yours, Lord. We surrender him." I felt a real peace, and fully expected him to be gone when we got back to the folks' place. (They were caring for him while we were in church.)

60

When we opened the door, everything was quiet. There was no crying. But Robert was not dead. He was sleeping peacefully. He wasn't whimpering, and he wasn't making sounds like he had been before. What happened? Then they told us that Dad Correll was talking to a neighbor and told him about the baby. The neighbor said, "Have you ever tried goat's milk?"

Daddy Ralph went out and searched until he found a place that sold it. He brought it home. They fixed a bottle and gave it to baby Robert. Almost immediately, he went to sleep. That was the turning point of his recovery. How glad we were that we had said yes to the Lord.

Kenosha, Wisconsin

As I look back on other occasions, I remember when we lived in Kenosha, Wisconsin. I certainly remember Armistice Day, for in November 1930, in the eleventh month, on the eleventh day, at twenty minutes after eleven, we welcomed Roger Merrill Correll. I had just gone through the longest delivery I had ever had, **thirty six hours.** What a blessed relief. Yes, now I could rest.

Mother and Dad were often with us when we needed someone, and we surely did now, for as usual, we had a house full of guests. But, alas, at this time we also had a house full of sickness. One young preacher had the mumps. Our three older children and some of the guests had the chicken pox. And here the lady of the house was in bed with a new baby.

I don't know how long before Robert, Rebecca, and Roselyn were fretting and crying, wanting to "scratch the itching." It is usually not a very serious time, and then it is all over. Well, it was like that for everyone but Rebecca. She continued to have problems and complained about her ear. The doctor discovered a "pox" down inside her ear. It went from wanting to scratch to infection. Then began a constantly running ear infection. There seemed to be no remedy. If doctors had only known then what they know now. For years, Rebecca had this problem, and with her ear full of cotton and pain that she couldn't describe, she was in tears many times a day. We were at a loss. What was the answer? We discovered when she went to school that she wasn't hearing as she should. They didn't have hearing aids for children in those days. Rebecca learned that it was better to let folks know you had a hearing problem than to think you were stupid or stuck up. She has lived with it all her life, and for years has worn a hearing aid in each ear.

Many years ago, when her youngest daughter, Kitty, was about six or seven, Rebecca was about to go out with her husband, Bob. She had her hair up on top of her head. Kitty said to her mother, "Mama, I can see your hearing aids." Rebecca replied, "Kitty, I can see your glasses." "But that is different," answered Kitty. Rebecca went on to explain that Kitty wore glasses to see better and that she wore hearing aids to hear better. I have thought of this when I hear the advertising for hearing aids making a big deal out of "you can hardly see them." It goes without saying, when your children suffer, so do the mother and father. I, of course, can never cover them all.

I would just like to add, when we have problems, so much depends on what we do about it. May I say, Rebecca went to Cuba in her sophomore year. She stayed with Mom and Dad Correll on the mission station. In spite of her difficulty of hearing, she learned to speak Spanish (that isn't easy even when you can hear) and she learned dress making. Most important, she learned to be able to make her own patterns by looking at the ladies magazine, making the sleeves like one, the skirt like another, etc., and putting them all together. This came in handy as she made most of the clothes for her six children.

Helen Rowena (Penny)

I was thinking of my baby girl and a dark day in her life. She graduated from Taylor University, majoring in education. Later she got her Master's Degree at Bowling Green, Ohio. She has taught school for over thirty years. She was even in the 1971 book, "Outstanding Young Women of America", and has received many awards and honors. But, the dark shadows came when she was thirty-three years old. She discovered a lump in her breast. The doctor put her in the hospital, the lump was removed and they discovered it was benign. While she was still in the hospital, there was **cancer down under her breast**. They took her to surgery again. What a dark day it was when she came out of the operation and was told it was a radical operation and they took the whole breast.

How she wanted her Mom and Dad. She didn't know it was that serious when they first examined her. We could not be reached, for we were on a missionary trip. The doctors wouldn't wait. We knew nothing about it until it was over. We were devastated. We couldn't wait to get home to her. All the while as I was remembering my "baby girl" (even if she was 33 years old), I was thinking back to when she was around five years old. She would wait for me to come and tuck her covers in after she had gone to bed. She would leave them off on purpose so I would come and sing, and pray for her and give her a good night kiss.

But my girl came through with flying colors after her dark valley and for years, she worked with the Cancer Association in demonstrating "it's not the end of the world."

More Cancer

But there are more rivers to cross. We got a call from our son, Roger. He was in his fifties at the time. He said he was going to the hospital for a very serious operation.

I took a plane as soon as I could get one to reach him before surgery. He was so glad to see me and we did get to have prayer before they rolled him away.

I am sure that a great many people experience that fearfully long, anxious waiting period that tests your faith. I sat with his wife and prayed, and thought, and remembered. I looked back to earlier days, when Roger was a little towheaded guy about two and a half years old. He was singing reverently with his eyes turned heavenward, "I'm longing to go, I'm longing to go. When the trumpet shall sound from the mansions on high, I'll leave without saying good-bye."

Then I remembered how he would sing on our radio program when he was ten. We called him Radio Rog. But then I remember the most wonderful night of all. I believe it was Easter of 1980. He called us late that night and said, "Mother, did you hear the bells ringing today?" I said, "You mean because it is Easter?" He said, "No, Mother, it was because both Dona and I gave our hearts to the Lord today." What more wonderful news could you get than that? And now the dark shadows had come.

It sometimes seems forever before you finally hear the results. The doctor came, in fact, several doctors came, as they told about the long procedure Roger had been through. Roger had gone into the hospital with the word he might have a problem in his bowels. But now the doctors were telling us (I won't try to give it in medical terms) that they took a portion of the bowel out which had a malignant tumor. Second, they took out the right kidney and a rib. Third, they removed the gall bladder.

There were other things I can't describe, but my heart bled as I tried to realize the suffering and pain.

That was in 1988. In 1989, he was back again with cancer of the bladder. Twice, he has been in for chemotherapy.

There is one good thing that came out of it. Roger had been hopelessly addicted to cigarettes, but the doctor said, "There is too much at stake for more cigarettes." Praise the Lord, he hasn't had one since.

Many prayers had gone up for Roger, and there was wonderful news. Time after time as he went back for tests, the answer came back, no return of cancer. Praise the Lord.

These have been a few illustrations of facing sickness, but when did we as a family face death?

Facing Death

We are still talking about my life as a mother.

It is strange, but I was thinking about something that happened back in the early 1930's when we were in Kenosha, Wisconsin. Our four older children were quite small yet. We lived in the outskirts of the city. We had a little dog that was loved by all. One day I heard such weeping and sobbing. Sidney Robert came running in, utterly grief stricken. "Teddy is dead, Teddy is dead," he sobbed. We all ran to the edge of the road where a car had hit their beloved doggie. For all of them, the pain was very real. We gently picked up the broken body of this little animal that had brought so much joy and fun to all of the family. We found a cardboard box that was big enough for him. We laid a piece of colored cloth in it, then laid Teddy in it. They gathered some flowers to put in with him. Then a hole was dug big enough for the box and it was gently put in the ground. We all stood around holding hands while the tears flowed down our faces. We thanked the dear Lord for letting us have dear Teddy for this long. We would miss him very much, but we were glad he was not suffering. And now, Lord, heal our hearts and help us to remember how much you love us. Amen. These little ones would know the pain of missing someone or something they had loved.

Our First Family Death

I remember the first time death struck our immediate family. Our daughter, Roselyn, had married one of the wonderful young men of our church, Norville Kellar. It was during the Korean war and "Bud" was in the Air Force, stationed in Texas. His job was that of a mechanic. Roselyn transferred to a hospital in Wichita Falls to continue her nurses training. Those were very busy but very happy days. Bud thought he would get to stay here for the duration and work on planes, but the day came when he got the word that he was to be sent overseas. They tried to cram a lifetime into a few days before their newly established home would be broken up. Then a soldier husband waved good-bye and disappeared into the sky. The courageous wife returned to her duties as a student nurse there in Wichita Falls, Texas. The future would be brighter and their hope of working hand in hand for the Lord would be fulfilled. But we don't always know the future or the will of God.

It was almost a year that Bud did his work with the 34th Bomb Squadron. He had achieved the rank of T/Sgt. and was made crew chief. I remember a letter I received from him that was so filled with exuberance. "Mom," he had written, "it won't be long until my time is over and I can come home to my sweet wife. I can hardly wait."

In the meantime, I had left for Europe to be on the Youth For Christ team. I had taken my daughter, Penny, with me. She wasn't twelve yet.

We were in Switzerland when I got an urgent message from my husband and a phone call. "Honey, we have had a very sad thing happen. Bud was killed in a plane crash in Japan. They were on a routine flight and hit the mountain in the fog. Roselyn is devastated. I am flying to bring her back home, but she needs both of us. Come as soon as you can."

We had conducted funerals and had comforted others, but this was our first taste of death to come to us as a family. Penny and I did return immediately, and how our heart bled for our dear Roselyn.

Sidney went to Texas and helped her to leave Wichita Falls. He drove her back in their car. At nights, he would hold her close as she sobbed and asked, "Daddy, why?" How do people face times like this without the Lord, when things seem so unfair, and their hopes and dreams crash in a heap? What does the future hold? It is very difficult, as many military wives know. You are grieving without a body there to touch. Then there is the wait and wait and wait, endlessly, until finally his casket comes with his body and his belongings are returned. Even now you can't open it to get just one more look and to say your good-byes.

Somewhere through the haze, there were bright moments in this time of sorrow. You did have the consolation that he was with the Lord. Inside this box was just the house he lived in. Some day they would be together again. God's promises never fail.

But we went through the funeral services and stood together by the open grave. We listened to the Military Gun Salute and heard the taps play their solemn notes. Who could take away the ache that was there? I felt it very deeply, and I was only the mother-in-law. But here are Roselyn's own words that she gave in thanking the many who had held her close during her time of sorrow. "I confess I asked the question many of you have asked, 'Why Lord?' But now I know it is not for us to know everything down here. I am thankful my husband was a sweet Christian. Someday I will see him again. I am glad I have that hope. Another thing, I believe I shall be a better nurse after passing through this valley. You can get pretty hardened to death when you are working around it every day. Now I believe I can do what the scripture says, *'Weep with those who weep.'* I want to be more compassionate to those who suffer. God bless all of you who have passed through the waters of suffering."

This was not the last time we would face deep personal grief. Just four years later, in 1957, we walked through the valley once again.

Our Eldest Son

We were so proud of our eldest son, Sidney Robert. When he was eight years, old he knew God wanted him for a **missionary**. He never lost his vision. He so enjoyed the visiting missionaries that came to our home and church. In fact, one of them, Dr. Harry Strachen of the Latin American Mission, invited Robert to come to Costa Rica and stay with the Latin boys there. This he did in 1942. He was there a whole year. He would go with the missionaries on their different trips. He learned so many things and wrote letters verifying that he so wanted to go as a missionary. And he wanted to go to a very **difficult place**. During that year, he learned Spanish **fluently** and that next year in high school, he took **first prize in the State of Ohio**.

In his senior year of high school, he had a goal to run the mile. To do this takes desire, discipline and determination! These were the key words in the making of a champion. Paul the Apostle said, *"Do you not know that those who run in a race all run, but one receives the prize? Run in such a way that you may obtain."* I Corinthians 9:24. It was

Robert's desire to be a **miler** like Gil Dodds. In his junior year, as he began his training, the coach said it would be up to him and his desire, for he was **not a natural born runner**. He had real discipline. He watched what he ate, went to bed early and sacrificed much of his social life to run, run, run. Very near us was McKinley Park, with its cinder track. Almost every morning, Roselyn went along to time him. I rode my bicycle around the track with him to encourage him. It was pure determination that caused him to never give up.

The day of the big event finally came. Each school had sent their top qualifiers. The University of Dayton stadium was filled with parents and friends from all over the city. Sitting with our family was Reverend and Mrs. Wendall Boyer (our associates at the Christian Tabernacle). The tension was too great and I just couldn't sit there and wait, so I got up and made my way to the finish line. After much anticipation, the race finally began. I beamed with motherly pride as Robert made his first lap around the field. I knew he didn't see me but **that was my boy** out there. I was about to burst. But then before you knew it came that last lap. My heart was pounding and pulse raced. Hanging over the fence as far as it was humanly possible, I saw him coming toward the finish line. He was a little behind the leader, then suddenly he began passing him. I screamed, "Come on, Robert. You can make it!" A few dizzying seconds later, it was over. **Our son, Sidney Robert, was the city champ.** When he came to where we all were, happy, exhilarated and exhausted, but with a darling smile on his face, he laughed and said, "Mother, I heard you scream over the whole stadium crowd. I had to win!" Needless to say, there was a celebration.

I give you the article that was in the Dayton paper:

Dayton's Fastest Miler To Become Evangelist
By Bob Gibson

"Gil Dodds, the Flying Parson, who has piled up mile victories hand over fist in the past few months of the indoor track season, has a counterpart in Dayton high school track circles. He is Sidney Correll, 17 year-old Fairview senior, who is just about as near a carbon copy of the nation's best as could be found.

Like Dodds, both Correll's mother and father are members of the clergy, preaching at the Christian Tabernacle and again like Dodds, Correll looks toward the ministry for his life work.

Last Tuesday, the bespectacled miler ran the fastest mile that **local cinders** have seen in well on to **five years** when he toured the four laps of McKinley park in 4:41.5, just three seconds over the city record of 4:38.

Correll's ambitions of becoming a minister are likely to be carried out for he has a punctured eardrum which will keep him out of the armed services.

Five feet, seven inches and only 130 pounds, Correll started running at Fairview last year. As a junior, he showed a natural ability in distance running and it wasn't long before he proved to be **the top miler in the Bulldog field.**"

The City Champ

It was a wonderful time with all the friends and loved ones. When things had quieted down, we quickly sent a cable to Sidney in South America. "Robert is city champ," the cable read. My husband would know what that meant. Sidney Robert wanted to go to Harvard. Sidney had said, "Son, if you win the City Mile, I'll send you to Harvard!" So now he had the good news.

In August of 1944, when Robert was eighteen, he went to Harvard. He was on Gil Dodds' track team. Things were going great, and then he injured his foot and could no longer run. Eventually he felt perhaps it was best, for now he could concentrate harder on his studies.

How can I tell in a few words the many things that followed for Sidney Robert? In the midst of his time at Harvard, a wonderful opportunity arose. He regretted keenly that he was not able to join the military because of a punctured ear drum. He thought it was important to serve in some way. One day he picked up his Harvard Service News and read an appeal to young college men to give their services to the war effort. They wanted some of the fellows to go with the American Field Service and drive ambulances. This was very appealing to him. He said, "I believe there are two practical things to be learned which will be of good use later in the mission field - first aid and auto mechanics. You know, Mother, the boys I meet will be badly hurt. Their vitality and, perhaps, morale will be at the lowest point of their lives. If I can say some word of encouragement to them and convey the peace of our loving Savior, then my work and even my life will have a real purpose."

He joined the group and we didn't hear from him for a very long time. When we did it was from Calcutta, India. I wish I could share some of his letters with you, but let me read from one in which he wrote, "Dad and Mom, for years I have had a goal of being a missionary, but something has happened to me here. After being constantly surrounded by the sick, needy and dying, I now want to be a **medical missionary** so I can help **physically** as well as **spiritually**."

After he returned to the states, he decided not to go back to Harvard, but to go to Wheaton College and become a pre-med student. Before leaving for school in August of 1946, he married his childhood sweetheart, Betty Oaks. They made a commitment, not only to each other, but also to the Lord and whichever mission field He chose for them to serve in.

After two hard years, Robert graduated "Cum Laude." The beautiful part was that my husband was the one delivering the Convocation address. He looked so grand, marching along all decked out in cap and gown, beside the president of Wheaton, Dr. V. Edmond.

Betty was in nurses training at West Suburban Hospital. The next step was for Robert to get into medical school. That wouldn't be easy, but he applied to several different schools.

He was finally accepted into two different medical schools. He chose the Boston School of Medicine. He was one of **75** students accepted out of **1500 applicants**.

The main reason he wanted to go to Boston was to attend the Park Street Church where Dr. Harold Ockenge was pastor. Robert had gone there when he was in Harvard. What a fantastic missionary church it was! The depth of spiritual and biblical foundation he received was equal to a formal theological training. Sidney Robert was also president of Inter-varsity. Betty continued her training, and graduated from Massachusetts Memorial Hospital.

Doctor R. S. Roseberry

About this time Dr. R. S. Roseberry was a guest in our home and church. He was a veteran missionary from Africa with the Christian Missionary Alliance. He told such fantastic stories of their work in what was then called French West Africa (later, after Independence, it was called Mali). But he told how great the need was, and pleaded for workers who would "catch the vision".

It just so happened that our son was home from the Boston school of Medicine. Dr. Roseberry asked him what his future intentions were. (Robert had mentioned that he wanted to be a missionary doctor.) So Sidney Robert said, "I have several places in mind, one of which is the Severance Hospital in Seoul, Korea. I have also been invited to the Lambie Hospital outside Jerusalem." Dr. Roseberry made a real appeal and said, "Son, we really need you in Africa." From that moment, the burden of "the dark continent" was laid on Robert's heart.

Sidney Robert Correll, M.D.

The time passed quickly and now another graduation day had arrived. Sidney and I drove to Boston. Betty was six months pregnant with Stevie, but she and I helped Sidney Robert get his cap and gown on for the big march. It was to be held in the great Boston Gardens. There were hundreds and hundreds of people there from all different groups.

The glorious day was June 8, 1953. At 10:30am, the great organ began the concerto in B Flat and went on to Bach's Prelude as the processional started. The graduates were coming while the organist, Samuel Walter, played the overture to the Occasional Oratorio.

What a sight to see, the ocean of caps and gowns. It was almost like being in church as those many voices lifted in singing, "O Worship the King, all glories above." When the sheepskins were being handed out, and Robert's class was coming, my husband stepped down close enough to get a good picture. Our son was now a medical doctor. Some of the other M.D.'s said, "Well, Correll, where are you going to hang your shingle?" He replied, "Where they really need me, in Africa."

Another M.D. asked, "Why waste your life there? You'll not even get enough to pay back your tuition." But our young doctor never lost his goal.

Betty had graduated with an R.N. degree. Then the baby, Stephen Ralph, was born. Sidney Robert went on to become a **surgeon**. Then after an itinerary in many churches across the country, they were ready for their journey. They had their farewell service at Christian Tabernacle in Dayton. What a service! He was trained as a physician, not a theologian, but what a message! His text was from Colossians, chapters one and two. There wasn't a dry eye in the place. The presence of the Lord just hung over the auditorium. He told how they meant business with God. "If God sees fit to take our son, Stevie, then we are prepared to give him. If the Lord takes Betty, she is on the altar. If the Lord should require my life, I am prepared to lay it down." Later, there was a beautiful farewell service following the church service.

His Last Message To Us

I would like to share what Sidney Robert said to his father and me just before he and his family left. We have always been very close. He said, "Mother and Dad, I am going to miss you so very much. You have been wonderful parents and I am so proud of you. I am so glad you raised me to love God and His work. Africa is a great distance, and it will be a long time before we can come home on furlough. If the Lord takes you or daddy in the meantime, we won't be able to come back. You have our love, and we will meet again some day." Our tears mingled. Part of our heart went with them, but we were at peace with their wonderful consecration.

On December 20, 1955, the young doctor, the young nurse and their little son left New York on the S.S. Rossville, headed for Dakar Africa. Church members, family and many friends were at the station to see them off. There is so much more I could tell you, but I wanted you to have this background so that you would know the extent of the loss when it came.

They were in Dakar for a year and a half. He worked in the French hospital there, doing more surgery in less than two years than many surgeons do in a lifetime. He worked in conditions our American doctors have never seen.

During that time they also had another son, John Richard. In their second year they moved to an area Sidney Robert had found earlier, a place at the **end of the world**, the village of Kenieba in Mali, Africa. There was no hospital within a radius of 500 miles in any direction. He was so needed.

Now let me go back to where I started, with our eldest son. I know all of this has been a story in itself, but at this point we are talking about death.

The big blow came when we received a cable from Betty, "Sidney Robert badly burned - **pray**." This word from the other end of the world left us in shock. The questions rushed in. **What happened? Where did it happen? Were others involved? How badly was he burned?**

The next day, we appealed to our radio audience. Hundreds were praying, all over radioland and among our church members. Sidney Robert was so important to the work. God just couldn't take him. So much depended on him. He had studied **twelve years to prepare to be the doctor for these people**. What about the hospital? We had been raising money to send to help them. Believe me, we cried out to the Lord. We were so positive we would get an encouraging word from Betty. But three days later we got the cable, **"Sidney Robert went to be with the Lord Tuesday morning."**

How could this happen? We were at home on the farm when the message was phoned to us. My dear husband fell prostrate on the floor crying out **"Oh, God, what a loss, what a loss! Oh God, why?"**

We had never sent a missionary to the field that was **better prepared** in every way. He had everything. He was a doctor, a surgeon, a linguist, a musician and a gentle, kind compassionate missionary. He had so little time to minister.

All the family came together immediately (except Rebecca who was in Louisville, Kentucky, and so distressed she could not get there). We all cried on each others shoulders and asked God to send the Comforter we so badly needed. The report of Sidney Robert's death was an item on the evening news, and friends began to call.

An interesting thing happened that evening I would like to relate. My husband remembered that we had a nurse that was about to leave to work with Sidney Robert in Africa. I believe she had been a Lt. Nurse in the Navy. Her name was Ada Yarnall. My husband went to the phone and called to tell her the sad news of Robert's homegoing. Then he said, " I know you are about to leave for Africa, but I wanted you to know that if you feel you would rather change your plans, we would understand." There was not a moment's hesitancy as Ada replied, "Dr. Correll, God called me to Africa, not Dr. Robert, so my obligation still stands. I am still needed there." That is consecration!

God met us through the night and gave us courage and strength. The next morning Sidney left for speaking engagements in the East, in Boston. He spoke with a bleeding heart to the young people in the congregation, giving them a challenge to "pick up the torch and carry it forward". There was a **landslide of young people** who made a dedication to the Lord's ministry. In fact, it was repeated in every service, from place to place.

In the afternoon I faced **my challenge**. Would I conduct my radio program, "Wings Over Dayton", or would I get the staff to do it? I knew I had to relate to the listeners that **what we had talked about for others worked for us, too**. I think we had our largest audience ever, for they had heard the news report about Sidney Robert's death.

So at two o'clock, I was right there. I will admit I spoke through tears that day. I read the scripture from John 12:24, *"Except a corn of wheat fall into the ground and die, it abideth alone. But if it die, it bringeth forth much fruit."* God just poured His blessing on the broadcast, and we had so much wonderful response to it. There are so many things I would like to tell, but there is neither time nor space.

Our son had been flown out by helicopter to the Government Hospital in Bamako, Africa, which was also the capital city. He was buried there with the understanding that we would come out and bring his body to the mission station. He would be buried between the hospital (which wasn't built yet) and the chapel. Dr. Correll and I flew there and brought his body back to Kenieba. We knew he would want to be buried there among the people he had come to know and love.

As we stood around the grave, we were surrounded by our missionaries on the station and so many Africans. They, too, were grieving over the loss. I will never forget one tall African man who said to my husband, "You lost a son, but we lost a father." One village's people had wept for three days when they learned their doctor was dead. He was the only doctor for so many miles. Before Sidney Robert passed away he told his wife, Betty, "Remember Philippians 1:21, *For me to live is Christ and to die is gain."* This verse was put on his grave in three languages, English, French and Bambara. Only heaven will reveal the gain of a life laid down.

The last day we were in Kenieba, we gathered around the grave once more and renewed our vows of consecration to the Lord. The missionaries, my husband and I all held hands and sang with tears, "How Great Thou Art"!

I have been talking about life as a **mother**. Before we close this theme, let me speak as a **grandmother**.

A Lovely Granddaughter

Our son, Kenneth (Kenny) Correll, came to live with us when he was **eleven years old**. His younger days were not the happiest, so we were delighted when he became a part of our family. I am sure there were many happy days in his growing up years, but I remember a day which was one of the most important and happiest days of his life. It was the day his daughter, Dawn, was born. She just seemed to fill his whole life. In fact, he was jealous of anyone else touching her. He didn't even want me to change his baby's diapers. He did it himself. The mother, Sue, just smiled.

Through the years, as this little girl grew up, there were many pictures taken of her, and she was the apple of their eye. They lived in St. Petersburg, Florida. A number of times when my husband would be in town, he would call and ask if Dawn would like to go to lunch with her grandfather? She always did. He treated her like a little lady, and after lunch he would say, "Let us just look at these pretty things over here. You pick out any thing you would like to have and we will buy it." She did, and it wasn't always cheap. (Smile)

A few years later she was going to Sunday School faithfully, every Sunday. One day her teacher asked her if she would like to give her heart to Christ? She prayed with the teacher to let Jesus come into her heart.

Dawn grew up. She got a job, and finally had her own apartment. She was **so beautiful**. When I would go to Florida I, too, would see her when I would visit with her parents. She was now in her twenties.

Then one day Sue called me, **"Mom, Dawn was killed in an auto accident today."** I guess one is never prepared for the "Grim Reaper". I hurt so much, for though I had lost a son, I had six other children. This was Kenny and Sue's **only child,** and she was in the prime of her youth.

As I took Sue into my arms before the funeral she said, "Mom, Dawn is with Grandpa now." My husband had been buried just the year before. Dawn was the first of the grandchildren to go.

74

In relating this story, I wanted to pass on to you a poem that I had read on my radio program, especially during the war. May it touch someone reading this who has felt bitter at their loss of an only son or daughter. I am thankful to say, though they were very sad, crushed and lonely, I don't believe Ken and Sue were bitter with God.

Where Was God?
The door bell rings.... A telegram
For which a father springs;
Then, white faced, sinks upon a chair,
Unable quite to face his wife
Who's spent the night in ceaseless supplication
For her son, their **only son.**

In bitterness he seeks his church,
And to his pastor speaks of
Pain and grief and doubt.
"You preach of God, His love and care;
Then why this loss, we cannot bear
Of this our son, our **only son?**"

"Where was God when death stretched forth his rod
To him we loved so well?"
"I think," the answer softly came,
"When death befell your son,
That God was in the very place
He was so long ago, When death befell
HIS SON, HIS ONLY SON."

At this writing, all seven of my children are grown (two of them are with the Lord). I have twenty-two grandchildren (counting Dawn in heaven), thirty great grand children and one great, great grandson.

I am thankful to report that all of our children have received Christ, and we look forward to the great meeting on the other side.

I'd like to leave you with this poem:

Are All The Children In?
Are all the children in? The night is falling,
And the storm clouds gather in the threatening west;
The lowing cattle seek a friendly shelter;

The bird flies to her nest;
The thunder crashes; wilder grows the tempest;
And darkness settles o'er the fearful din;
Come, shut the door and gather round the hearthstone.
Are all the children in?

Are all the children in? The night is falling;
When gilded sin doth walk about the streets.
For, at the last it biteth like a serpent.
Poisoned are the stolen sweets,
Oh parents, guard the feet of inexperience;
Too prone to wonder in the paths of sin!
Oh, shut the door of love against temptation!
Are all the children in?

Are all the children in? The night is falling,
The night of death is hastening on a pace
The Lord is calling, "Enter thou thy chamber,
And tarry there a pace."
And when He comes, the King in all His Glory,
Who died the shameful death, our hearts to win,
Oh, may the gates of heaven shut about us,
With all the children in!

By Elizabeth Rosser

Last family picture taken before Robert and Betty left for Africa

Leaving for Africa

Dawn, Sue and Ken

77

This picture of the Correll family was taken in 1946, in Dayton, Ohio. We had a radio program each Saturday called "The Happy Family". The back row is Helen, Sidney and Roger Merrill. The front row is Rebecca Ruth, Roselyn Maybelle, Helen Rowena (Penny), and Sidney Robert. The baby in arms is Michael Richard Todd.

Sidney Robert became a missionary doctor and served the Lord in Africa. He had two children. He lost his life in a gasoline expolsion there.

Rebecca had a family of six children besides getting a business degree, and works in a bank.

Roselyn had four children and became a nurse.

Roger had three children and became a Certified Public Accountant.

Penny got a Masters Degree and has taught school for over thirty years. She has two children.

The baby, Michael, studied music education as a major in college. For years, he was a musician and entertainer. He has two children. He dedicated his life to the Lord's service. Since the death of his father, he is not in his father's arms as you see in the picture, but is walking in his father's footsteps as president of Correll Missionary Ministries.

Chapter 12

My Life As An Ordained Minister

What is it to be ordained?

*"And He **ordained** (appointed (NKJ)) twelve that they should be with Him and they might send them forth to preach, and to have power to heal sicknesses, and to cast out devils."* Mark 3:14.

*" You have not chosen me but I have chosen you, and **ordained** you that you should go forth and bring forth fruit."* John 15:16. To **ordain** is to set apart. Christ gave them authority.

As I am writing this I have referred to my "Star Book for Ministers". It is pretty badly worn by now. I was interested in what it said under the title of ordination. Chapter 13 says, "It must be kept in mind that ordination does not make a minister of Christ. It endows him with no gifts, graces or capabilities which he did not before possess. Nor does it impart any ecclesiastical authority; for those who ordain have none to give. **His call to the ministry must be from God.**"

The ceremony of ordination is a recognition of God's divine calling to the work. It is also an approval of the church's action and of one's entrance upon the duties of the office. Of course, it is needed as far as the State Government is concerned. The minister must be ordained and registered with the state to be able to perform marriages, etc.

The secret is God's call. Many a man or woman has gone into the pulpit as a vocation or maybe to fulfill a parents wish, such as, "Son, I would love to have you become a preacher like your grandfather." But the most important thing is to have that constraining urge as the Apostle Paul had when he said, "Woe is me if I preach not the gospel." It is an overpowering assurance that God has called me and I dare do nothing less! **It has been this fact** that has kept me going straight on in the face of any opposition down through these many years.

I do not minimize ordination. It was a very special day when I knelt along with others at the Angeles Temple to receive the "laying on of hands", to be ordained a minister of the gospel. It is true that I was young, but I felt God's hand upon my life. I thought of Mary, who was ordained of God to bring Christ into the world. I felt I was being set aside to bring **that Christ to a lost and dying world.** Through the hands of those ordaining, I felt the hands of the Blessed Lord saying, "Go and I will be with you."

Why was I being ordained at the time and my husband was not? Because he was still in Bible School. I had already graduated. We were now pastoring a church that needed recognition from the state to fulfill all its duties. There were young people waiting to be married. (I will tell you more of this later.)

My husband certainly under stood that. Let me say right here, in case you think my husband was intimidated, that Sidney went on to graduate, be ordained, receive a doctorate (which I never did), and Sidney later received an FRGS or Fellow of the Royal Geographic Society because of the excellence of his missionary films. Just because I had my ordination did not mean I usurped authority over my husband, for **he always was head** of our home and the church. Our first pastorate was there in Fullerton, California. We were there for one year and a half. I cannot remember once attending a board meeting, except to sit and observe. I could have, but didn't wish to. I can still remember how amazed I was at the respect those board members had for my husband. Even though he was much younger than any of them, there was never a note of dissension. My husband was a very special man. If this were the story of him, we would need volumes to tell it all, but this is my story, or the story of both of us as a team.

Paul, the apostle, was a very educated man, (he had sat at the feet of Gamalial), we don't find him mingling with the theologians or men of wisdom or the super educated. But he emphasized this: *"For Christ sent me to preach the gospel: not with wisdom of words, lest the cross of Christ should be made of none effect."* 1 Corinthians 1:17. Read the whole second chapter of I Corinthians.

Christ Sent Me To Preach. Wow! Where Do I Begin?

Let's start when I was sixteen years old. I had been in Bible School one year. During the summer, the students attended tent meetings. That year the group I was with was to go to Pasadena, California. That was very handy as I was still living there. This was in 1924. Everything was ready to open and I was to preach that very first night. You don't have to be ordained to preach! I don't remember what my text was, but I know there were converts.

The thing that made that night special is that **69 years later**, I was to meet a man in Van Nuys, California who had been in that meeting. He had gone with his parents that night to the tent revival. He was among those who wr to the altar and received Christ as his Savior.

80

For these last many years, he has been a deacon in the Church on the Way. But that night in Pasadena, he was 16 years old and I was 16 years old. When we met in California, we were both 85 years old.

"Preach the Word. Be instant in season and out of season." II Timothy 4:2. Preach the Word! How powerful! When Sidney and I began ministering in Fullerton, California, that was our motto: Preach the Word! Not our own wisdom or fine sermons, but God's Word is what a hungry world needs.

We were still in the tent, holding meetings and speaking every night. I would preach one night and Sidney would preach the next. We took turns leading the song service. The crowds kept coming. God kept blessing.

There was a group of people who had been so faithful, who said, "We want a regular church." So they helped us find a hall or store building right downtown on Commonwealth Avenue. We moved from our little home I told you about earlier to an apartment upstairs over the Hall. On Sundays we used our apartment as Sunday School Rooms.

One of our greatest opportunities was our street meetings. We held them right on the main corner of the city. The crowds grew larger each time, which was resulting in traffic jams. But did they run us off the streets? No way. The Chief of Police dispatched a special officer to that corner to direct the traffic, so the crowds could stand and listen, yet not disrupt the passing cars. As a result of that, not only were there many converts, but the special officer's son and daughter came to our services and were converted. Later, they went to Bible School. Best of all, the policeman and his wife also were converted. Can you believe what happened next? **The Chief of Police** himself was converted, and did a fantastic job of cleaning up some of the problems of the city.

There were pastors in town who would shake their heads and say, "How can they do it? They are just kids. We can't get that kind of crowds!" Maybe it was I Corinthians 1:27, *"But God hath chosen the foolish things of the world to confound the wise."*

In our meetings, I played the guitar and Sidney played the banjo. Later, Sidney took over the guitar, and it was his companion (next to me). He carried it around the world many times, and finally started taking the ukulele since it was easier to carry.

We had a packed crowd for every service at the hall. The church members said, "We must build now, we can't go on like this." So a lot was purchased and plans were soon under way for our first church (the first of many). Sidney and I drew up the plans for our dream church the way we thought it ought to be. It was to be built with donated labor. It didn't have posts in the auditorium, so there must be trusses. We figured on the platform, choir room and prayer room. Curtains were shown around platform and pulpit, the way they should be. We thought we had figured everything down to the smallest detail.

The lumber was on the lot when the men came to work on July 1, 1926. We had asked one of the carpenters to be in charge. We were thrilled and beaming. The carpenter looked around and said, "Where is the material for the foundation?" What foundation? You don't need foundations in California, do you? I guess we could be excused because we were eighteen and nineteen years old. We were thinking **basements** were not needed in California. All the men went home while Sidney got sand, gravel and cement to pour a foundation for the church. It was kind of silly, but many people have made no provision for Christ in their life and He is the foundation. "On Christ, the solid rock, I stand. All other ground is sinking sand."

Since we were going to be in a new church, we moved to a lovely four room house at 316 Wood Street. That is where our son was born. Incidentally, last year I went by and took pictures of the house on Wood Street, and I had the privilege of preaching in the beautiful **new** Foursquare Church and telling them how the church was started 67 years ago.

I wish I could tell you more of the wonderful times we had in that year and a half, but down in my husbands heart was the urge to pioneer. He wanted to do hard things for the Lord. He would say, "Honey, things are too easy here. We are liable to get into a rut and someone else can carry on here. Let's find a place where it is hard." After all, we were getting $25 a week. I wonder, if we had known then what we learned later, if we would have been so quick to move on. Those wonderful days in Fullerton were the sweet preparation for the storms that were to follow.

Sidney followed the convictions of his heart and looked for new fields to conquer. We heard of a little town further north in California called Pasa Robles. Two families had called Headquarters, requesting someone to come and start a church. They had nothing to offer us, no building to use for a church and no house to live in. But they wanted a church.

The dear people of the Fullerton Church pled with us, in tears, to please stay but, for some reason, we just couldn't. Our zeal was greater than our wisdom. We resigned and gave the church to other pastors.

With a six month old baby, a Ford car, a grandmother to support and very few belongings, we said good-bye and headed north. Pasa Robles was between Los Angeles and San Francisco. We were filled with anticipation and adventure. We found a little cottage on a corner, which must have been waiting for us. It wasn't large or spacious but, with the lovely things the Fullerton church had given us, we made it comfortable. The furniture wasn't much, but we weren't choosy.

The next thing we needed was a meeting place. There were no church buildings available. The only thing we could find was a building that had alternated between being a **sulfur bath house** and a **saloon**. This was prohibition time so it was now a bath house. What a mixture of smells - sulfur and stale beer!

We completely renovated it until it was quite a nice place to worship. The fact that the city needed the church was not disputed, but who would pay the price? The hearts of the people were adamant! Every tenth house was a "bootlegging joint". We advertised our meetings, but few people came. We decided we would just go hold a street meeting. Sidney played his banjo and I played the guitar. We played and sang and played and sang. People would deliberately walk on the other side of the street. Windows were lifted so people could listen, but when they heard it was gospel music, they slammed them shut like we had a plague or something. Sidney yodeled. A few people stopped, then rushed on. Were we discouraged? Yes. Would we give up? Never! There had to be a way. We remembered our training, "If the people don't come to you, go to them." We moved down in front of the pool hall. It was filled with men who were smoking, sneaking a drink, playing cards and pool. When we started to sing, they began to file out until the pool hall was almost empty. They listened attentively until they heard our testimony, a short message and an invitation to our meeting house. Surprisingly, a number of them followed us to the hall.

Our crowds began to increase. We were very happy that we were finally getting the interest of the people. A revival was in progress. A number of notable people were being converted. The offerings weren't much (as we certainly didn't have a paying church), so Sidney began to saw cord wood to sell. He got $4.00 for a stack of wood 4 feet high and 8 feet long. (I remember him saying, "My aching back!")

Even though we didn't have much ourselves, we always believed in hospitality. When a stranger, out of work, came by and was hungry, we couldn't turn him away. We shared what we had. Strangely though, the next day there would be another one, then another. We came to the conclusion there must be a mark on our front gate.

One night a poor soul needed sleep, so we fixed him up with a bed. In the morning he was gone, but he had left us some **cooties and bed bugs.** We were beginning to get wiser. We still had the wood pile where Sidney sawed wood. So instead of my husband doing all the work, when a stranger came by, we suggested he chop a little wood. It was amazing how the hungry stopped coming to our door.

We had discovered that our little son, Sidney Robert, needed goat milk to survive. It was forty cents a quart, so Sidney started looking for a goat. He found a beautiful valley with a broken down ranch house and large pens of bleating goats. Then he found Old Man Bell. Sure, he had some dandy goats and he would fix him up. Old Man Bell said, "By the way, would you like a job herding goats? I'll **give** you two goats if you want to start working for me." He said he had an old drunk that had run off on him, and he needed help. He said he would give Sidney **twelve cents an hour for a 12 hour day**. Sidney thought, "Well, that is not very much, but it's a way to get milk for the baby," so he accepted the job. Old Man Bell hadn't even asked him if he had ever herded goats before.

My husband has gotten into some funny situations before by acting on impulse. So, here he was with two goats to milk. Who was going to milk them? **I WAS!** He had to go herd goats and fortunately, as a girl, I had milked goats.

Later, Sidney tried to describe what it was like to herd five hundred goats over mountains, thickets and brush. He thought you tried to kept them together, like sheep. This was not so! These goats literally climbed the low California scrub oaks. They would scatter in every direction. He would look and look and could not find them but, in the evening, they all came home. (He did lose a few of the kids to some mountain lions that were in the area.)

In the meantime, I was taking care of the church, preaching, milking goats, and also taking care of the baby and my grandmother.

Several weeks later, the original goat herder came back. The sun was just setting when he came toward the cabin. He gruffly introduced himself as he sat down. Sidney had a roaring fire going and had fixed some corn with bacon strips cut up in it. The man sniffed the food and proceeded to help himself. He looked around the cabin and came up with a bottle of whiskey. He saw Sidney's guitar and demanded he play. Sidney strummed a bit on the guitar and this guy was leering at him.

Finally, Sidney understood what the herder was trying to say. He snarled through his teeth, "I'm going to **kill** you!" Never having been killed before, he didn't know what to expect, but he was getting plenty scared.

Feeling he might soon die, Sidney decided he better do something important right now! He got out his Bible and started reading scripture on hell fire. He described hell in every lucid and factual way he could. The goat herder began to cry, so Sidney got him down on his knees and prayed for him. The man promised to go straight. In fact, he went to the door and threw his bottle out into the dark.

I could go on, but that was Sidney's last day herding goats. He went to Old Man Bell and reported. Bell laughed and said, "I knew he would be back." Needless to say, Sidney was very glad to be back home. We were certainly getting an education in the "School of Hard Knocks". The wood cutting and the goat herding was behind us, and our baby was getting better.

We now set about in earnest to build the church, not a building, but a congregation. Our dedicated chapel was now being filled, and we were having a revival. Sidney appointed board members to get involved and assist us. This led to the first real testing with a board member. There was one board member who felt it was his duty to keep the preacher in his place.

(Remember Sidney was not even 20 years old yet.) In Fullerton every board member was like a father to us. What a shock and surprise to meet a man whose sole purpose was to make life miserable for the pastor. You could not please him. Sidney would work so hard on his sermons, and after every one this man would criticize. His punishing blow would always be, "With out holiness no man shall see the Lord."

The payoff came after several months when Sidney decided it was his special duty to call on this board member and pray with him. So he got in the old Ford and drove out through the Pasa Robles mountains and came to the board member's farm. He was in the field with three head of mules. Sidney walked across the plowed ground behind him when, all of a sudden, something terrible happened. The mules became contrary, but it wasn't only the mules that began to act up. It was the board member who was always saying, "Without holiness, no man can see the Lord." You should have heard that man cuss. Sidney had heard "mule skinners" cuss when he was a boy, but **no mule skinner ever used those words more fluently than that board member.**

For a few moments Sidney stood riveted to the furrow, then he turned and ran back to the car. He was not afraid of that man any more. Arriving home he grabbed his Thompson Chain Reference Bible and got his sermon for next Sunday morning. As he preached, he fastened his eyes on this old hypocrite and preached the stormiest message on the text "Without holiness, no man shall see the Lord." Strangely, the board member never used that scripture on him again. In fact, Sidney never lost the man from the church but he became his friend. (That was my husband's way of doing things. He attempted to win even his enemies without compromising his stand.)

The Lord gave us many wonderful experiences there in Pasa Robles and things were now moving, even in this difficult and almost impossible town. As I said, we were having a revival. I suppose our most outstanding convert was the mystery woman from the mystery house.

There was this questionable house with a high fence around it. The place was only one street south and a block and a half west from where we lived. Whenever anyone talked about it, it was in hushed tones and whispers. You see, these were prohibition days and there weren't wide open doors to get liquor or drinks. You had to know someone, or someplace where bootlegging was done.

How many times we had seen staggering men and women coming out of the gate of that house? You had to know the "password" to get in. There were strange rumors of homes being broken and lives being wrecked, all centered around this woman. Mrs. McNeal was regarded as public enemy number one.

The law just didn't seem to do any thing about it, whether it was sneaking it during prohibition or getting it through the open swinging doors. The youth were being enticed and ruined by it. But the greatest weapon against it is prayer. So the Christians joined us and we prayed, "Lord God, break up this joint! Please, Lord, souls are going out into eternity lost and without You. Please Lord, do something!"

How beautifully the Lord answered prayer. Each service in our chapel building ended with a glorious altar service, with men and women finding God.

I will never forget this one night when the place was packed. People were venturing to come from all walks of life, from the homeless in the streets, to the business people. Tears were flowing freely in repentance and rejoicing. Several drunkards were kneeling at the altar. Then someone whispered to me, "Guess who is here? Mrs. McNeal!"

She was not only at the meeting, she was at the altar. **Miracles do happen!** We were singing the old song,

> "Oh happy day, that fixed my choice
> On Thee, my Savior and my God.
> Oh may this glowing heart rejoice
> And tell its raptures all abroad.
>
> Happy day, happy day
> When Jesus washed my sins away.
> He taught me how to watch and pray,
> And live rejoicing every day.
> Happy day, happy day
> When Jesus washed my sins away."

About that time I heard someone cry out, "Oh, Mrs. Correll, Mrs. Correll, did you hear me? Did you hear me? Do you know, Reverend and Mrs. Correll, this is the first time I have sung for twenty years? I haven't opened my mouth to sing since I was a girl. I got away from God and I have lived an awful life." She stood and faced the audience. "I don't need to tell you people the kind of a life I have lived. You all know me. But, oh, I have met God tonight and it is all different now. This is the first time I have been happy in years. I have been living in sin and leading others on the same road. I have caused plenty of grief in this city, but from now on, I am going God's way." What a blow to the devil. This is what we had prayed for, but never dreamed it would happen this way.

After the meeting we talked to her. She said, "I know it is asking a lot, but I would like you to come by my house. I want to talk to you about my future. I will fix a little lunch and then I want you to help me pray." What would Jesus do? We knew for the Bible tells us what He did. Isn't it wonderful that Jesus is a friend of sinners? We never gave a thought as to what people would think seeing us go into this mystery house. I will **never forget** the sensation when we ventured to go see the mystery woman. The old gate **squeeeaaaked** as we entered. We did not need a password. The place was hung with heavy drapes and filled with sweet smelling incense. We had eaten in some strange places, but this topped them all. Big dogs guarded the place. Our eyes bugged at everything we saw as we remembered all the things we had heard about this place. We had to pinch ourselves to think we were actually here. We were rapidly becoming educated and enlightened.

Finally she sat down and with tears in her eyes she said, "Oh, I have never been so happy. I feel like I am just beginning to live. Here is what I am up against. This was, of course, my bread and butter. Now, do you see all these empty liquor bottles?" (There were rows of empty ones.) "I get them filled with that awful stuff (moonshine liquor) and then I sell them. I will certainly not fill them again but what should I do with the empty ones? Should I sell them?" I suppose she could have sold them, but I was surprised to hear my husband say, "Why, Mrs. McNeal, I will buy them." I was flabbergasted and I thought, **with what?** I could not believe he said that. However, I was to learn never be surprised at what my husband does. Sidney asked her what she could get for them? I think it was ten cents and that was a lot of money in those days. She looked as startled as I did, and said, "Oh, Reverend Correll, you will buy them?" "Yes," he said, "under one condition. We take them down to the old riverbed and break every one of them on one of those big boulders and shout, 'Hallelujah', as loud as you can with every one you break." I knew he did not have time to think that one through, but her eyes beamed as she said, "Do you mean that?"

We went out the back gate, down the pathway with her as she carried baskets full of dirty old liquor bottles to a very remote area. We found a big boulder with a deep hole beside it, and we watched as she threw the first bottle and shouted, "Hallelujah!", then the second bottle and "Hallelujah!" Before she got through, we were all shouting, "Hallelujah!" with every bottle. I don't remember how we paid for them, but I am sure we did.

This story has a grand ending. Mrs. McNeal became one of the finest workers and singers in the church. Instead of sending folks to hell, she was giving them a helping hand to glory. She got a good, honest and legitimate job and became a fine citizen, all because she met Jesus. Like the woman at the well, she received the Living Water.

So much was packed into this year, but the Lord must have felt we had done enough work in Pasa Robles. We did have a real work going, and I learned later there were two or three from there that went to the mission field. I don't believe we were ever in a place very long, but that there were those who had been called to the Great Commission. That was the big concern of my husband's heart all his life.

Chapter 13

Whittier, California

It was good news to know someone else was coming to take our place in Pasa Robles, and we had been called to the lovely Foursquare Church in Whittier, California, which is near Los Angeles. We didn't realize it then, but this would be a pattern for the next few years to come. Pioneering, or starting a church, and moving on. Once again, we had a lovely building, a beautiful choir, **a salary**, a nice home, some very wonderful members and we did not have to do a thing but step in and take over. How refreshing!

Another Trip To Colorado

We were just getting settled in our new church in Whittier when we got a telegram from Dad Correll, who was now in Colorado, saying, "Have rented dance hall for revival meetings. Can you come?"

Let me bring you up to date on this story. Do you remember when Sidney went to Colorado for the funeral of his Aunt Cecil? Shortly after that, Dad and Mom Correll (Ralph and Stella), went back to Colorado from California to help take care of the two little girls, Barbara and Dorothy Lee. They also wanted to lead all the recently converted relatives into Christian growth, because there were no churches for miles.

Mother and Dad were real prayer warriors, and each day they would go out to the old buildings where the hay and grain were stored. How they would pray for God to move the hearts of the people in that area!

Not too far from the farm was a huge barn that was used for barn dances on Saturday nights. People would drive for miles to attend. Sidney's brother Carroll was only 16 and still living with the folks. However, when Carroll became involved in those Saturday night fights (which they always had), Daddy Correll got so mad at the devil he started really praying for the Lord to **send a cyclone** and destroy that barn off the face of the earth! He would say, " If there can't be any churches to help our young people, why do we have this dance hall that is destroying them?" Then the still, small voice of the Lord spoke to him and said, "Why don't you hold a revival meeting in the dance hall instead?" He had never thought of that.

He got up off his knees, found the owner of the dance hall, and said to him, "Mr. Clevenger, why couldn't we rent your dance hall for every night of the week except Saturday for a revival meeting?" Dad was prepared for an argument, but Mr. Clevenger studied him for moment and replied, "Well R.H., I don't know any reason why you can't." It was as simple as that. Isn't it interesting how God prepares the way when we pray? And that is when Dad sent us the telegram asking us to come to Colorado.

Sidney and I talked it over. Sidney felt that because we had been in Whittier such a short time, it may not be wise for him to go. However, he said, "Why don't you go?"

Mom and Dad agreed, and I was willing, but I gulped a little when I remembered it was only two weeks to our wedding anniversary. But **God's work always came first**, so Sidney wired them to tell them I would arrive the following week. At that time, our son, Sidney Robert was just ten months old. I packed my clothes and the clothes of my baby, and we took our first journey together. This time it was Papa who stayed home with the church and I was on a mission. He would not be completely alone because my grandmother was staying with us.

It was my first experience being on "the old farm". There are lots of funny stories I could tell you, but let me stick to telling you about preaching.

As we drove through the countryside, I couldn't believe it. There was a large cardboard poster with my name on it. In fact, it looked like it was on every telephone post in the county! This was indeed virgin territory for the Lord. No one could remember when there had been a meeting like this!

You couldn't help but wonder if people would come. What did they know about these kind of services? But when the opening night came, people streamed in like they came for the big dance, only more so. Night after night, the crowds got bigger and bigger. One thousand people would fill that old dance hall. I wondered, "Where did they learn to sing like that?" I guess it was my turn to be surprised. They must have learned those songs somewhere.

Although I was there with a new message each night, it was God who sent conviction like I had never seen before. People were coming down the aisles before I had finished preaching, crying out for mercy, with tears streaming down their faces. The whole countryside was aglow with God's praises.

The ironic thing was that, every week as the revival crowds got bigger, the dance hall crowds got smaller, until the dances were finally discontinued altogether. Eventually, the barn was used to store grain and hay.

Daddy Ralph had asked God for a cyclone to blow that dance hall away. Instead, God sent a revival and cleansed it from the inside out. What a demonstration of "Preach the Word! Preach the Word!"

By the way, at the time of this writing, Reverend Gary Curtis is ministering with Dr. Jack Hayford at the Church On The Way in Van Nuys, California. His mother, Blanch Curtis, was one of the converts at the dance hall revival meetings!

Returning Home - A Desert Experience

It had been a blessed time and my heart was full of joy. I said my good-byes, and with my little son, I took the train and headed home after an intensive month. The pangs of homesickness began to take over till I thought I couldn't stand it, for we were not going directly home. We were going by way of the "narrow gauge" railroad to Montrose, Colorado, to visit my mother. (One of the rare occasions.)

This was a very beautiful part of Colorado. I had lived in Montrose when I was a small child. Mother took us up to the Little Blue River, where we rode horse back and fished for trout. I think I caught close to ..... well, a large number anyway. Though I was enjoying it very much, and the scenery was SO gorgeous, it didn't outweigh the anxious desire I had to get back to my husband. So, because my mother was going to drive us back to California anyway, I said, "Mother, do you mind if we just head west now?" While in Montrose, Robert cut two more teeth, so he was fussy.

Talk About Desert Experience!

As we journeyed, we came to the great California Desert. This was in the late summer of 1927. Quite different than driving in the 1990's. We drove at night to escape the extreme heat. The heat waves would roll through the car like waves from an ocean, leaving you sticky with sand. We had no air conditioning. Service stations were 100 miles apart. There were no refreshment stands. In the middle of the desert, we had a flat tire. What a nightmare! On top of that, Robert got an earache. The road was thick gravel in places and it was hard to drive. Earlier, there had been a cloudburst in the mountains. The water rushed down to the desert and washed the road out. We had to make our own road. We came to a long stretch of desert which seemed like the loneliest place on earth, especially at night. It was thundering and lightening in the distance. Would we ever get there? We pulled to the side of the road and slept an hour. Oh, how we welcomed daylight and the California state line.

We ate breakfast at Barstow, and from then on, we had paved roads. It was like the golden streets of glory. Needless to say, my husband went into spasms of joy at our return. Homecomings are wonderful. Heaven will be like that.

"The trials of the earth will seem nothing
When we get to the end of the way."

One of the greatest joys Sidney and I have had, after being separated for the Lord's work, was the wonderful talkfest we always enjoyed upon our reunion. We would talk for hours, and then have a time of prayer to thank the Lord for His watchful care over us while we were absent from each other.

Moving On Again

There are many lovely stories we could tell about our time in Whittier. They were precious and gracious people. We were doing just fine, until my husband went to an auditorium in Los Angeles and heard the challenging speaker, Dr. Oswald J. Smith of Toronto, Canada. He was definitely a man of missions. Dr. Smith spoke about the urgency of getting the message out before the second coming of Christ. He gave his famous slogan that has stirred so many hearts, **"Why should any man hear the Gospel twice until every man has heard it once?"**

Sidney was so moved when he came home that he relayed the message to me, "Honey, why should we stay here in California and preach to people who are surrounded with fine Gospel ministers, when we could witness to the hungry hearts in Colorado? I can hear them crying out to us, 'Come over and help us.'" Dad and Mother Correll, who were still holding down the fort, encouraged us to come.

John 4:35 says, *"Lift up your eyes and look on the fields; for they are white unto harvest."* So, for us it was "Go east, young man, go east."

We gave the news to people who loved us and wanted us to stay. It meant once again leaving a comfortable nest, a salary, and a certain amount of security in Whittier. But this time our goal would not be to settle down, but to **evangelize**.

So we packed our things and got into our New Whippet car (another sign of our affluence over the model T Ford). We headed east, stopping en route to see the Grand Canyon and witness the wonderful handiwork of the God we were serving. Oh, incidentally, I was pregnant with our second child, but we never let that stop us.

When we arrived in Colorado, we began our meetings in the old school house that Sidney had attended in his youth. His former classmates came and brought their families. It was almost like doing foreign missionary work, because the power of God was foreign to them. We hung up gasoline lanterns for lights, made a pulpit, and the people squeezed into the school desks. They kept coming until they filled the school to the point where others could not get in. Conviction was great, and people were converted nightly. I can still remember one man who was blond and over six feet tall. He started for the altar and fell face down.

We went from one school house to another. We never worried about the crowds being there. They were so hungry for God, they came and filled the place up. Now, let me tell you another interesting story.

The Oyster Stew

All of our needs were pretty well met as far as bed and board were concerned. However, no offerings had been received. They had never been taught to tithe, but some of the people felt we ought to have a personal offering. Instead of taking an offering they decided to have an event called an "oyster stew", and give the proceeds to us after the expenses were paid.

Our policy had always been to accept **free will offerings** only, as the people gave from their hearts. But this was their idea, so we told them to go ahead. The ladies worked like beavers, to get the dishes, tables, milk, canned oysters, etc. The perspiration dripped from their brows. Finally, supper was ready. We took our entire family, Mom and Dad, Maxine, Sidney and myself and little Robert, as we all loved oyster stew. At 15 cents a bowl, we spent $1.35.

After it was over, the ladies came to Dad Correll and said, "Ralph, we don't know what happened, but things are higher than we anticipated. After all the bills were paid, we just have $2.00 left." Daddy thanked them for their fine efforts. But on the way home, we were hilarious with laughter. We were seeing for the first time how it worked to **pay God's bills man's way**. After taking out the $1.35 we paid to eat, we had exactly 65 cents.

We have enjoyed wonderful fellowship and covered dish dinners many times since that first oyster stew, but it was the first and last time we had a dinner to pay God's bills. What we started out believing was still true. God's work done in God's way will not lack God's support.

Our school house meetings were followed by big baptismal services at the nearby irrigation ditches, but we felt God was leading to bigger and better things for Him. Why not the city of Sterling? It was the largest city in Northeast Colorado.

Before we tackled this, it was back to the grainery for prayer. God had used this humble prayer room to answer many prayers. Once again, we seemed to get assurance that God was behind our move. So Sidney and Dad went to Sterling the next day, and prayed, "Where do you want us, Lord?"

They passed a large **skating rink** that was about to be torn down. It was built three feet off the ground. The sides were boards part of the way up, and then the rest of the way up, they were canvas. But it had a nice auditorium inside. They estimated it would hold 800 people. Do you get the picture?

They found the boss of the outfit and asked if it could be rented. A price was agreed upon and then next they went to the lumber yard and ordered lumber for the platform and seats. Sidney and Dad asked them to deliver it the next day and send the bill to our post office box.

It was an incredible and outrageous step to take. It was the middle of February. Snow was on the ground and there were five huge room furnaces that needed **coal**. All arrangements were made including newspaper ads. We made a sign that stretched across the entire building. After they rented the post office box, **they didn't have a dollar between them**! (I am afraid they couldn't do that in this day.)

It was not just faith, it was God's timing. It was 1928 and we were told there had not been a revival there since Billy Sunday's.

Opening night arrived. The sign read "Correll Evangelistic Party". Our team consisted of Sidney, myself and Dad Correll. Mother Correll was our prayer support. Sidney's little sister Maxine got her start in gospel work that night at the age of 14.

We were staying at an old ranch house in Proctor, Colorado, which was twenty-five miles from Sterling. We hadn't enough money to get a place in Sterling. We would leave the farm early in the afternoon because we needed to build the fires in the furnaces to warm the building.

So much was at stake. We not only wanted a revival, but **we owed** all those start-up bills! Even some of our relatives doubted our sanity at such an undertaking. And even though we had prayed about it and had confidence in the Lord, I will admit we also had first night jitters.

We had hired the Sterling Municipal Band and they began playing one-half hour before the meeting time. It was snowing and we began to wonder if anyone would come. Soon they started to file into the building and by the time we walked to the platform there were around 400 people. Some had driven for miles. The people were a little cold those first few nights, not only physically but spiritually too. As they began to enter into the singing and listen to the warm messages for the body, soul and spirit, their hearts warmed and they began to be receptive.

Daddy Ralph had the first breakthrough of converts when twenty came forward and received Christ. A night or two later God blessed my message when twenty-five came forward. Then one night Sidney preached a stirring evangelistic sermon. He called it "The Death Valley Limit and the Glory Express." There were thirty-five who came forward. Some of them were **railroad men**. After that, the meetings began to grow. We had huge children's meetings and that brought many more adults. Even though the building was only supposed to hold 800 we were having 1000 in attendance. For the several months we were there, we took offerings in our meeting and **every bill was paid.**

Since this story is about **the lady preacher,** let me tell you what happened to me one night. It was my turn to speak. It was only about five or six weeks before the birth of my daughter, Rebecca. I wore a cape, so many were not even aware of my condition. We had driven 50 miles (round trip) each night for the meetings and it was cold. There was no place to rest in the building and I was taking an active part each evening as well as playing the piano.

I didn't feel well but I got up to preach anyway. My sermon was on Belshazzers' feast from Daniel 5. I was describing the momentous and elaborate occasion, and the handwriting on the wall, "MENE, MENE, TEKEL, UPHARSON". Suddenly, I became ill. I stopped for a moment and put my head down on the pulpit. Sidney got to his feet, assisted me to a chair, and checked to see if I was alright. Then he went to the pulpit and went right on from where I left off and **preached my**

sermon. Needless to say, that was my last sermon until after my daughter was born.

We had been in the skating rink over three months and felt it was time to bring the meetings to a close. The people came and surrounded us and said, "You can't leave us now without a church. We are just beginning to grow." So we agreed to either help them get a permanent building or build a church building. Then we would send a request to Headquarters and ask for a Pastor to carry on the work we had begun.

We prayed about it and felt God's hand was in it. Sidney began taking pledges toward a church building. Daddy Ralph was acquainted with the Banker and suggested we get a loan. Sidney said, "No, wait awhile. See what God does."

The next day a gentleman came to see us. We noticed he had been coming to the meetings night after night. He would sit by one of the furnaces then leave without talking to anyone. He said, "God has been speaking to me about this church you want to build. How much do you think it will cost?" Sidney said, "If we build it Tabernacle style, it will cost around $2500." (Remember this was in 1928.) The man replied, "Now I know God is in this. That is **exactly the amount He told me to give**, or loan indefinitely without any interest." Then he told of a dream he had. He saw a table spread with fine linen and sparkling silver, but no food. A voice said to him, "Why don't you put your money where the food is, not just in form and ceremony?"

He loaned the $2,500 as he had said. Wonderful! A host of men came to donate their labor and in several weeks, the lovely Tabernacle was ready for dedication. An old prize fighter (who hadn't received Christ yet) worked almost every day and sang the loudest, "We'll work till Jesus comes."

We had given our best and the church building was finished. A lighthouse was built on the front instead of a steeple. A fine young couple, Paul and Lola Royer, had come from California to become pastors of the new flock. We felt our work was still "Pioneer Evangelism."

Partings are always sad, but this one was even sadder. Sidney and the other members of our family were not only leaving the people we had learned to love, but they were **leaving me**, to await the birth of my baby. Sidney had arranged for me to stay in the home of Mr. and Mrs. Vernon Hamilton, a couple that were converted in the meeting.

This was incredible. In three months we had names and address of **400 converts**. 70 young folk went to Bible School. How many are now Missionaries? Only God knows. **God is so good.**

Update

Mr. and Mrs. Vernon Hamilton later went to LIFE Bible College and graduated. They had two sons who graduated from LIFE, as well. All four became pastors.

Chapter 14

Trinidad, Colorado

We had a letter from a lady in Trinidad saying, "This railroad and mining center needs a revival. Please come!" We accepted it as God's voice. Lead on, oh Lord, lead on.

"Trust in the lord with all thine heart: and lean not unto thine own understanding. In all thy ways acknowledge Him and He will direct thy ways."

The city of Trinidad, Colorado, is nestled among the Great Rocky Mountains. Sidney and Daddy Ralph had gone on ahead to prepare the way. They had great expectancy in their hearts as they were met by a handful of friends who were eager to get started with our meeting.

We were going to use a tent loaned to us by a friend. Obstacle number one appeared when the lot they had planned to use could not be obtained. The man across the street who owned the lumber yard objected, saying he believed the tent was a fire hazard, and he was able to secure a restraining order from the Chief of Police.

Obstacle number two happened because the tent had already arrived and they had to pay rent on it. The men went to see the owner of the lot and he said, "If you can get the lumber man to withdraw his complaint, you can use the lot." Excitedly, they rushed to the lumber yard, only to find the owner had gone to Denver. They felt they just had to have this particular lot. So they prayed each day for five days. Every day they went to see if he had returned. On the sixth day, alas, they were told that the lot had been sold.

Discouraged, tired, and dismayed, they began looking for another location. They had to get that tent out of storage. That very day, the Fire Chief came to Sidney and Dad, telling them he had decided to withdraw his objections. He had arranged a lot for them right in the heart of town! They lost no time in rounding up some friends to help them unroll the tent and put it up. The benches were made, the advertising was out, and it was the day to begin.

Would you believe it, it **rained that very first day** and **the tent leaked like a sieve**. In the summertime, it rains almost every day. In fact, Daddy Correll declared it rained harder inside the tent than it did outside. But after the storm was over in the afternoon, the sun came out and the sides of the tent were rolled up. The dust had settled and the seats were washed clean. And in one hour, it was dry and clean as could be. **Here is the real miracle.**

This lot had been used as a dump for cinders for many years. There was a layer of 10 to 15 feet of **cinders,** so consequently the water just drained right through the sawdust we had used, through the cinders, leaving it dry and beautiful. The lot they had prayed so hard to get at first was **clay soil**, and when it rained it was a sticky, muddy mess. Our meeting would have been ruined, but instead we had **eight wonderful weeks**.

"Lean not unto thine own understanding . . . He will direct thy paths." Sometimes it is good when God doesn't answer our prayers.

In the meantime, Sidney drove back to Sterling to be with me when our baby Rebecca was born. I was so glad he was able to be there. When he had to get back, he took Mother Correll, Maxine and our little Robert back with him to Trinidad.

When Rebecca was two weeks old, I took her to church with me to the New Tabernacle in Sterling. I had a chance to greet the people and say a last good-bye, as I took the train that afternoon for Trinidad to be reunited with rest of the family. My poor baby Rebecca travelled in that smoky, dusty, hot ride for 500 miles.

But what a joy to be together again. Now there were two more members to the team, Sidney's brother Carroll and his wife Inez. Carroll used his beautiful singing voice, and preached. Inez, also a LIFE graduate, preached and assisted in the meeting.

We didn't get a salary in those days, but the people surely did provide for us. They would come to meetings loaded with groceries. We never went hungry. One thing happened in the meeting that put the fear of God into the crowd. Two young men came to the meeting to ridicule God. They made fun of everything, tried to cause trouble, and made quite a disturbance among the people. One night, they drove by the tent and they were quite drunk. They stopped in front of the tent, mocking and yelling obscenities. Screaming and shouting, they drove on one block. They went over the bridge and were killed.

"Be not deceived, God is not mocked. Whatsoever a man soweth, that shall he also reap." Galations 6:7

One Sunday evening as we had our song service, the people were singing so beautifully, especially the children. They were singing with great gusto, "My Sins Are Blotted Out I Know." We had heard that chorus on the radio coming from a Chicago radio station just a couple of weeks before.

After the service a tall, handsome young man came up to us and said, "I was so surprised to hear you singing my chorus." I asked, "Oh, is that so? Which one was that?" "It was 'My Sins Are Blotted Out I Know.' The problem is, you didn't have it quite right! Here, I will sketch it out for you." He started writing notes out on a piece of paper, saying, "By the way, where did you learn the chorus?" We answered that we had just heard it on the radio station from Chicago. Then he told us, "That was my program, and I only wrote that song a short while ago. I couldn't believe I was hearing it clear out here."

Then we asked him to play it for us. When he sat down at the piano and hit the first chord, we had no doubt he was telling us the truth. Then he told us that his name was Merrill Dunlop. He was the pianist and organist at the Chicago Gospel Tabernacle. Then he said, "Isn't it strange how 'little things' can sometimes mean so much." He went on to tell how he happened to be in our meeting.

He and his mother were on their way to California. Because it was Sunday evening, they thought they should go to church somewhere. As they came within a block of the tent, they had a flat tire. While the tire was being fixed, they saw the tent and decided to attend. That's when they heard his song that had originally been sung in the Chicago Gospel Tabernacle on the Back Home Hour. It went over the air waves to Colorado and here we were passing it on. We had a lovely visit and time of fellowship.

The friendship which began that evening became a very precious one which has lasted for years. As you will read in our story, we were in Kenosha, Wisconsin, a few years later pastoring a church. We wanted to renew our friendship with Merrill Dunlop, so we went to the Chicago Gospel Tabernacle where he was the pianist and organist. The pastor at that time was the famous Paul Rader. Then later, Merrill was associate pastor with Clarence Erickson. Merrill was not married when we first knew him. He would come to Kenosha to visit with us, and went ice skating with us and our young people.

One day Merrill asked Sidney to be best man at his wedding to his lovely bride, Lenore.

I am so glad and humbled to have had Merrill Dunlop as my piano teacher also. He taught me what we called "evangelistic playing."

This was truly a lasting friendship, for fifty years later Merrill asked Sidney to attend their fiftieth wedding anniversary. After the reception, Merrill and Lenore were not able to leave right away, so they asked the news commentator **Paul Harvey**, who was also a guest, if he would drop Sidney off at his hotel on his way home. Wow, what a luxurious ride in his limousine to his hotel! Sidney really appreciated it.

But that wasn't all. Merrill and Lenore drove all the way from Chicago to Charlotte, North Carolina, to attend Sidney and my **sixtieth** anniversary on June 19, 1985. Isn't it something what a flat tire can do? (Or was it just a flat tire?)

While in Trinidad, we had our third wedding anniversary on June 19th. We climbed the high hill overlooking the city and took inventory on how good God had been to us. Then I had a little surprise for him. I slipped the brass wedding ring off his finger. It had a thin layer of gold that was wearing off. I replaced it with a white gold ring that cost me $11.00. I had saved a long time to get it. Sidney was always saying such lovely things to me, and I wanted to show my love in giving something to him.

When our allotted time was up and we had to return the tent, the people who had become wonderful, faithful friends said, "If you can't all stay, can't some of you stay? We need a permanent church!" So, Mother, Dad and Maxine found a building and stayed to pastor the church. Carroll and Inez Correll were invited to go to a new meeting in Cortez, Colorado.

Don't Quit

When things go wrong, as they sometimes will
When the road you're trudging seems all uphill.
When the funds are low and the debts are high,
And you want to smile, but you have to sigh,
When care is pressing you down a bit -
Rest if you must, but don't you quit.

Life is queer with its twists and turns,
As everyone of us sometimes learns,
And many a fellow turns about
When he might have won had he stuck it out.
Don't give up though the pace seemed slow -
You may succeed with another blow.

Often the goal is nearer than
It seems to a faint and faltering man;
Often the struggler has given up
When he might have captured the victor's cup;
And he learned too late when the night came down
How close he was to the golden crown.

Success is failure turned inside out.
The silver tint of the clouds of doubt,
And you never can tell how close you are.
It may be near when it seems afar;
So stick to the fight when you're hardest hit
It's when things seem worst that you must not quit.

author unknown

Our 3rd anniversary

Chapter 15

Denver, Colorado

Never will we forget those months of ministering in the beautiful Barns Auditorium in Denver, Colorado. It seated 800 people. It was a very modern building.

What a lot of wonderful people; we discovered so many lovely friends. First, a committee led by Brother Anderson took Sidney and me out on a shopping spree and outfitted us from head to toe. Believe me, we needed it. They also took our two children, Sidney Robert and Rebecca, into their hearts.

We had a nice apartment to live in, and we had **a salary.** Hallelujah! We actually had money left over to buy things with. But best of all was the spiritual awakening in the church. Thirty souls came to the Lord the very first service we had in the auditorium.

We had so many wonderful memories from there. We were still in our early twenties, but it seems like our life was a series of valleys and mountain tops. We were certainly on the mountain top here. Well, after all, we were in Denver, which was called "The Mile High City."

I will never forget one of the biggest responses to an altar service I ever had. It was after I had preached on the rich man and Lazarus. People streamed from every part of the auditorium to the altar. This was long before Billy Graham. What a sight to see!

Dad Correll's Famous Sermon

There is another memorable service imprinted in my mind. Dad and Mother Correll (Ralph & Stell) had been pastoring in Trinidad, Colorado, since our meeting there, but they came by for a visit.

We announced a special Sunday afternoon service for them. That was not really a very likely time to have an enthusiastic meeting, so we were amazed at the wonderful crowd. Daddy was excited and really steamed up for the occasion. He had been reading an account of Voltaire, I think, who had declared as he ridiculed the Bible, "One hundred years from now, the Bible will be an extinct book! All people will be atheists and know there is no God." Then Daddy Ralph's excitement was out of bounds when he read the account that not only was **the Bible *not* extinct** one hundred years later, but **the very home of this atheist was now the center of a Bible publishing house!**

That day, Reverend R.H.Correll preached a sermon that would have made the leading evangelist proud. He was the defender of the faith with a burning heart. I can hear his voice shouting now in that great auditorium: *"The fool hath said in his heart, there is no God."* (**Psalms 14:1**)

Jeremiah (verse **32:17-18**) said, *"Ah, Lord God! Behold, Thou hast made the heavens and the earth by Thy great power and stretched out arm, and there is nothing too hard for Thee."*

Then the psalmist shouted (Psalms 139:7-9), *" Whither shall I go from Thy Spirit, or whither shall I flee from Thy presence? If I ascend up into heaven, Thou art there: if I make my bed in Hell, behold Thou art there. If I take the wings of the morning, and dwell in the uttermost parts of the sea; even there shall Thy hand lead me and Thy right hand shall hold me."*

John the beloved said (John 1:1), *"In the beginning was the Word, and the Word was with God and the **Word was God**."*

Isaiah declared (verse 40:8), *"The grass withereth, the flower fadeth; but the Word of God shall stand forever."*

Psalms 119:89: *"Forever, O Lord, Thy Word is settled in heaven."*

Jesus said in Matthew 24:35, *"Heaven and earth shall pass away but My Word shall never pass away."*

Do away with the Bible?? Did you ever stop to think what a gigantic job that would be? Let us start at the church. Get every large pulpit Bible, and gather all the Bibles from the pews. Go through the Sunday school rooms and the reading rooms, taking all the Bibles. Then go to the homes. How many Bibles do you have? Don't forget the trunk in the attic. Bring them all out and burn them with the church Bibles. Will this destroy the book? No, no, it has only just begun. Now, go to the libraries. Gather the Bibles, the study books about the Bible, the Bible story books, the millions of books with Bible quotations. Then go to the schools and universities. Even if not read in school, they can be used as a reference book. What about the book stores and the religious sections in department stores, even the economy cut-rate stores?

Hurry! Hurry! As you wipe your brow, you look like a man at the seashore with a broom, seeking to sweep back the waves of the sea! Have you forgotten the judge's chamber and the court rooms that use the Bible to swear in a witness or a President of the United States of America? And then there are the museums and all the original manuscripts. Only a **fool** would declare the Bible to be an extinct book.

Even if you were able to collect all the above, is your job complete? No, a thousand times no! You have only just begun!

Have you thought of the cornerstones of buildings, large or small, which have a box that has been placed in it? Most every one, among other precious memories, will have a Bible nestled there securely. You would have to tear these buildings down and destroy them to make the Bible a forgotten book. Even the graves would haunt you, for many a saint has been buried with his faithful Bible in his arms. But that is not all. What about the missionaries in the remotest areas of the world, from the highest mountains to the tropical forests? They not only have a Bible, but the nationals have God's Word in their own languages. You would have to search out all these ambassadors of Christ around the world and get all their translations.

If you were able to do this impossible task of gathering up the physical books, would you have completed your task? Never!

What about the people that have committed the Bible to memory? Psalm 119:11: *"Thy Word have I hidden in my heart that I might not sin against Thee."* There are many that know the whole Bible by heart. You would have to destroy all the people with the Word in their memory.

What a gigantic task, trying to destroy God's Word. But you, Voltaire, are not the first who tried to accomplish this through the ages. Bibles have been gathered and burned, translators have been martyred as were Latimer and Ridley. As the fire licked up around their legs, Latimer cried out, "Be of good cheer, Master Ridley. We shall this day kindle such a flame by God's grace, in England, as I trust will never be put out!"

All of this was too much for that Sunday afternoon crowd and spontaneously, **as one man**, they leaped to their feet. They filled the auditorium with thunderous applause and ringing cries of "Hallelujah!"

Yes, there were many wonderful memories of our Denver ministries. It was a mount of transfiguration. Frankly, we felt like the disciples. We could have built a tabernacle and stay there for years. However, for one of the first times in our ministry, we faced arbitrary authority, and at the Annual Convention and Preachers Meeting in California, without our knowledge or consent, another pastor was appointed to take our place in Denver, and we were sent to Michigan.

Chapter 16

From Denver, Colorado, To The Slums of Grand Rapids, Michigan

"There is no disappointment in Jesus." That is what the song says, but frankly we were heartsick and sad as the old train rumbled along the track from California to Detroit, Michigan.

We had so wanted to return to the Barns Auditorium in Denver. We had enjoyed such a wonderful time there. It wasn't easy when someone else had been put in our place. That is when it is hard to claim the scripture of Romans 8:28. How could it be working for good when we were sent by the General Supervisor who said we were needed much more in Michigan than Colorado?

So many promises had been made to us about Michigan - the nice church, the glorious success, etc. But this didn't seem to lift our spirits. Sidney Robert was three and a half years old, and Rebecca was nine months. They were good travelers as we covered the many miles, once again going east. We finally resigned ourselves to the fact that God must have a reason. We would give it our best, whatever the future held.

We arrived in Detroit in a raging blizzard. What a cold, miserable trip across the state to Grand Rapids, Michigan. We tried to huddle close to keep from freezing. It was one disappointment after another.

I don't know who got their wires crossed, but the fine, successful church, paying a good salary turned out to be a crummy little mission hall in a part of the city where only mission type people would go. Besides that, the church was $500 in debt, and had no hopes of getting out. We began to realize the Lord had sent us to the **mission field**. So we became missionaries as we moved into two upstairs rooms.

It was located in the slums of the city, where everything that could happen, did happen. When I did my washing, I had to put a tub on the gas stove to heat the water. Then I had to carry it to the bathtub and there, on my knees, I washed on an old fashioned washboard. I had to hang the clothes around the room to dry. In the several months that were to follow, I threw my hip out of joint and had to stop and push it back in again. On top of all this, we became aware that our third lovely child was on the way. I am amazed when I remember the joy and the courage the Lord supplied us. Sidney worked and prayed hard to make a go of our mission church. He did a lot of advertising, such as putting out handbills from door to door.

But even though we got the people, they had no money to pay bills. It was just hopeless, that is all. Maybe this would be a good time to quit! But that was not part of our make up. The Lord would see us through.

As soon as the weather warmed up in the spring, we stepped out by faith. We got another tent, sixty by ninety feet, and went to Greenville, Michigan about thirty miles away. Sidney practically set the tent up alone, pounding in the stakes with a sledge hammer. He got several boys in the neighborhood to help him pull up the two large center poles. For food, he rationed himself to ten cents a day. He would slip in the back of a pool hall and get two five cent hamburgers. (Does anybody remember when you got a hamburger for five cents?) We didn't know a soul in town, so after the tent was up, Sidney would dress up in his good clothes and go from door to door, advertising the meeting.

When the day came to open our tent revival, we got in our cheap car that we had been able to buy and drove the thirty miles for the service. We had a fairly good crowd, but they were very conservative people, not easily enthused. We sang and played and preached. Our children were an added attraction just being there. The audience began to thaw and be blessed. Folks were beginning to receive Christ. The meetings gained momentum. Finances loosened up, so we soon could pay our bills. But, right at the peak, an **epidemic** hit the city. Many public places were closed; people were afraid to venture out.

Our crowds grew small but, hoping against hope, we plugged on. Sidney spent many of the nights with the tent, watching in case of storms. I drove the sixty mile round trip with the two children. Relief finally came from the epidemic, and the people were beginning to come to the services again. We were all set for a real revival! Zero hour!

The biggest storm of the season approached. I hurried home with the two children, gave them a bath and put them to bed. Then I stood staring out the window into the night, praying as lightning split the sky and the thunder crashed till it shook our building. The rain poured in torrents. I don't believe I slept a wink. I could only think, "What is happening to my dear husband?"

Eight o'clock the next morning came with my bedraggled, drowned looking man, my husband. He had battled the tent continuously during the violent storm, as it pitched and lurched like an angry elephant. Stakes began to snap out of the ground. The quarter poles were jumping

110

up and down. He was furiously swinging the sledge hammer in the driving rain and tying the ropes to the stakes. Then the final heave came as the center pole crashed to the ground, just missing Sidney. The sixty by ninety tent, ripped to shreds by the wind, now lay on the ground. Sidney, weary and bruised, crawled under the canvas and slept the sleep of total exhaustion. In the morning, as he awoke, he said he felt a presence. It was the heavenly Father (or was it his own Dad?) who laid a hand on his shoulder and said, "It will be alright, Sidney. Don't worry."

He was one discouraged boy, though, as he sat there in the kitchen and told me what had happened. "It's all over! Everything is lost! We have nothing coming in, and now our personal debt is over $1,000. The tent can't be fixed, and I have just been informed that the lot has been sold."

In just a little while, the man who owned the tent came by and demanded his money. This was the last straw. You know, it never occurred to us to ask the organization for assistance.

The old enemy of our soul jeered, "Now, how are you going to get out of this? You will have to quit."

But just as we hit an all time low, who should drive up from California but Dad and Mom Correll. Certainly it was divine providence. They loved us both and encouraged us. Sidney took Dad over to look at the wreck.

On the way home, they passed the bridge on the Grand River. It was under construction, and a sign had been posted that said "men wanted." They stopped the car, found the boss and inquired about work. "We understand you are hiring men. We would like a job." The boss coolly looked at my slender husband and answered with a tone of disdain, "Yes, we are hiring men!" Sidney snapped back, "Well, you are looking at two of them and we want a job now!" It worked, amazingly, and they were hired.

They were to return that night by twelve o'clock. The catch was that each had to have a pair of hip boots and neither of them had any money. They came home to report they were bridge builders. Sidney took his beautiful Olds trombone (which he then played) to a pawn shop and got money to buy boots.

That night they went to work, and I do mean work! Twelve long hours of it. Their first job was to saw pilings in the bottom of the Grand River. They had to saw the piles under six inches of foul smelling water. It was a nasty, back breaking job. Ever time they stopped for a breath or to straighten their backs, the devil-possessed straw boss would swear and cuss at them and tell them to get moving. Sidney so wanted to please, and he wasn't used to this kind of treatment. Dad would say, "Oh Sid, don't pay any attention to that old fool. You're doing okay." They worked until they saw stars (which were not in the sky). Would twelve hours ever pass? Would their backs break? But they didn't give up. The whistle finally blew. What a relief!

God had mercy on them. Their shifts changed and they didn't have to be back for twenty-four hours. They struggled home, showered, ate, and fell into bed. Sidney slept for twenty-two hours without waking. Did they quit? Never! They were both back at their jobs the next day. They received $7.00 for a 12 hour day.

On payday, the man who owned the tent was right there to collect Sidney's check! He had no hold on Dad, so we lived off the money he made, and worked on other accounts.

How could all of this have been in God's plan? Day after day they worked. They let their light shine. The whole ungodly bridge gang began to show real respect. They saw how they worked and kept their cool, in spite of ridicule. The men learned they were preachers, and would seek them out for a chance to talk.

The job Sidney and Dad were doing now was tamping down the cement as it poured into the coffer dams. It was discovered, when the wooden frames were removed from around the coffer dams, that Sidney and Dad's concrete walls were the smoothest, with fewer holes showing.

Finally, Daddy was teamed with another partner and Sidney had another man to work with him. This, too, was by design, because now Sidney had someone to preach to. As they stood in the freshly poured cement above their knees, working the cement with their boots and smoothing the sides of the coffer dam with wooden ladles, Sidney began telling him the way of salvation. It was only days before his partner asked him to pray for him to be saved.

Some years later, Sidney met this same man. He had since graduated from Bible school and had become a pastor. How strange that even from this "working pulpit", there was at least one that went into the ministry, and another worker who also received Christ.

Daddy and Sidney worked six weeks on the job, twelve hours a day, paying on the huge debt. **The tent man got all his money**, even though it took several years to do it.

The Lord had given us happy hearts, and on the evening of our fourth anniversary, we walked through the park in Grand Rapids, eating popcorn and thanking God that He had given us each other and the multitude of blessings.

The Tide Changed

The tide changed as we received a telegram from evangelist Essie Binckley Locy, asking us if we could come for revival at the Majestic Theatre in Waukegan, Illinois. Talk about a message from heaven - this was it! We returned the wire, "Happy to come."

The next day when Sidney and Dad went to work and told the boss they were leaving, this man who had been cussing, vitriolic, and mean, almost wept. He said, "I can't tell you how I regret to see you both go. You have changed the whole atmosphere around here. Believe me, we will miss you."

We all felt another class of hard knocks had been passed, bringing glory to God. With our two children and Mother and Dad, we went to Waukegan, Illinois, and the Majestic Theatre.

Oh yes, with Daddy's money, we paid off Sidney's trombone in the pawn shop. So we were back in the business musically, also.

Chapter 17

Waukegan, Illinois to Kenosha, Wisconsin

From bridge building in the Grand River, the Lord built a bridge for us from the valley trials to the high peak of revival in Waukegan, Illinois. It was good to have our evangelistic party, which consisted of Mom, Dad, sister Maxine, Sidney, and myself, together again. As we began our meetings in the beautiful Majestic Theatre, with the red carpet down the isles and a huge stage, we could look out over the wonderful crowd, and Sidney and I could sing with real enthusiasm, "I walk with the King, hallelujah." Sidney played his trombone, and I played the piano. We all took turns preaching. Mother Correll took her turn preaching to us at home.

We would be out on the street corner at Genessee and Bevedere, telling of Jesus and witnessing at every opportunity, but the thrill was the wave of revival as, night after night, souls came with tears, confessing their need of Christ. People came from many cities around the area, including Zion, Illinois, Kenosha, Wisconsin, and even farther north in Wisconsin. When the six weeks were finished, there were a number who dedicated their lives to full-time service and went to Bible School. Among them were Ray Davis, Erby Freeman, Ingar Larson, Margaret Schott, Judge Morley, and others. We were in contact with them for years, still working for the Lord.

We made wonderful lifetime friends and carried away precious memories. But now that the six weeks were over, what next? We had no definite orders or commitments, so we had our family prayer together and asked God for guidance, and followed the example of Abraham of old in Hebrews 11:8: *"He went out not knowing whither he went."* Sidney and Daddy started out toward the north to Wisconsin. While driving through Kenosha (just over the Illinois line), they saw the 63rd Street sign, and remembering a lady named Mrs. Vingren had invited them to come to her home, they whirled the car around and went to the Hugo Vingren residence. The dear Swedish family welcomed them with open arms and invited them in. Before talking about their desire for us to come and start a church in that city, Mrs. Vingren set before them some very delicious split pea soup with hamhocks. It was the first time Sidney had ever eaten this, and he enjoyed it. It became one of his favorite dishes. Oh yes, and that good Swedish coffee - he was introduced to the fact that the coffee pot is always on the stove. (This was before our modern gadgets.)

The rest of us were staying with the Fred Schott family in Zion, Illinois, who had begged us to come to see them. While we were enjoying their hospitality, Sidney and Dad finished their snack, and we learned of the desire of, not only the Vingrens, but also others who were eager to have some spiritual refreshing in their city. So Sidney and Dad began to check on a building that was available. They found and leased the Lincoln Theatre which had been vacant for some time. There was lots of work to be done.

We're from Kenosha.
I said Kenosha.
That great big busy town.
Right in the middle of the USA,
Between the New York Harbor
And the San Francisco bay.
Where the wonderful east
Meets the beautiful west.
That's the best place to be found.
We are singing so loud of it
Because we are so proud of it.
Kenosha, my home town.

This song was sung many times with great gusto and enthusiasm by the young people God gave us in this city. Kenosha was the home of American Motors. (In those days it was called Nash.) Almost everyone worked for Nash. This city was to completely change our style of ministry. We were actually to stay here over five beautiful years before moving on.

As I look back, two things were predominant there. First, a glorious ministry with young people, and second, we found our stride of what a church can do in missionary work around the world. Of course, another good reason for staying could have been our fast growing family. For the ladies who like statistics, we started in Kenosha on September 3, 1929. (Will we ever forget it?) Sidney Robert had just had his third birthday on August 15. Rebecca (born in May) was around 14 months old. October 14, 1929, Roselyn was born, and less than 13 months later our son, Roger, was born, on the 11th day of the 11th month, in the 11th hour, in 1930. Well, in December that year I was 23 years of age.

Believe me, we were quite a family! Even though these were the depression years, and money and food were scarce, and there was a lot of work with a family of children, people referred to us as the "happy family." We thank God for every one of the children. We were young enough to grow up with them.

Now, because I was very involved with the church work, it would be fair to say that I could have the liberty to be a mother and preacher at the same time, only because of Armenda Farris. She was only fourteen when she came to live with us, but she was very mature, and with tremendous responsibility, she cared for the children with love and wisdom. I shall always be grateful for her loyal service, and I have recently told her so, as we had dinner together even as I was writing this story.

But, wait a minute. I didn't tell you about our beginning. On the first night, September 3, 1929, when Sidney and Daddy got back and told us of renting the Lincoln Theatre, we were excited about our new venture. We had a roundtable discussion as to how we would proceed. We wanted to do something different than the old cliche, "Come to an Old-Fashioned Revival" or "Come to the Correll Evangelistic Campaign." So we made a big sign for the front of the theatre which read "Come to the Correll Jubilee Party, October 3 at 7:30. It is free!" We found all kinds of excuses why we shouldn't use "revival" or "campaign." It wouldn't do any harm to try.

Eagerly, we waited for the opening night of our Jubilee Party. We had worked hard to get ready. Daddy Correll went to Kenosha in the afternoon to make sure the building was warm, and to take care of last-minute details. We were still staying in the home of the Schotts. Sidney, Maxine, Mother Correll, and I arrived just in time for the evening service. As we drove along in the car, we prayed earnestly for a good crowd on this first night. The scripture says, *"Ask largely that your joy may be full,"* so we asked for 300-400 people. We were not known here, and no churches were sponsoring our services. As we turned the corner and drove up to the front of the theatre building, we noticed a large crowd of people standing on the outside of the door. Our first thoughts were, "The door must be locked." Where was Dad? The door was unlocked, and we went into the lobby. We stood and gazed in dismay. The roar and noise inside the building was terrific. Opening the door to the auditorium, there were 300-400 people all right, but they were a mass of howling, screaming children and young people. Standing for a moment, dumb with amazement, we finally saw Dad Correll leaning

117

against the piano, making no effort to stop the noise. Sidney ran to the platform and began to talk.

No one heard a word he said. He was greeted with loud cheers, boos, screams, and stomping of feet on the floor. He motioned me to go to the piano and play, but they only stomped more and clapped their hands. Sidney motioned for Maxine, Mother, and Daddy to come to the platform. Daddy refused; he was worn out. He had been fighting this since six o'clock. Sidney was perspiring, and his wing collar and bow tie were beginning to wilt. (Remember the wing collars?) He asked mother to pray. She shut her eyes to block out the commotion but had no success. She prayed under great stress, but only the Lord heard her. A few men, including heavyset Mr. Tocklin, were trying to clear the kids from the building, but when they put them out one door, they ran around and came in another. These were not ordinary children. They acted like they were inspired by the very demons of hell. The adults who were there and all of us agreed there was only one thing to do—call the police! The police were not long in arriving, and soon every child, unless he was accompanied by his parents, was removed. The police used their motorcycles to clear them away from the streets. It was just as though a hurricane had passed, and now that wonderful peace had come at last.

We didn't have much zest to continue the service, but, believe it or not, there were 35 or 40 adults still there. We proceeded with our service, dispersing with most of our singing. Then Sidney preached his heart out. I don't think it was the sermon he had prepared but, though he was very tired, God blessed him. When he had finished his sermon he asked if there were those who would like to come to the altar and pray with us for our own needs or for their own needs. There were a dozen or more who came forward. We had a wonderful time of prayer, and as we dealt with each one of them individually, we learned that seven of them had definitely given their hearts to the Lord. What a happy ending to a hectic evening. This was the beginning of a wonderful ministry in Kenosha, Wisconsin.

Later that night, at home after our service, we began to analyze the reasons why we started with a riot. Our first decision was to go back to the good old word "revival." If it was good enough for John Wesley and D. L. Moody, it was good enough for us. There was a reason for the mobs of children that night. They had always come to the Lincoln Theatre to see a show or other amusement. They expected a jubilee, and we had said it was free. There really was jubilee in heaven that night for the seven souls that found the Lord.

Chapter 18

A New Church Is Born In Kenosha, Wisconsin

If you should ask, "What was the secret of five wonderful, productive years of ministry in Kenosha, Wisconsin?" I would say it had to be prayer plus a burden for souls. *"The effectual fervent prayer of a righteous man availeth much."* James 5:16.

Some time ago, I received a letter from Margaret (Schott) Claxen saying, "How well I remember when you stayed in my home in Zion, Illinois, just before opening in Kenosha. Sidney was so burdened, he fasted and prayed for three days."

Shortly after our meetings began with that fateful opening at the Majestic Theatre, we moved into a small apartment above the theatre. This had now become our church. We had a prayer closet, which we used for personal prayer.

Perhaps the first significant revival began with the children. It was children that had disrupted the first meeting, so it was glorious to have such good response to our special children's meetings. It was almost a young church in itself. The seed sown had brought a wonderful harvest.

Speaking of children's conversions, it was in the Kenosha church that our eldest son knelt at the altar when he was six years old and received Christ into his heart. His sincerity was verified when, at seven years of age, he led his first soul to Christ. He loved attending prayer meetings, even all night prayer meetings. He may have slept on the bench part of the time, but he tried. Then at eight, he knew God wanted him for a missionary. You have already read how he completed his call. Rebecca also remembers that, at age four, she gave her heart to the Lord. She still remembers it was Mrs. Brinkman that prayed with her. Didn't the Lord say, *"Suffer the little children to come unto me and forbid them not,"* in Luke 18:16?

A Mother's Prayers And Love

Only when we get to heaven will we know the full results of mothers' prayers. One of the classic examples was Olga Sorensen, a wonderful redheaded Danish lady. She found the Lord after coming from Denmark. She had three fine but very mischievous sons, Edward,

Paul, and Wally, and a good husband, although none of them were living for the Lord. How fervently and earnestly she prayed. One day her fun-loving sons heard her and schemed to play a prank on her. Coming home that day, they heard her praying in agony of soul, praying for her boys with tears on her face. Quietly they slipped up behind her with the huge family dog. They put its paws on either shoulder and it nuzzled her cheek. She cried out, "Oh Lord, the devil has got me!" Her sons doubled up with laughter. But you didn't discourage Olga Sorensen. She prayed, and then put some actions to her prayers.

Olga came to one of our first meetings in the theatre. She enjoyed the meeting, but she fell in love with Maxine, Sidney's sister. She said, "Lord, I would like to have her for a daughter-in-law." At home she said to her oldest son, Eddie, "Son, I saw a very pretty girl in church tonight. I would like to have you see her. If you will go, I will give you a dollar!" In depression days that was a prize you couldn't turn down, especially if there was a pretty girl. He came to church. He got the dollar. He fell in love with the girl. The mother got a daughter. As he came to the meetings, he dedicated his life to the Lord. He went to Bible school, and on Maxine's nineteenth birthday, they were married. Eddie and Max pastored a church for several years, and then went to Cuba as our missionaries, where they stayed for eighteen years until Castro uprooted them. They still continued to serve the Lord together until Edward Sorensen went home to be with the Lord. Maxine is still part of our ministry today.

Olga prayed for three sons and a husband. All her prayers were answered. We will tell you about Paul and Wally later. I tell this story to encourage mothers to never give up!

Other Mothers' Prayers

Olga was not the only mother who prayed fervently. There was a very interesting situation in our young church. We had a wonderful children's work, and more than fifteen teenage girls. I formed a girls chorus called the Joy Bringers. They were wonderful, but it didn't seem fair. Where were the boys? The mothers who had sons began to intercede for their sons. Mrs. Fred Block had four handsome sons. Mrs. Staneck had one. Mrs. Buss had three, and other mothers began to join in. We prayed as though everything depended on God. Then we worked as though everything depended upon us. The mothers said to me, "You have got to help us. We can't get the boys to come to church. Why don't **you** invite them?"

I wish I had the fervor of soul winning today that I had then. While mothers prayed, this lady preacher went on the attack. It might be mealtime in the evening or before breakfast. We were there to use every persuasion and reason to get them to church. I assured them how desperately we needed their help, or as a last resort, we reminded them there was a judgment day and they had better be ready! I wouldn't recommend these tactics today, but we meant business with God. Several of the boys told me later that, when they saw me coming in the front door, they went out the back.

Then it happened. Several of the boys would come and sit on the back row. Conviction was strong in the meeting. One night Richard Block couldn't take it any longer, and with his face as red as fire, he started for the door. God just turned him around and he ran down the isle to the altar. This was when we were in the little brown church. He fell on his face full length, crying like a baby. When he got to his feet the burden was lifted, and his face was all aglow. There was a huge spot on the carpet that was wet with tears. What rejoicing! What a night! It was the beginning of answered prayer.

Herb Tocklin was a fine artist, poet, and a baseball player. What a pitcher! He came to church and sat by Richard, and when the altar call came, Richard pushed Herb right out into the isle and down to the front, and there was boy number two. He had an outstanding conversion. Then Leonard Block came, and there was another pool of tears spilled at the altar. His girlfriend Muggs had stayed in the car. She was rebellious and wouldn't even come in. Her curiosity got the best of her when she could hear things going on inside. When she saw the joy on Lenny's face, she wilted and knelt to receive Christ. They were later married, and were a part of the church. Fred and Cliff Block were special to me, for they were in my children's church. They were soon teenagers. Then Paul, Rueben, and Clarence Buss came to the Lord. Time, space, and memory prevent me from naming all the boys. Oh yes, there were Clyde and Cliff and Royce Greisen. I would love to tell you about their conversions, but we had enough fellows to form a men's chorus. We called them the Gideon's Three Hundred. We didn't have that many, but it sounded like it. I wrote a theme song for them from chapter 7 of the book of Judges.

Gideon's Three Hundred

Gideon's three hundred onward, we are fighting for the right.
Christ has washed our hearts and filled us,
With the heavenly gospel light.
We have left behind the fearful, in this battle over sin.
Not by might, nor power, but by my spirit saith the Lord.
The victory you shall win.

Chorus:
Hear the trump of God resounding, the pitchers crash
The lamps are burning.
The enemy is in confusion.
The Lord has won the **victory**.
Gideon's 300 onward, lift the bloodstained banner high.
We'll never let the standard touch the ground.
We'll gain our honors by and by.
(Sorry I don't have the music to give you too.)

Those Quiet Hours

It is one thing to win a person to Christ, but it is another thing to lead him to maturity. We had special concern for our young people. My job was getting out and rounding them up. But Sidney had an amazing ministry in their spiritual growth. Much of this was accomplished through what we called quiet hours. Sidney would have confidential talks about what God expected of each of us in our everyday living. It was a teaching ministry. I would hold a vesper service. Then, while songs and prayers continued, one by one, the young people would go into Sidney's study for personal prayer and consultation. Two of those young people were Ruth (Vingren) Hollis and Betty (Soderburg) Boyer. When asked to describe what the quiet hour meant to them, they said, "Those were the times we really took inventory and were scared to death to do anything wrong during the week, for we would have to confess it at the quiet hour." It was a combination of fear, of not wanting to displease the Lord, and of respect because Sidney cared and was concerned. As an illustration, Ruth remembers when she and one of the other girls had a falling out and weren't speaking to each other. It finally came out in quiet hour. Both girls asked forgiveness, cried on each others shoulders, left the meeting arm-in-arm, and became the best of friends. Betty said, "I believe that was the foundation that helped me to be a pastor's wife, and to have an understanding of things one faces in the ministry." Both of these girls have been lifetime friends, both became pastor's wives, and I am still in touch after all these years.

Our Prayer Tower

As we are talking on prayer, I dare not pass up our prayer tower, which was a little room in the church. The ladies signed up for two-hour shifts during the day hours, and the men signed up for the night hours. Once a week, as many others are doing today, we prayed for church requests of members, friends, and especially missionaries around the world.

I guess Herb thought he was Daniel. He was praying so the Lord would be sure to hear him. At three o'clock in the morning, the door of the prayer room opened up and there stood two policemen. He tried to explain, but the police took him down to the station. When they were convinced he was just praying and not drunk, they let him go. They admonished him to pray more quietly at that time of the night.

Prayers At Six O'Clock In The Morning

For years, we had a prayer meeting at six o'clock in the morning. Working people would come by on their way to work. Concerned church members came. The scripture was read, but it was mostly a time of prayer. Hattie and Walter Block were a young couple in our church. You could always depend on them to be in church and prayer meetings. Walter was a young businessman, concerned about what God wanted from him. One morning, everyone had gone except Walter and Daddy Correll. (We took turns leading the morning prayer service. Today was Dad's day.) Only the Lord knew the battle that was going on in Walter's heart as he stayed on his knees. He had dedicated his life to the Lord, but as a businessman, how much should he give God? Should he ask God to be a partner? In final, desperate yielding to the Lord he cried out, "Oh God, I give you everything I have. The devil is not going to defeat me. It is all yours, Lord, all yours!" With the tears streaming down his face, he began taking off his watch and laying it on the bench. He removed his ring, his wallet, and emptied his pockets, turning them inside out. Then he slumped forward with his head in his arms and sighed a peaceful sigh. Daddy was sitting quietly while God was dealing with Walter, and when he finally looked up, Daddy slapped his hands together and said, "Well, praise the Lord, Walter! God surely did a work on you, didn't He?" A yielded Walter said, "Yes, He can have it all!" Daddy Correll said, "Walter, God sees your heart, but I don't think He really wants you to give up your watch and these other personal things. But if you really want to invest your money, I am sure there is a place for it."

Walter Block remained true to his consecration that morning, and it was the beginning of a beautiful miracle. It would take too long to tell of the steps of advancement, but to the glory of God, Walter invented the curtain stretcher with the little balls on the tips to keep from sticking your fingers (before nylon curtains). His business became known as The Quaker Stretcher Co. During the war, they made army cots, and with the coming of television, he manufactured and sold TV trays. If your tray says Quaker, it was a Walter Block production. He went from a one-room work shop to a huge manufacturing plant that covered acres of land in Antioch, Illinois.

Today, both Hattie and Walter are with the Lord, but only heaven knows the large contributions Walter gave for the Lord's work. He never wanted his name mentioned, but I know he gave thousands to the work of our missionary ministry alone, let alone many other projects that have helped the work of Christ. All because one man dedicated his all in an early morning prayer meeting.

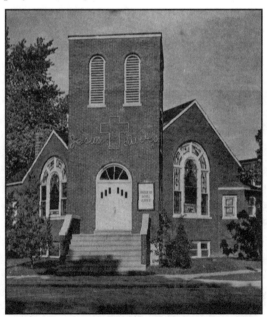

Little brown church

Chapter 19

Kenosha

"Therefore, whether you eat or drink, or whatever you do, do all to the glory of God." I Corinthians 10:31

In the cool, cool, cool of the evening, the air was crisp and invigorating. The moon made a wonderland of the Lincoln Lagoon in Kenosha, Wisconsin. The lake was frozen deep, and snow and icicles covered the surrounding trees, but in the stillness, there was movement. It was the skaters, gliding along with such beautiful grace and ease. Well, that is, unless you're a beginner. Then you had your ups and downs! Ice skating was one thing that made the cold season easier to bear.

Our church young people had grown up on skates, so they skated well. To become involved with them, we learned to skate also. Roy Davidson was one of our expert teachers, but I will never forget one evening as he was demonstrating his circle maneuver. Leaning far to the side as he approached us, he came a couple of inches closer than he intended and clipped the bottom of my skates, and I promptly sat, plump, on the ice.

These were beautiful, clean cut young people who were very keen and sharp. You would be proud of them anywhere, but there was something special about them. They had a goal to excel for Jesus in whatever they did, and Sidney would drum into them to put yourself on record! They used every opportunity to witness for Christ. We would all gather at the end of the lagoon and stand, making a big circle with our arms around each other, and we would sing songs and choruses in beautiful harmony.

The other skaters would gather around to watch and listen, asking, "Who are these young people?" The happiness and radiance of our young men and women bore real testimony in the city.

Music, Music, Music

Music had always been a part of worship from the Israelites, the Psalms, the disciples. As our young people came into the church, we insisted that they sing in the choir or play an instrument. We got a man from the local music store to come and lead the band. Sidney played trombone. I played trumpet, Herb played the bass drum, Cliff Griesen played the snare drum, and Mr. Tocklin played the bass horn. We would decide the instruments we needed, and then recruit the young people to learn them. Ruth Vingren Hollis groans about having to learn the clarinet.

We had the good fortune to get a fine young man who was an excellent trumpet player, Wesly Gallup, to join our group. He was so efficient that he not only played first trumpet, but took over the leadership of the band. It was that same urgent desire to excel that took the struggling beginners band and transformed them into a stirring marching band. The object was always new challenges. We would go to nearby cities for crusade rallies. Music always helped to bring the people in. There were the young people, who would have the musical program and give bright, shining testimonies. Then they would also try their wings with a short message. They were being involved and felt the thrill as they helped to pull in the net of converts.

The next challenge came as an extended tour of different churches. This trip took us through Illinois (Danville, Urbana, Decatur and Kewanee) and Fairfield, Iowa. We always had a parade through town, with an invitation to come to our meeting. The young people stayed in different homes and had some very interesting experiences. At one home, the lady became very angry when she learned she wasn't going to get **paid** for having the two young men stay in her home. She put them **out,** and they slept in one of the team's 1926 Chevys. They then drove around until they saw our car. They came to the door and our hostess invited them in to have breakfast with us.

We had a meeting in Fairfield, Iowa at the Billy Sunday Tabernacle. It was so hot it was unbearable. During the parade, the head of the bass drumstick flew off. On another occasion, Cliff Griesen's snare drum fell off the stand and rolled down the aisle, and Cliff chased after it. Back at the big tabernacle, which hadn't been used for quite a while, there were hundreds of bats inside. It was the boys' job to get rid of them in one way or another. Whatever the hassle, the enthusiasm of the meeting and the presence of the Lord were always a blessed reward.

The Ball Game

Another interesting experience was in Urbana, Illinois. The morning after our meeting in the church, the young people went out to the park to get some exercise and play a little ball. A group of fellows from the neighborhood came out and struck up a conversation. They learned that our group was a church group, so they challenged them to a game. They no doubt thought that these kids, being religious, were a bunch of "sissies" and would be easy prey. They wanted to appear real tough, so they said, "We're not going to throw underhand. We're going to pitch overhand, that is the way we play it here!"

Herbie said, "Well, okay, if that is the way you want it." Herbie sent Arminda Farris out in right field, as they were short of boys. Cliff Griesen was the catcher. They played with a 12-inch soft ball and they called it "kitten ball". The game started. What the neighborhood fellows didn't know was that nineteen year old Herb Tocklin was a semiprofessional pitcher. He could have curved that ball around a telephone pole if he wanted to. Those boys who challenged this church group were very surprised and chagrined that day when they couldn't even get a single hit, and Herb struck out twenty one players. They quit after the seventh inning. They had enough. Our young people felt good, because they had excelled for Jesus.

Eastern District Supervisor

Sidney was the supervisor of the whole Eastern District of The Foursquare Gospel Churches, from the Mississippi River to the Eastern Sea Board. It was a big job, plus pastoring our church in Kenosha.

Many of the wonderful new graduates from LIFE in California had come to our headquarters. If there were no openings at the moment, or calls for evangelists, our place was always home. We loved it that way.

This was in the early 1930's and a real depression was on. Money was very hard to come by. How well I remember one thing we were thankful for was this big house the Lord had provided, and a huge garden. It was filled with **cabbages** and **tomatoes**. So for our large family, we ate tomatoes and cabbages day after day, served in every imaginable different recipe. We had day-old bread to go with it and a few other things. But there were no complaints.

I would like to mention just several of the young couples who were our preacher guests. There was Howard Courtney and Vaneda. They had driven back with me from Los Angeles to Kenosha, Wisconsin. (Well, we did drop Vaneda off at her parents place. They were not married yet, and she came later.)

They were to be married in the little brown church where we pastored. Vaneda had paid $3.95 for her wedding dress. As they were

127

getting ready for the ceremony, which was to be that evening, my husband said to her, "Vaneda, don't you have a wedding veil to wear?" When she said no, Sidney said, "Come on with me, you must have a wedding veil." They rushed to the department store, arriving just ten minutes before closing time. Fortunately, they found a veil and dashed back to the parsonage. Later at the ceremony, she looked very lovely. (We kept the veil to use at other weddings.)

It was a momentous occasion. Sidney read them their vows. I was the matron of honor, Daddy Correll was best man, and little Robert was ring bearer.

I loved hearing the Courtneys tell about their first church in Racine, Wisconsin, and about how our church came to their rescue with a food shower (which turned out to be mostly **peanut butter**). We had some wonderful memories of ministry together.

But now for an update: Howard Courtney became Dr. Howard Courtney, and his wife also became an ordained minister. Howard became the supervisor of all Foursquare churches for twenty-seven years. Then he, along with Vaneda, were pastors of the Angeles Temple in Los Angeles for many years. They are still preaching and ministering in churches, and have been married over sixty years.

Nat and Lois Van Cleave also came to Kenosha. Sidney sent them to Wausau to start a church, and he married them there on June 8, 1930. Some years later, they went to Puerto Rico as missionaries. Returning to the states, Nat became Dr. Nathaniel Van Cleave. It would take much time to tell all the ways God has used them. For one thing, he became a district supervisor in California, as well as a beloved professor at LIFE College.

I wish I could tell you of many other precious young people who started their ministry there in Kenosha and lived a lifetime for God.

Kenosha Bible School

We had been constantly sending our young people to Los Angeles to Bible School, but we felt we could open doors for many more who were not able to leave home. So we started our own Bible School, and Howard and Vaneda Courtney (whom we just told you about) would drive over from Racine, where they were pastoring, to assist us in teaching and in the administration of the school.

If we had the time, I could give you a history of ministers, missionaries and Christian workers and their children (who followed in their footsteps), who came out of this school.

Is The Day Of Miracles Past?

The senior Corrells had spent a great deal of their time in pioneering new churches, as we had done before coming to Kenosha. Because of difficulties they had getting permission for tents, Daddy Ralph conceived the idea of a portable tabernacle. The roof was steel, with steel posts and framework, and the sides were still of canvas. This was much less of a fire hazard. We asked Mom and Dad Correll to come for a series of special meetings, and we put the tabernacle up on 23rd Avenue.

In this particular week, Sidney was going to preach on salvation. I was going to preach an illustrated sermon on heaven. Daddy Correll was to preach on "Is The Day of Miracles Past?" This was my day for the "illustrated sermon". Daddy Ralph went to the tabernacle in the afternoon and put up some wires to hang a star in the peak of the roof. He used a tall ladder set on the platform by the pulpit. When he climbed up the ladder to stretch the fine wire together in the middle, the wire snapped, and dad lost his balance and came down head first. He hit his arm on the pulpit and his nose on the edge of the steps. Naturally, he was stunned for a few minutes. Even before he hit the floor, his mind was saying, "Now see what you have done! Didn't you tell the people last night you were going to tell them about the God of miracles? Now what are you going to do?" He felt terrible and was numb all over. He noticed his arm stuck out in a funny direction. He took his good arm and felt his face. All he could feel was a bloody mass. Believe it or not, he got to the car (he was alone there), and drove the five blocks to our house with one arm. Mother Correll came to the door and saw the blood streaming from his face. His pain was unbearable. She put him in a chair and sent for Sidney and me. Many others came in, some from the official board, and witnessed his arm broken at the elbow and his nose smashed almost completely off his face. I'll never forget Hugo Vingren saying, almost with nausea, "Oh that nose, that nose!"

Sidney rushed him to the doctor. Most of the doctors had left town for the convention. Two were leaving, but stayed to help. They took X-rays (which we kept for many years). They showed the arm clear out of the socket, and some pieces of the bones broken off. They said,

"We can set your arm, but you will not be able to stand the pain and relax your arm at the same time. We will have to take you to the hospital and give you an anesthetic." Daddy Correll said, "No, set my arm right here and now." He quoted II Corinthians 12:9, *"My grace is sufficient for thee, for my strength is made perfect in weakness."* The doctors gave daddy one look and, while one quickly grabbed him and held him from behind, the other started pulling and setting his arm. Daddy was able to relax, and there was no pain. The doctor told Sidney afterward, "It's a good thing your father is a minister, because he will never be able to use his arm again."

Sidney brought him home and put him to bed. All night long daddy was praying and repeating scripture. *"All things whatsoever you shall ask in prayer, believing, you shall receive."* Then mother heard him say, "Thank you Jesus, you have healed my nose." He said it was just as though a hand took hold of his nose, lifted it up and put it in place, like it was putty. He could breath again through both nostrils. He knew it was God's hand. He said, "Lord, if you can heal my nose, you can heal my arm." He began taking off the bandages. His arm was supposed to be put in a cast the next day. He began working his fingers, lifting his arm above his head, praising the Lord.

The next morning I took him back to the doctor to see about his nose. The doctors hadn't returned from their meeting, and daddy said, "Helen, what are we doing here? God has healed me." We went back home. He removed the bandages from his face and **all that was left of the injury was a little red line** that would be covered by his glasses. Later that day he shaved with the arm that had been broken. He dressed and went to church and preached his sermon, "Is the Day of Miracles Past?" He repeated the scripture he had said in the night. He pounded his elbow on the pulpit. It sent shivers up our spines. People crowded around to see the X-rays. People who had seen him before testified to it. **It was a miracle.** The arm the doctor said he would never use again, was used the very next day as he helped others paint the steel on the tabernacle. He later helped to take the tabernacle down.

"There are many other things," John 21:25. It would take books to tell all about those five years in Kenosha. These were years of foundation building and a time of maturing, for we, "the kids," were growing up.

We had moved from the little brown church to the huge old Methodist Church downtown. We had some big conventions there. We finally bought a lot on which a new church was to be built. It was not all "sunshine and roses". We had many exciting experiences, as we have related, but let me close with two difficult experiences that both Sidney and I had.

The Board Of Deacons

Will we ever forget? I don't remember how the Board of Deacons was elected. Even though I was not a member, I did know it was a battle ground. A meeting might be called on a Sunday night after service, any time, any place, without any preparation. It was true, Sidney and I were aggressive, enthusiastic and would tackle anything. We must have been a problem to some of those men, for I am sure we did things they had never done before. There was almost always a point of contention.

I would say we had been in Kenosha a year and a half when the following happened. God had given us so many unusual blessings, especially through the young people and the ministry of prayer. One night, the board meeting was held in our home. Suddenly, this one dear member of the board, a Swede who had the reputation of being very spiritual and someone they all looked up to, almost knocked the wind out of Sidney's sails. He turned toward him and, in a very harsh voice, said, "Brother Correll, I don't like the way you preach. You make faces. You're no pastor. Now Helen, your wife, is the real preacher. You should let her do all the preaching. However, I have decided that it is time for you to leave. God has spoken to me." You have to understand, the old timers felt he was the **authority** of God and they would never oppose him.

Nothing like this had ever happened in our ministry before. Sidney felt he did not have the power to oppose the man, so not knowing what to do, he stood up and went out of the room to the porch. With his heart crushed, he looked up to the stars in the sky and began to weep tears and more tears. He struggled in his despair. Suddenly he thought, "If the Lord could speak to this board member, why couldn't he speak to me?" So he asked the Lord if it was His will that we move on, and if our time was up here? There was **nothing.** That settled it. He got up, walked into the room and put his arms around this dear brother. (You could see a slight smile on his face as he could almost see us on the next bus out of town.) Sidney looked quietly into the brother's eyes and in a kindly voice said, "I'm sorry, I would like to please you. I would like to go, but you see I can't, because **God hasn't told me** to go."

Wow! Like a clap of thunder, the brother shouted at him, "I have had much experience in these things, and when I say a preacher goes, he goes!"

Two or three weeks went by, and Sidney continued to preach. The board member was in every service. He would scowl at Sidney, but to the glory of God, my dear husband kept the sweetest spirit and never let bitterness take over. As always, he had a wonderful Godly love. You will have to admit, it wasn't easy to preach under those circumstances.

Then it happened! The third Sunday, right in the middle of Sidney's sermon, this man stood up. (It was in the little brown church.) He started down the aisle toward the pulpit. Sidney was stunned, and thought, "Dear Lord, he is going to throw me out bodily?" At the foot of the steps, the man turned around to face the congregation, and to all our amazement, he was weeping. Then he said, "I must say something. I have sinned against this young man." He turned toward Sidney and said, "Brother Correll, I ask you to please forgive me." Then again to the audience he said, "I have set a bad example to you as a people and I ask you to forgive me." He then fell on the altar, weeping. Sidney had worked very hard on his sermon for that day but he never finished preaching it. Everyone ended up at the altar.

Years later, when Sidney would preach in nearby cities, this dear brother would meet him with tears. He would throw his arms around him and say, "Brother Correll, what we need today is an old fashioned Holy Ghost revival like we had in Kenosha." As Sidney preached, this dear brother sat and smiled.

To Ruin Or To Save

Speaking of board members, I feel I want to tell something that happened in our very early ministry. This book is not just a story to be read, but perhaps lessons to be learned as well.

Sidney was on a mission board. During one of these meetings, there was the unpleasant duty of examining a young pastor, as there were some serious accusations brought against him. When the young man was confronted by the chairman, he stood up, confessed his sins and wept like a baby. He asked for forgiveness, and assured the board that this would never happen again. He was asked to leave the room. In Sidney's mind, there was nothing to do but to back the young man up and to love him. It was a blockbuster when the chairman said, "Well, what he has done before, he will do again. I move that he be dismissed." And, just like that, he was no longer a pastor. He was brought back into the room, and when the resolution was read to him, he cried like a wounded animal and made his way to the door. Sidney was stunned at such a reaction, and he went running after the young man. He followed him down the aisle of the church where he had thrown himself on his knees, crying out to God in such a piteous manner. Sidney knelt beside him, putting his arm around him and praying with him. Then suddenly the young minister rose to his feet and walked out the door, and my husband never saw him again.

This single incident stayed in my husband's mind and heart, and he solemnly vowed to God that he would always do everything in his power to fulfill Galatians 6:1, *"to restore such a one in the spirit of meekness, considering thyself lest thou also be tempted."* And to the glory of God, he has helped more than one minister to know God's forgiveness and be restored to ministry without public embarrassment. What would Jesus do?

Helen's Taste Of Bitterness

The incident happened toward the close of our Kenosha Ministry. It had been such a blessed and fruitful time. The old enemy never likes that.

There was a young couple who had been in Christian work, but were away from the Lord for awhile. They now appreciated our giving them an opportunity to minister once more.

We wanted to give them different responsibilities. We mentioned that we had a six o'clock morning prayer meeting and we took turns being in charge of it. We had to be in Milwaukee, Wisconsin, preparing a citywide meeting for a nationally known evangelist, so we turned the rest of the services over to this couple. Shortly, we started getting feedback of stories being told about us, our lack of spirituality, our dress wasn't becoming and our preaching wasn't deep enough, etc.

It was then that I found I was more carnal than I realized. Every time I would hear some of these criticisms, instead of rejoicing as the scripture said, I was **furious**. After all, we had tried to help **them**, and they turned and knifed us in the back, saying all these things about us.

Once you allow these things to fester in your heart, they grow out of proportion. I very well remember the resentment that had built up

133

in my heart toward these associates. I am relating this story to show what I learned from it.

I have had unusually good health all my life and am so thankful. I've just had one problem. While in Wisconsin, I would have "quinsy" of the throat each year. I finally had my tonsils removed.

At the time of my story we were staying in a hotel in Milwaukee, where I was the pianist at this citywide meeting. Sidney was in charge, leading the singing, etc. I became very ill, and my throat swelled and swelled. I had no tonsils, so there was nothing to relieve the pressure. I had to write notes as I could not talk. I was getting worse and worse. Finally, a doctor was called to the hotel room. He took one look and said, "Something must be done **right now**!" He got a scalpel from his case and, without any pain killer, put that knife through the tissue in my throat until I thought the knife would come out the back of my neck. Then I leaned over a basin and the green, ugly infection poured out like a river. As the doctor stood there and looked he said, "Do you know there is enough poison there to kill three people?"

When he was gone and I laid back on my pillow with unbelievable relief, the Lord whispered to me, "Do you know what that poison was? It was all those feelings you've been storing up against others." I asked the Lord to cleanse my heart as well as my throat.

In the years to come, I heard my husband preach one of the finest sermons he ever gave on the effect of bitterness and hate and anger in the physical and spiritual body. How many people have ill health because of it? No wonder it is more important to let love have it's perfect way in our lives. There is no room for **hate** and **love** in the same life.

Actually, the Lord might have used this to help loosen the strings that tied us so tightly to the Kenosha church as God was saying, "It is enough." In other words, this was God's time for us to leave.

We had such a wonderful time in Milwaukee that the people said, "Why don't you stay and open a church here?" When the meetings were over, we did begin preaching in one of the halls of the city auditorium. We couldn't have services during the week, so we had morning, afternoon, and evening services on Sundays.

It was interesting to read one of my old letters I wrote, dated August 30, 1934. "We have three services on Sunday. We have doubled in attendance every service in the last months. We have received no personal finances, but last Sunday we received enough offerings to pay all the back bills and leave us in the clear. This coming Sunday is our love offering! We have some wonderful people here, and we believe we are going to have a great church."

Depression days were still on. We were never quite sure when we would eat, but **nothing** mattered except the Lord's work. We never went hungry.

"Trust in the Lord with all thine heart, and lean not on thine own understanding. In all thy ways acknowledge Him, and He shall direct thy paths." Proverbs 3:5-6.

Chapter 20

Ministry In Milwaukee

Sidney and I searched the city for a permanent location, and finally we found it. It was a former department store, right on the corner of a main street, with transportation right outside the door, and plenty of room for all our needs. We thought, why not? After all, during our first ten years of ministry we had pioneered in a former sulfur bath house, on street corners, in a narrow store building, a skating rink, a dance hall, country school houses, and of course, conventional church buildings. Paul the apostle talked about *"the church in thy house"* in Colossians 4:15, and I have always loved the song that says "Where Jesus is, 'tis heaven there." Surely Jesus would be with us in a department store building.

Finding the building was just the start. We needed seats for the auditorium, a platform, a baptistery, and other things. Though it was a gigantic job, we changed the store building into a presentable church auditorium, with flags and banners. It became an exciting place! We had plenty of rooms for Sunday school, and the showcase windows out front made a wonderful place for displays. With the help of a professional artist who wanted to do something for the Lord, those windows became a work of art. People would stand for a while, admiring the windows before they even realized they were looking into a church. Many strangers attended the services; many were converted and stayed with us.

We had a choir, and as I think back, I am amazed at our courage and daring. For the Christmas season of 1934, we chose to perform the magnificent oratorio, Regem Adorate. What breathtaking music! We searched for volunteers for the occasion, and one of these was Paul Sorensen from Kenosha, Wisconsin. (Remember Olga Sorensen's three sons?) He hadn't been converted yet, but through this singing ministry, **he found the Lord.** Even if nothing else but Paul's conversion was accomplished in Milwaukee, it was worth it.

As I am writing this, I like to bring our readers up to date. Paul went to Bible school, and married a wonderful wife, Henrietta. Later, both of them were our associate pastors in Dayton, Ohio. My husband sent them to fill in for a church in Canton, Ohio, where they ended up staying and pastoring for over 30 years. They are retired now (supposedly), and though still on a daily radio program in Canton, they find time to spend in Florida, not just vacationing, but pastoring a church in a mobile home park.

Back to Milwaukee. As always, we found problems here as everywhere. If we had not been seasoned pioneers by now, we could have found many reasons to quit. For one thing, Milwaukee was not an easy place to preach the gospel! It's a beer town, and not especially receptive to Christian work, and we were in a largely unchurched area. Another big problem arose when the weather became cold. Our large auditorium was great in the summer and early fall, but in the winter it was a different story. The old radiators around the building were constantly breaking down, even as we urged them to give more heat. When it was really cold, we resorted to holding service in one of the smaller rooms.

The work of the church was a full-time job, and yet Sidney had an even bigger task. He was supervisor of the Eastern District for the Foursquare Gospel. He helped start and oversee many churches, and had a number of young pastors under his care. It would have been impossible to carry on both ministries if not for the fact that **God made us a team.**

At this time, our family consisted of Sidney Robert, Rebecca, Roselyn, Roger and two nieces, Dorothy Lee and Barbara Gentry. We had a glorious climax to the year 1934.

Worldwide Missionary Trip

With the coming of the new year, Sidney had an invitation to go around the world to minister to missionaries. At the time, he was 27 years old. Once again, our consecration was put to the test. We couldn't both go, so I would remain at home, caring for the family and the church.

He was to leave on the Japanese ship <u>Hyia Maru</u> from Seattle, Washington. I went with him to see him depart. On one hand he was excited, for this was his first missionary trip, not to mention his first sea voyage around the world; on the other hand, he was sad for both of us. We stood in the fog and mist, and kissed good-bye with tears flowing. He boarded the ship, and we waved till the ship faded into the fog. The old fog horn sounded a sad refrain, and I had to rush to the station to catch my train back to Milwaukee. I took a book with me to keep my mind occupied on the lonely trip home. I read <u>The Magnificent Obsession</u> - what a book!

Arriving back home and getting into the routine of responsibility, there was plenty to keep me busy, but I waited eagerly for the letters I was sure would come. I would like to share a bit of both his and my letters during this time. Histories are often written from letters, and following are quotes from our letters.

Quotes From My Letters to Sidney

January 30, 1935

My Own Precious Loverboy,

Today you are halfway across the ocean, but I hope you receive this in China. When you left, my heart was filled with anguish and loneliness, but the peace of God came to the rescue... As I arrived home in Milwaukee, the children were fine, glad to see me back of course. They loved the little things you sent them... As to the church, I know there is victory because the battle is hard. I set aside three days for fasting and prayer. I have prayed much for you honey... I miss you so much but we have shown the Lord we love Him best of all. I know you miss me but we can't think of that... I have a water baptismal service Friday. The pastors from Racine are going to help me... Good-bye for now.

February 15, 1935

Dearest Sweetheart,

Today you have been heavy on my mind... You are in China now. You no doubt had a glorious meeting with Brother Paul Stephens, you have shed tears of joy. Your heart has been filled with new emotions, your soul has been moved afresh for missions. Didn't I picture it right?... Oh honey, I know you know my heart... I haven't been able to keep back the tears as I think of you... But I know how much this trip will mean to you.

Sunday was a wonderful day. What new enthusiasm. Sunday we had a full house. So many strangers. God did bless. I preached an illustrated sermon on "Gateways to heaven." If the weather permits, we will be needing more chairs as each Sunday the number has increased.

139

Sunday night, even though it was a great day, I was so lonely. After I got the family to bed, I put a pillow on the floor before the radio, turned on the music and thought of my beloved... One of the songs was "Just a Wearying for You." I know it was played just for me... If I were in your arms, with my head upon your shoulder, we could talk, and talk, and talk . . . Good-bye dear sweetheart. I love, love, love you.

There is not enough room here for all of his letters to me, so let me give you the highlights. He wrote from China. (This was before China was closed to missionaries.) He gave some very vivid descriptions of India, also. He brought back many pictures to help tell the story of his travels. His letters were filled with wonderful expressions of his love for me. He never lacked for words, as he told of his loneliness, too. But there was a crying out of his heart for the teeming millions he saw.

For instance, he described walking down the streets of Calcutta. He saw babies being born right on the street, and he knew they would live there all of their lives. They would sleep on newspapers on the sidewalk. They would not know what it was to have a full stomach.

But the thing that jarred his sensitive nature the most was the wagons that drove through the streets in the early morning. The men on the wagons would pitch the bodies of those who had died in the night onto the wagons like they were cord wood. **No one cared for the body or the soul!**

At one point, he had almost reached the limit of his ability to take seeing the diseased, starving, emaciated bodies every where he looked. The last straw came as he looked upon a woman whose face was so eaten away with leprosy that all that was left was a gaping hole. Her mouth, nose, and eyes were gone, and she made a croaking sound as she lifted up ugly, disfigured hands hoping for a morsel of food from anyone. Sidney clasped his hands over his face and ran as he cried out, "Oh God, I can't stand any more!" The missionaries took him home, where he was almost overcome. **He never did get over the hurting needs, both spiritual and physical, of a lost world.**

Then I wrote to him and brought him up to date. "The Sunday school has grown. We now have 12 girls in the girls' chorus. They look sweet in their white dresses with the violet corsages. Seven new members joined the church. Oh yes, we are going to have an orchestra. The Bradigan boy (violinist) will conduct it. Several were converted Sunday night. I preached on 'Fireman, save my child.' It snowed

Saturday, and I went out with the children and slid down the driveway on the sled. Maybe not too dignified, but we enjoyed it."

Then I heard from Sidney. He told more of his experiences in India. He traveled the length and breadth of India on $75.00 as he rode the train fourth class, which was unheard of for an American! His money from the states never caught up with him, and he told of a number of escapes he had. But God was with him.

Sidney wasn't the only one who was plagued with financial difficulties. Back home, we had crowds of people at church, but the winter expenses and bills were greater than our offerings. I had hoped we would get the funds so I could meet him in Europe and travel back with him, but that was another dream that had to be set aside.

As I reread my letters to him, I recalled my busy life making sick calls, practicing with the girls' chorus, preparing sermons, and keeping house. One particular Monday I wrote, "Today I went on a real cleaning spell. I cleaned the kitchen, scrubbed the floor, cleaned the cupboards, the ice box, the stairs, the basement, etc. Many times I read or wrote until the wee hours of the morning. Then I went to prayer meeting." I have mentioned this part to show that it is possible to go beyond the strength that even the Lord gives you. I have had wonderful health, but I was to find that there is a limit.

For this story, let me quote from the letter I wrote my grandmother in California. "My dear Grammie . . . Just a couple weeks before Sidney was to get home, I had a nervous break down. My first experience and, I hope, my last. I got so tired from both my work and Sidney's that I found my mind getting foggy. I sent a telegram to our dear friends, Bill and Bea Wildman, to come and hold a revival meeting. The very day they got there, I was out with one of the girls from Kenosha. We were going to make a pastoral call on a church family. I was so tired I couldn't drive, so she did. When we got to the house, I couldn't get out of the car. I just started to cry (which is unusual for me). I cried until my strength was gone, and then I went into a coma. For several days I was lifeless. My hands and feet were cold, my right side partly paralyzed, and I had no appetite. I worried about the church, but the church family was so kind. They took me to the home of our very good friends, the Oslunds, who lived in Kenosha, and I stayed there until it was time to go to New York to meet Sidney."

Everyone insisted that I was not able to go to New York, but I was adamant. I would go to meet my husband if I had to crawl to get there. Upon hearing of my being sick, Mother Correll immediately came to take care of the children, so I knew they would be alright while I went to New York. It was finally arranged for someone to drive me, and I would rest on pillows in the back seat during the trip.

The big day arrived. Sidney was on the maiden voyage of the world's largest ship, the S. S. Normandie. The ship was given a glorious New York welcome, with the fire boats shooting great sprays of water in the air, and whistles blowing. What a celebration!

Even though the ship arrived in the morning, the passengers were detained all day, initially because of the parade, and then size of the ship was somewhat of a problem. The ship was so large, it was difficult to accommodate it at the pier. Then the passengers had to endure the red tape of customs. I was about to get frantic, with my beloved so close and still I couldn't see him. I had no confirmation that he was even on the ship!

Finally, I saw him coming through the line. I ran and flung myself into his arms, weeping hysterically. He was puzzled at this kind of welcome, as he didn't know I had been ill, or have any idea what I had been through. (Communication wasn't what it is today!) Yet despite the tears, it was a wonderful meeting, and having him back was just the medicine I needed. He hugged and hugged me and kissed the tears away, and I felt so safe there, locked in his arms. And I was so grateful that the Lord had given me this wonderful man to lean on. Suddenly, somehow, all was right with the world!

Chapter 21

The Move From Milwaukee To Cleveland

"Now unto Him that is able to do exceeding abundantly above all that we ask or think, according to the power that worketh in us. Unto Him be glory in the church by Christ Jesus throughout all ages, world without end. Amen." (Ephesians 3:20-21)

Sidney had asked me if I would go to Cleveland, Ohio, to conduct a revival service. John Hoffman, a board member and Sunday School superintendent of a Foursquare Church there, had written and requested Sidney to send someone to fill in, as they were without a pastor. Sidney felt it would be a good change for me, as I had worked so hard in Milwaukee while he was on his missionary tour. He was very much involved in our department store church, doing all the things I had been unable to do alone. I was feeling better physically now, and he felt it would give me a new inspiration. He didn't know how true this would be.

When I arrived in Cleveland, I was met by John Hoffman and his family. Mrs. Hoffman was a real southern cook who made delicious biscuits every morning. They had two sons and four daughters. As I listened to their southern conversation, I was captivated. It was love at first sight, first with the family, and then with the congregation.

I discovered that most of the congregation had come to the city from Tennessee. We loved the Swedish people and the German people we had been ministering with these past years in Wisconsin, but there was something so alive and refreshing about these Tennesseans. Sidney was right; this was a new inspiration. I spoke night after night, and saw God's Spirit moving in their midst. The weeks went by, and I didn't want to leave!

It certainly wasn't the building that made we want to stay, as it was just a hall in a rather run down area. Why did I feel so at home here? I wrote to Sidney of how I wished we could move here. He reminded me of the fine people and the large building there in Milwaukee. We owed it to our own congregation to stay. Sidney had always made the decisions in the past when we made our moves, but I couldn't get over the tug in my heart to stay with these warm, friendly people.

In his next letter, Sidney reminded me, "Honey, we are responsible for so many young pastors, and we have always had an Evangelistic Center. How could we have it in the location where you are now?" I responded, "But why do I feel like this if we are not supposed to come?" Finally Sidney wrote back and said, "If you can find a suitable building in a better location, we will see what God works out."

The Cleveland congregation was overjoyed, and they began to pray in earnest, constantly urging me to come.

Looking For A Building

One day, as John Hoffman and I were looking for a location, we stood at the intersection of 93rd and Euclid. On one corner was the famous Cleveland Clinic. On the corner across the street was a magnificent Gothic cathedral. I was immediately captivated. There were a number of other such churches in Cleveland, but the difference was, this one was unoccupied!

What a building! Why was it not in use? Right then and there, I set out to find determine the reason. I did find that there was a congregation that met in the basement of the church. Also, in warmer weather, the upper part was sometimes used for a series of services. I discovered that the big drawback in having services year round was the heating of this huge building. When the Methodists had built it, the city had piped the heat through underground pipes from their huge furnaces. The Clinic and many other of the city buildings had access to it, but for some reason, the Methodists had moved elsewhere and the heat was shut off. The impossible hurdle was the fact that a $700 to $800 deposit was required to turn it back on, over and above the monthly heating bill. We certainly needed God's help!

Surely God was able to move this mountain. The Bible had said, *"Now unto him that is able to do exceeding abundantly above all that we ask or think."* I felt we just had to have this place. Talk about an evangelistic center! We had never had it this good.

The Lord gave me courage, and I went to the city officials and unashamedly asked them to waive the deposit so that this lovely building could be put to use. I almost felt like I was David, and this task was a giant Goliath. But, praise the Lord, the impossible happened! It was so exciting I couldn't wait to write Sidney, so I sent a telegram!

Meanwhile in Milwaukee, Sidney was ministering full time in the church, besides overseeing many other pastors and churches. Our people were quite stunned when they heard the news. What they thought had been a three week evangelistic meeting turned out to be a permanent parting.

It would take too much space to tell all the details of getting ready to move. Mother Correll was in Milwaukee with our four children plus our nieces, Dorothy Lee and Barbara. Daddy Correll was away, building another church and placing a pastor. Then there was Florence Brinkman.

When we first went to Kenosha, Wisconsin, Florence was 11 years old and in my children's church. She was very talented, and shared in the music. Five years later, we had moved to Milwaukee. Florence was 16 and had graduated from high school. Her mother asked Sidney to pray that Florence would find something to keep her involved until she was older, as her mother felt Florence was much too young to go to college. While Sidney was on his world trip, he wrote to Mrs. Brinkman from China. (Florence still has the card.) He asked if Mrs. Brinkman would be willing to let Florence come to Milwaukee and be his secretary, as we had no one to help. Mrs. Brinkman was very strict, but felt God was in it, so she allowed Florence to come. So Florence became part of the team in Milwaukee, and was a great blessing in all the work Sidney had to do. But, when she heard about the move to Cleveland, she was distressed and was sure her mother would never let her go that far away. However, God still had His hand in the situation, and Mrs. Brinkman again gave her permission. What a wonderful help Florence was to Mother Correll in getting ready to move!

Back in Cleveland, we were really working to get the church cleaned and in order before the big day. All the necessary business and paperwork had been completed in order to rent the church and have the heat cut back on. We were making preparations for a grand opening, when Sidney and the rest of the family arrived.

Sidney was more than pleased with the building and the location. In the time to come, we would hold some very large conventions in that building, including people not only from the states but from many foreign fields as well.

While in Cleveland, Sidney took time to continue his schooling at the Western Reserve University. As usual, we had a constant flow of national evangelists holding meetings at our church, as well as missionaries who ministered. We also had a radio program, and that's where I would have the opportunity to have my first ministry on the air.

I want to tell you about John Hoffman's family. They all came to church except for the youngest son, Clifton. This was a real concern to his folks, and they asked us to pray that God would get hold of their son. Clifton was playing in the night clubs. He was a darling, happy-go-lucky young man with a guitar and a charming smile, but he had no time for God. We not only prayed, but helped to answer those prayers. We asked him if he would be willing to chauffeur me on some important calls I had to make. He worked at night, so being available to me during the day was no problem. The sermons he missed in church, he got in the car! That didn't bother him, he just laughed it off and didn't come to church. I began cautiously to mention the darling secretary we had with us. He seemed interested and intrigued, but still didn't come to church.

Finally, one night he came to church. He met Florence, and began to show a little interest in her. But when Florence became aware of that interest, she became quite hostile and said, "That egotistical Southerner needn't think he can melt my heart."

Well, Cupid kept on working, and to make a long, wonderful love story short, Cliff had a glorious conversion and dedication, and a love affair with the Lord. Cliff and Florence had a beautiful romance, and were the first couple to be married in our lovely Gothic cathedral.

Update

At the time of this writing, Cliff and Florence have been married 57 years, and have ministered together in song and message around the world, and are still active for the Lord in our missionary ministry. Florence still smilingly reminds us that she never did get to college.

Chapter 22

From Cleveland To Dayton, Ohio

Reverend Bert W. Bruffett and Reverend Bessie Bruffett had been in Dayton for eight years. They came from California to hold a meeting in the Old Jewish Synagogue on Jefferson Street. The crowds grew and grew until there was no longer room for all of the people. The meetings were moved to the memorial hall, which seated several thousand. There was a real moving of God's presence in revival and healings. The Bruffetts and the congregation continued to meet at the memorial hall for two years. Then the people insisted that they needed a church home, so the Bruffetts rented the old United Brethren Church on North Main Street, which became known as the Christian Tabernacle. What a wonderful foundation they laid, as the church was established.

By the end of the eighth year, the Bruffets felt their work was finished. Being quite concerned as to who would take over, they called my husband. Bessie Mae said, "Sidney, we have gone about as far as we can go in this rented building. It may be sold at any time. What this church needs is a new building of its own. We know that you are a supervisor over many churches and are a very busy man. We also know that you have been responsible for pioneering and building churches, and raising the needed funds. We just feel that you are the man! Bert and I would like for you and Helen to come and take over the pastorate here."

Sidney's heart began to pound and he felt the excitement of a real challenge. But then he said, "Helen and I have been a team for years in our ministry. She is so happy in Cleveland, I'm not sure she will want to leave. Why don't you ask her to come down for a day and see if she feels the same 'bells of assurance' in her heart that I feel."

He came home and told of the wonderful meetings, the church, the vision, the possibilities, the challenge of building the new church. Yet all I could say was, "But we just can't leave Cleveland."

However, at Sidney's suggestion, I took the train to Dayton. Sidney stayed in Cleveland and preached. I tried to relax, but my heart felt a rebellion. It seemed like even the wheels of the train were saying, "You won't like it. You won't like it."

I was met at the station by some of the officials of the church. The ones who came to meet me were the only ones who knew why I was there.

As we came to the old church building, I realized that it was certainly no comparison to our magnificent structure in Cleveland. The people poured in and filled every nook and cranny of the edifice. The huge choir took its place and sang like angels, and the people lifted the rafters with their singing. A male quartet stirred my soul.

I didn't know what it was, but something was different. A joy bubbled up within me until I didn't know whether to laugh or cry. The bells **were** ringing in my heart.

As I spoke to the congregation, I was unusually blessed. I felt as though I were transported to another world. It was the same in an afternoon meeting, and again that night. The whole day, I felt that joy in my heart. When a group took me back to the train, I cried when I said good-bye and I cried most of the way home.

Sidney met me at the station and couldn't wait for my reaction. I looked at him and, with a tearstained face, I said, "What else can I say but yes to you, my dear, and yes to the Lord?" Sidney wrote Reverend and Mrs. Bruffett and told them we would plan to come to Dayton around Palm Sunday (which was four months away). We would resign the Cleveland church the first of the year, then go to Dayton in March.

We had a big Christmas program ahead of us in Cleveland, which included my favorite oratorio, Regem Adorate (written by Aimee Semple McPherson). I will never forget Cliff Hoffman as the serpent, slithering into the Garden of Eden.

With this wonderful spot on 93rd and Euclid Streets, the sky was the limit for opportunities. Any pastor would be glad for the opportunity to minister. But once again, it wasn't easy to tell the church that we were leaving. Our stay there was about one and a half years. We made some very wonderful, lasting friends.

About the middle of January, Sidney and I booked passage on a German freighter which was loaded with a cargo of lumber. We set sail for Panama to visit the missionaries there. This was my first missionary journey. How we did enjoy that trip together. One of my favorite adventures aboard was to walk along the lumber, forward to the very prow of the ship. Even when the waters were rough, and the ship dipped up and down, we would stand there with our arms around each other. We leaned as far into the mist as possible, feeling the waves dashing across the deck behind us and tasting the salt spray that filled the air. The more boisterous the sea, the greater our enjoyment. I can assure you that most of the sensible people were back on the enclosed decks or in their cabins when it was rough.

148

It was a real adventure going through the Panama Canal, seeing the lakes, the rivers and the locks, etc. The best part was meeting the missionaries. Arthur and Edith Edwards were in charge of the work there. We crossed the isthmus again by car. I certainly remember sitting on plank benches in the little Panamanian church that we visited, with the grass roof and the open sides. We learned to sing songs (phonetically) in Spanish, even if we didn't know what they meant. We knew the tune. I remember singing, "When the roll is called up yonder," using my hands in rhythm to **kill the mosquitoes**, slapping my legs, neck and arms. It was worth it all to see the yearning eyes of those seeking Jesus.

One day Brother Edwards said to Sidney, "Our national pastor, from the village of Pajanal, is here, and says they are waiting for me to go up for a service. They have converts to be baptized and babies to dedicate. It is a pretty hard trip, but it would be a wonderful chance for you to see pioneer work that really is primitive." Without hesitation Sidney said, "Yes, I would love to go." I spoke up and said, "Oh, I would love to go, too. I am a pretty good walker." Brother Edwards looked at me with a sympathizing smile as he said, "You'll have to walk about 20 miles, mostly up a mountain. None of the missionary ladies has ever tackled it." I replied, with determination in my voice, "Brother Edwards, if Sidney can make it, then I can, too." Sidney knowingly agreed, "I think she can make it, if it is alright with you."

The car was packed with water jugs (of boiled water), hammocks, lunch for the journey, a load of Spanish tracts and other paraphernalia, and we were off. The missionary, Sidney, a couple of national pastors and I left. We had to drive one hundred miles first. Believe me, that car was **not** the lap of luxury. It seemed like it was barely holding together. It was on this trip that Sidney and I decided one of our first missionary projects when we got to Dayton would be a **new car** for the Edwards.

On our journey, we threw out gospel tracts to people along the highway. The people would run to pick them up, often sitting down right there to read them. The missionary told us that the pastor of this very church where we were going was converted by reading a tract. He had walked this long way from the mountain, on his way to Panama City. He got one of the Gospel messages and read it. The name of the mission was on it. He came and asked if there were more of these wonderful words. He was converted. He stayed to study the Bible, and went back to tell his people about it. He wanted Brother Edwards to come with him, but he said, "We don't have workers, you do it." That was how the church was started.

It was getting dark when we came to the village where we would leave the car and start to walk. We ate some food and drank some water. Twenty national Christians had arrived to escort us up the mountain. Each of us took a flashlight. The men picked up the luggage, and we began the trek. It was necessary to get as much of the mountain climbing done during the night as possible, because the morning brought a very hot sun. It was an eerie feeling, trying to follow one of these Panamanian men over a narrow trail, single file. I just missed stepping on a snake which slithered across our path. I confess that it crossed my mind that I might have been a little hasty in my boldness for this journey.

When the moon arose and the stars began to brighten the sky, it became very exhilarating. We stopped to get our breath, and Brother Edwards pointed out to us the Southern Cross, a constellation whose four brightest stars appear as if at the tips of a cross. We curved back and forth as we climbed the mountain. The Cross seemed to move ahead of us, and we thought of the song, "With the Cross of Jesus, Going On Before."

It was beginning to get light as we reached the top of the mountain, which became like a plateau. As we walked along on level ground, the heat was almost unbearable. Our next experience was crossing **four rivers**. My gallant husband held my hand to help me, and finally one of the Christian boys took my other hand. We came to a hut about a mile from the pastor's home. Brother Edwards hooked up his hammock, crawled in and, with hardly a word, was sound asleep. Sidney and I sat beside the stream, took off our shoes and put our feet in the cooling waters to ease our tired muscles. We laid back onto the grass and dropped off to a sound slumber. I don't know how long it was before the national pastor woke us to say we had one more mile to go, and it would soon be time for the evening meal.

We made it! The pastor's home had a palm thatched roof and grass walls on two sides. The furniture consisted of a plank bench around the walls. The cooking was done outside over a fire, with three large rocks to hold the huge iron pot. The pastor's wife was stooping over it, cutting up different things to put into it. I was curious, and said to the missionary, "I wonder how she makes that? What is in it?" I never forgot the answer Brother Edwards gave me. He said, "One of the first things you learn as a missionary is to **never ask questions**. You eat what is set before you. It might be better if you don't know." I also learned what great lengths these people go to in order to entertain the missionary. They had walked miles to get a card table to eat on, a table cloth, two chairs, china bowls and silverware. They had none of these. They sat on the ground, ate out of calabashes, and carved out their own spoons; but it was their desire to make the guests at home. (Incidentally, I was the **first** white woman they had ever seen in the area.)

We were just a short distance from the jungle. It was now dark, and you couldn't see what it was like. My mind kept wondering what wild animals were lurking close to us. A couple of lanterns were lit and hung on pegs at the edge of the roof. The wife was just putting the bowls of food down in front of us. Suddenly, something brushed past my legs under the table. I almost upset the whole dinner. It was only the family dog.

When we had eaten (and it wasn't too bad), we noticed people were beginning to come. They had walked many miles for the service tomorrow, but they wanted a meeting tonight, also. We learned many things on this trip. One interesting sight was the women who carried their babies in a sling on their back, but the tied ends were across their forehead. When they arrived, they simply took the cloth off their head and hung the sling with the baby on a post of the hut. The babies slept peacefully. The women cried with joy in seeing a white-faced Christian sister in the Lord.

Sidney and I sang and gave our testimony (through an interpreter). The interpreter spoke, and the people just sat there. So we started all over again. We sang, testified and preached. **They didn't move**. Finally, Brother Edwards said, "They are here for the night, we might just as well go to bed." So he got out our hammocks, hung them on pegs across the room, and we had our own swinging beds. Needless to say, we slept with our clothes on. We were so tired, I think we could have slept standing up.

When I awoke, the pastor's wife was sweeping the dirt floor with her homemade broom. It really did look clean but I don't know why she bothered, for the chickens walked through, the dogs ran through, and the goats came in and out. I was amused as I peeked through the net of my hammock at the proceedings. Oh yes, some of the people were still there. They must have sat up all night. Others had gone to the river to wash up. When Sidney woke up, he said, "Well, honey, let's have a banana." Hanging from the ceiling was a whole stock of bananas.

This was Sunday, and the people came from everywhere to this building built by the Christians. Their testimonies would stir your soul.

There was a water baptismal service, and a dedication of babies to the Lord. But the highlight of the trip was the wedding! For years there was no clergy, Protestant or Catholic, in this area, so it had been customary to choose a mate and start a home. As Christianity came to their village, they felt keenly that they wanted God's blessing on their lives, so the missionary would come and perform the ceremony. What a wedding we saw! The couple had ten children! This was a sacred moment. The couple marched into the church, and the children were their attendants. The groom stood there with a coy, boyish smile. The bride had a veil made out of a curtain. She came to meet him with a tender blush on her face. The missionary read the ceremony, not leaving out one word. When they were pronounced husband and wife, the American influence was included, and he kissed the bride. The crowd sent up a cheer.

The saying, "What goes up, must come down," reminded me that we had another 20 miles to walk back, but I was glad I went. I felt the missionary vision that my husband was so burdened for.

Someone brought us a parrot out of the jungle. They asked if we wanted it. I thought of the kids at home and said, "Yes." It could speak Spanish. They said that "Corre, corre," meant run, run. The people told us it was just as well we didn't know some of the other things it said.

We put it in a cage in amongst our other luggage that went to the stateroom on the ship. What a wonderful visit we had there. With tears and waving, and invitations to come back, we leaned over the rail of the Japanese ship and shouted our good-byes.

We arrived in New York Harbor, and passed the Statue of Liberty. I don't know when we became aware of the **fury** of the Japanese Captain when he learned we had **a parrot aboard.** No one had told us we couldn't bring the bird into the U.S.A. We didn't know about parrot fever, and the possibility the whole ship could be quarantined! First, they were not going to let us take it off the ship. Second, if we did keep the parrot, it would be necessary to stay in quarantine a week or ten days. I wanted the bird. So because Sidney had to get back to the Cleveland church, **I stayed in New York until that bird was out of quarantine!**

When I arrived home, the children were delighted! I don't know why, but they named him Parson. In the morning we would greet him with, "Good morning, Parson." We tried to get him to say "Praise the Lord," but he must have had the wrong kind of training. The children would sing to him "The Man on the Flying Trapeze." They would sway back and forth as they sang. Soon, he was saying, "Ohhhhhh, he goes through the air with the greatest of ease." The children would go into gales of laughter. Then he would begin all over again, "Ohhhhhh, he goes through the air with the greatest of ease, ha ha, ha ha." He never did learn the rest, because the kids couldn't stop laughing long enough to finish it.

Good-bye To Cleveland

Frankly, it was not easy for either Sidney or me to leave the big city on the shore of Lake Erie. Sidney had really been putting down roots also, and it was with regrets that he would be leaving his studies with Western Reserve University. He had been majoring in History and Literature, which was a lifelong love. Also, it was the first time in ten years of our ministry that we were free of financial pressure. The great depression was winding down, and the war economy was gearing up.

But Dayton! We packed the car and started toward our new adventure. We left the children to finish out their school year. Mother and Dad were there to take care of them, of course. I said, "of course." I wonder if we took them for granted, or if we really made them feel how important they were to our ministry. Mother Correll was a disciplinarian (the kids sometimes thought too much so), but we knew they were well cared for.

As we neared the city, we could see the skyline. Today there are many tall buildings, but I think when we went, there was only one. There was a sense of destiny as we stopped the car. We got out and knelt by the side of the road. We cried out to God to use us in this city. I can honestly say that there was never any turning back in our consecration. "All for Christ" was our life.

In just six weeks Sidney would be thirty years old, and the following December, I would be thirty. It was all in God's timing as on Palm Sunday, March, 1937, we began our ministry in the Christian Tabernacle in Dayton, Ohio. This would be home for us until February of 1960.

Chapter 23

Dayton, Ohio - Building
Christian Tabernacle

A Prayer Meeting That Lasted For 100 Years!

"Pray without ceasing." **I Thessalonians 5:17**
"Let us arise and build." **Nehemiah 2:18**

Wow, that was some record! It is a historical report of the Moravians, founded by the disciples of John Huss at Hurn Hut. They had a place of prayer where the believers took turns, two at a time, in a continuous circle of prayer. They prayed around the clock, night and day, year after year, for a century. This was their secret of a great missionary movement. They believed in the command of the Lord, *"Go ye into all the world and preach."* Their goal was that one out of every ten members should become a missionary. The other nine were responsible to back the one financially. No wonder they covered the whole world, including the Indians of North America.

Since that time, many churches have emulated their example in a ceaseless chain of prayer. There are places where women pray two hour shifts by day, and the men pray by night. This has always been followed by a stream of blessings and glorious answers to prayer.

We are so grateful that we had this prayer opportunity in our early Christian life in the Angeles Temple of Los Angeles, California, where prayers were said day and night. It was a hallowed spot. So when we pastored in Kenosha, Wisconsin, the prayer tower became the powerhouse to back a fruitful ministry.

Realizing the tremendous responsibilities we would have in building a new church in Dayton, Ohio, we felt the first need was a place of prayer, with everyone having his or her share. A room was set aside in the basement of the old church on North Main Street, which was available night and day.

The time had come to arise and build. The lots were paid for at Herman and Best Streets. The building we were in had been sold. Both Sidney and I had poured over the blueprints with the architect and the building committee. Now, the problem before us was financing.

Building churches was not new to us, as we had experienced this from the very first church in Fullerton, California, just after we were married. In our pioneer ministry we would start a work, build a church,

155

get a pastor installed and move on. But this was different. We had to think on a larger scale. It would be a beautiful, light brick structure with all the modern facilities. In fact, it would be the **third air conditioned church in America.** It would seat a thousand people, with a choir loft and a platform clear across the front. We just couldn't wait! It is true, we didn't have a building fund, but these people knew how to give and, with **a loan from the bank,** so we thought, there would be no problems.

Sidney, in all his dealings in building, had never been denied a loan, so he went confidently to the Building and Loan Office and asked to see the president (always go to the top, he would say). He met the president and explained about our fine congregation, and how it was necessary to vacate the building we were now in at our present location. Our lots were paid for and now we needed a loan to get started. Then the **bubble burst**! Sidney's enthusiasm was shattered as the president looked him in the eye and very coldly said, "Young man, don't you know church loans stink?" Feeling stunned and crushed, Sidney walked out and down the street with mixed emotions. Then he remembered that he was a representative of the Most High God, and his spirit arose on the wings of faith. Right there at Third and Main Streets, with people passing on either side of him, he looked up into heaven, raised his hand, and said, "Oh Lord, God of heaven, You and I will build that church without a bank loan!"

As he walked home, he felt like he was walking three feet off the ground. They would see what God could do. He called the building committee together and told them his story. He shared with them the enthusiasm of a **venture of faith.**

The next Sunday was May 15, 1938. Sidney contacted our choir director, Dorothy Griffeth, and asked her to bring her cat to church. This was quite an unusual request, but she complied and brought the cat. My husband had a sack handy and put the cat in the bag, then brought it to the platform. He said, "Today is a very momentous day. We are going to let the cat out of the bag." With that, he opened the sack and out jumped the cat. You better believe he had the attention of the whole congregation. He announced, "It is time to arise and build!" He described the challenge for the whole congregation to pray, to have faith, and to work and sacrifice for the glory of the Lord. He told them of the bank's refusal to give a loan, but he reminded them that God is able to do great and mighty things.

First the basement had to be dug. It would be 64 x 110 feet long. As he presented the need, Mr. Clarence Christian, of Sand and Gravel, stood to his feet and said, "I will furnish all the sand and gravel you need." My husband caught his breath and then replied, "Mr. Christian, do you know how much sand and gravel that will be?" He answered, "I ought to, that's my business." Praise the Lord, what a mountain had been removed! We had a builder in the church, Ed Wetzel, who took over the building responsibilities. He had a couple of men that worked with him, and every man who was not working elsewhere made himself available to help.

It was pay as you go for materials and labor. Each Sunday, Sidney would stand in the pulpit and present the amount needed, which varied at times from $1,000 to $10,000 a week. Many times, the direct response started slowly, but as the Holy Spirit moved, it would come flooding in. It would be like the enthusiasm of a touchdown at a football game, **and the goal would be reached.**

This was not a one-time thing; it had to be repeated week after week. How could these people keep giving? Critics would say, "You'll drive all your congregation away if you continue these methods." But do you know what? Instead of loosing our congregation, our crowds got bigger and bigger. People came for miles, out of curiosity. "What amazing thing is this that is happening?" Then they would get caught up in the spirit of it and end up giving. The remarkable thing was, not once did Sidney present a goal **that was not met.** What about preaching? Who couldn't preach after a victorious manifestation of giving and sharing?

It did bother my husband a bit when he realized that he was getting a reputation of being a "money raiser". A few jokes were going around such as, the boy down the street had swallowed a nickel and his folks were desperate. Someone said, "Quick, go get Brother Correll! He's good at raising money." What the people did not realize was that Sidney paid a price. Every Saturday night, he stayed at the church, in the prayer tower, agonizing before God for the test that was in front of him. Every week, the devil would torment him and say, "This week, you'll never make it. You will fall on your face, and you will be embarrassed," but Sidney would travail in prayer until a witness came. Then, as he would face the congregation that morning, his faith never wavered, and the need was met.

All this time, our membership was growing. The Sunday School membership reached 1,001 as they crowded into the church and the adjoining houses. People drove for miles as our slogan advertised, "The church that is worth driving to". How faithful were the Herbert Van Tilburgs, who drove each Sunday from Sidney, Ohio.

Moving day came October 17, 1938, and our first service in **our new basement church** was October 23 of that year. Dr. and Mrs. Charles Leaming were there for the service. Immediately after church, we began a Bible reading marathon (reading the Bible aloud from Genesis to Revelation without stopping). Different ones took turns reading. It was completed the following Wednesday night.

The very next month we had our first wedding in the new church. It was on Thanksgiving Day. Margaret Schott, who had come from Zion, Illinois, to help in our parsonage with the cooking and housekeeping, was getting married. She married Larry Claxon.

For the next several years, we deferred going on up with the building. We now had a place to go. The people could have a rest. Of course, the "San Ballats and Tobias" of Nehemiah were around to spread the word, "they will never finish the building. It will always be a basement church."

Update

I saw Larry and Margaret Claxon recently, and they have been married for 56 years.

Charles and Audrey Mieir Arrive

In September of 1939, Audrey and Charles Mieir came from California to be the first of a number of fine associate pastors who would minister with us. What a terrific addition they were to our Christian Tabernacle staff in Dayton, Ohio.

Shortly after they came, we switched our radio program to a new station. For many years, we had a daily program from 2 to 2:30pm, which was called Wings Over Dayton. We moved the family broadcast to Saturday, and Audrey became known as our beloved "Aunt Audrey."

What a music department we had with the Mieir's, with choirs, trios, etc. We were so fortunate to have the colorful ministry of these dynamic song writers. Among the many songs was one that is sung around the world, "His Name Is Wonderful." After Audrey left Dayton, she led many famous choirs, including the one that sang in the Hollywood Bowl. She had many years with the beloved Phil Kerr (who also visited Christian Tabernacle). Audrey was also written up in Who's Who of American Women.

How grateful we were for this dedicated couple, and we could say, "We knew them when . . . " They were faithful, tireless, inventive and cooperative with their multiple talents. Charles was the less vocal member of the team, but he was invaluable. I think his nobility was really manifested when he would laughingly say, "God didn't call me to preach, he called me to look after Audrey and her ministry!" She was quick to say, "I would never have made it without Charles." They were still practically newlyweds when they came to Dayton.

Update

I had dinner with them several months ago. We are **all** in our eighties.

Something New Is Added

I began to realize our family was growing up all at once. Before long, they would all be gone. I felt an intense desire to replenish the nest and have a baby. When I voiced the idea to some of the ladies in the church, they assured me I had fulfilled my duty and anyway, I wasn't as young as I used to be. This didn't convince me. My baby, Roger, would soon be ten years old. I had gotten quite heavy, so I began a reducing program and had a vigorous swimming schedule at the YWCA several days a week. Then came the delightful news, I was going to have a baby.

The following months, I just never felt better. I never had a sick day, never missed a service at church, never missed a day of my half-hour broadcast. In fact, we had just finished a program and Audrey was sitting at the piano, when I said, "Hey girls, I think I am about to go to the hospital. I have that feeling." We sat there and laughed like crazy. I did go to the hospital, and the next day, Saturday, my baby came. Helen Rowena was born on September 28, 1940. I had shocked both radio and church friends, church friends mainly because I kept losing weight all the time I was gaining(?). What a joy to both my husband and me to have this new baby. She was a darling.

Church In The Basement

In 1941 we were still having church in the basement! We had been concentrating on evangelism. Nationally known evangelists from coast to coast ministered in our glorified basement auditorium. We had a harvest of souls and missionaries.

Each year, we would go to Camp Maranatha, in Muskegan, Michigan for our youth camp. In 1941, after the camp, we took a small house trailer and our four older children, and went to Mexico for a vacation, as well to visit missionaries. We could write a book on that trip alone! It was a wonderful time.

We were living in Dr. Cameron Townsend's home in Cuatla, Mexico, when Sidney tuned in to an international broadcast. He heard the stunning news that Hitler, with his Nazi troupes, had marched into Poland. He was galvanized into action. He found a telephone and called Fred Gray, who was the treasurer of the church in Dayton. He said, "Brother Gray, I want you to order the steel for the church **now**. Have them deliver it immediately." Mr. Gray followed instructions exactly. Sidney, the children and I left the next day for Dayton. Only God knew that Pearl Harbor was just ahead. Two weeks after the steel was delivered, all steel was frozen for the duration of the war. The steel was erected on the building, but it stood as an unclothed skeleton for the winter.

The following Easter, Reverend Thompson of the West Indies Mission from Cuba, was with us, as well as Reverend Vernon Gortner. Both were special speakers. Sidney raised $5,400 to get the building moving again. Bricks were not crucial to the war effort, so we started up with the walls. During June and July, we had a rooftop revival. The floor was laid and chairs were brought in. The choir was there, and Reverend A. Earl Lee and Rhoda Lee, from California, were the evangelists. They preached every night for weeks. During the day the brick layers laid the brick, and at night we held services. The people came, not only for the meeting, but to see how far the workmen had gotten that day. It was a unique and wonderful experience.

One other vital item, conduit for wiring our church for lights, was frozen. We prayed for and received another miracle. Someone found rolls of electrical conduit in a warehouse that was not under government restrictions. God had provided for us again.

The opening service of our completed auditorium was held on September 20, 1942. Dorothy Griffeth sang "Open the Gates of the Temple".

The following Sunday, the choir had their new maroon robes on for the dedication. Dr. Oswald J. Smith of Toronto, Canada, was our special speaker. How appropriate, as our church was definitely a missionary church.

How beautiful the church looked. Approximately one third of a million dollar edifice, dedicated **without a mortgage**. The well known

Dr. Paul Rudd called it the miracle church. Dr. C. M. Ward said it was the only great evangelistic center he knew in America that was built during the war years. God is good!

The Happy Family Broadcast

Audrey and Charles Mieir

Christian Tabernacle - Dayton, Ohio

Chapter 24

Dayton Missionary Bible Institute

"Go ye into all the world and preach the gospel." Matthew 28:19.

With our new church completed, we faced a another challenge in those fruitful forties. We had scores of young people who had volunteered for full time missionary service. Doors of opportunity had opened, but before we could send out workers, there had to be preparation.

"Study to show thyself approved unto God, a workman that needeth not to be ashamed, rightly dividing the word of truth." II Timothy 2:15.

It wasn't just a Bible school we needed, but a school that was **missionary oriented**, that breathed with a passion for a lost world. So in spite of our busy schedule, we added one more responsibility.

On September 22, 1941, the Dayton Missionary Bible Institute was born. Thirty-six students enrolled. The class was named "The Harvesters." There was a special benediction over the class that very first night as they began to sing:

> Lord give a vision, burning within,
> Of sinners dying, lost in their sin.
> We've a commission, Jesus to teach.
> I'll do my part Lord - others to reach.

Reverend Charles Leaming gave a stirring address. Reverend Herman Walters introduced the faculty, giving the subjects and goals they expected to accomplish. As the students stood to be dismissed, they launched on their three year journey by singing prayerfully, and with real meaning, "I'll go where you want me to go, dear Lord."

I would like to thank Mary Jane Search, Veda Mae Salyer and Reverend Crawford Jones for the well-kept record of names, dates and activities that make it possible to tell this story.

It was not a story of an organization, but an organism that was alive and vibrant, that bore fruit through the years.

Classes were conducted in the Christian Tabernacle of Dayton, Ohio, but the interesting thing is, Dayton Missionary Institute was not limited to our local area. As if by a magnet, students were drawn from far and near.

Barbara Monroe came 6,000 miles from Nova Scotia. Louise Stepula was from Detroit, Michigan. Doris Smith had a marvelous healing before coming from Iowa. Roy Gifford and Johnny Van Heart were from New York State. Erna Harder was a farm girl from Nebraska. Norma Stoffl left the windy city of Chicago to come. Al and Olga Fast hailed from the state of Minnesota. Betty and Milton Dresselhaus were on their honeymoon, coming from Beloit, Wisconsin. Jess and Irene Nicholson traveled from California. On and on they came, plus the local students.

Update

As I look back in retrospect and see these names I know, I realize that so many of these dear graduates have spent a lifetime in a foreign country or home ministry. They have now retired, yet not retired. If they haven't been transported to glory, they are still active for the Lord.

School Dormitory

With all the students coming from other states, we needed a place for them to stay. A lovely, spacious old house was purchased, and the young folk called it "The Senguele House". The name was from an African Tribe, meaning, "the senguele never turns back." There was a large living room which was a perfect place for class get-togethers, games, singing and fellowship. It was also great for Christmas parties, with everyone sitting around the warm, crackling fire in the fireplace.

The first graduation was in 1944, and Dr. Rhoderic Morrison came from California to give the Baccalaureate Address. The second class was called "Pilots", and the third was "King's Messengers".

During the fifth year, as more students came, we realized we did not have room to expand without a building program. Sidney was much too busy to get into that, so we prayed to the Lord to show us the answer. Dr. Correll became very excited when the invitation came to amalgamate with the Bible College in Kansas City under the direction of Dr. Walter Wilson. He was not only a noted, magnificent Bible teacher and a precious soul-winner, but a very dear friend.

So as new students came to our school, they were transferred to Kansas City. Only Eternity will reveal the wonderful harvest of these dedicated young people.

Chapter 25

Cuba

Doors Close; A Great Door Opens

"When you pass through the waters, I will be with you; and through the rivers, they shall not overflow you. When you walk through the fire, you shall not be burned, nor shall the flame scorch you."

Let me give you another scripture: *"'What are these wounds between your arms?' Then he answered, 'Those with which I am wounded in the house of my friends.'"* Zechariah 13:6.

I suppose there isn't a pastor who couldn't say, "I know what you mean." When everything seems to be on the mountain top, then wham! It seemed we had been going from one mountain top to another. Was it pride on our part because we had worked so hard to have the **largest missionary offering** in all the sister churches that year? God had been **so good.** I will go into it only enough to give you the picture. One of the officers who was over all the fields seemed to get the idea that he needed to bring us, or Sidney as a supervisor, down to earth. He was heard to say, "Sidney is getting too big for his britches. We need to bring him down a notch." So, at the annual convention, Sidney was dismissed as an official of the organization. It seemed our world had crashed. I wept for ten days, for I thought that was the end. This was many years ago, and I only mention this to encourage some pastor who might be going through the same thing. Remember Joseph?

Joseph must have though it was the **end** when his brothers sold him into Egypt. Then, years later, when Joseph was **next to the head** of all Egypt, his brothers faced him in great fear. He said, *"But as for you, you meant it for evil against me; but God meant it for good,"* Genesis 50:20. Even Christ went through this in John 1:11, *"He came unto his own, and his own received him not."*

All of this happened right in the midst of building our new building. In 1940, Christian Tabernacle became an **independent** or **interdenominational church.** We had gone through this deep valley. We had faced disappointment and bewilderment, but oh, how our church was growing. Our building was going up, but we found ourselves with no outlet for our **missionary vision,** and we still had young people in our church who desired to be missionaries. For Sidney, having no missionary program was like being a fish out of water. I saw a man sometime ago whom I had not seen for forty years. He said, "I remember the first sermon I ever heard Dr. Correll preach. It was a missionary sermon." I replied, "My brother, the last sermon he preached was a missionary sermon."

Where do we start? As we waited on the Lord, Sidney's attention was directed to the coming annual missionary convention in Toronto, Canada. It was conducted by Dr. Oswald J. Smith. He went to the meeting and joined hundreds of mission-minded people. His soul was blessed and inspired. They were so kind to him. A wonderful fellowship began between Sidney and Dr. Smith, which would take them into many missionary meetings as a team in the years that followed.

When Sidney returned, he was renewed with the gospel message to "go." He preached a sermon that glowed with excitement. Shortly, we had our first **very own missionary conference,** which began on May 12, 1940. It was Mother's Day and Sidney's thirty-third birthday. We took our first **faith promise commitment** for the year, and it totaled $2,650. We felt real victory.

My husband said one day, "Honey, get your things together. We are going to Cuba." Cuba! Why Cuba? He said it was our only open door at the time. This was during World War II, and missionaries were restricted from most parts of the world. However, Cuba was right at our doorstep.

While in Toronto, Sidney received an invitation from Dr. Elmer Thompson, of West Indies Mission, to visit their mission station in Los Pinos, Cuba. So we packed the car and were on our way. I was six months pregnant with little Helen, but that never stopped me. The church and the family were in good hands, for we turned everything (even our kids) over to Charles and Audrey.

The building program would be well directed by our most excellent executive secretary, Beatrice Wildman.

We drove to Key West, Florida, boarded a ship (car and all), and headed for the Pearl of the Antilles, Cuba. We passed the Morro Castle and entered the Havana harbor. That morning, as we drove through the city and out into the tropical country side, it was love at first sight! We loved the tall royal palms waving in the gentle breeze, the banana trees, mango trees, papaya trees and the lush green everywhere. The people were so friendly.

We arrived at the West Indies Mission and discovered a fantastic ministry. There was a huge auditorium, filled with over 1500 singing, happy Christians. What precious days these were. We visited palm-thatched churches in the remote areas, as well as having fellowship with them at the home base. Sidney counseled with Dr. Thompson, asking if there was any place on the island that had not been reached with the gospel. We had young people ready to send to the field. The answer was, "Yes, the west end of the island had not been evangelized." It was an open door. We got in our car and drove westward, to the end of the island. We came to the town of Caimito. There we selected our first missionary site. When we went back to Dayton, Ohio, we called the church together and, after much prayer, **World Mission** was born. (This was 1940, six years before it became **United World Mission**.)

October 7, 1940, we sent out our first missionaries, Esther Batson and Mr. and Mrs. Louis Grossnickel, to Cuba. Going to a new country usually poses real problems, one of which is usually learning the language. However, this was not one of little Esther's difficulties, as she was the daughter of missionaries.

I must tell you Esther's story. In the midst of her missionary endeavors, there came a young Spanish man who was eager to learn English. He asked if Esther would help him because she spoke both languages. She agreed. When they came to conjugate the word "amor" to love, Ramon found himself getting sidetracked and telling her about his wonderful country of Spain. He told her that he was a prince and that he was looking for a princess, and he wished to escort her away on his noble white steed to his great castle on the hill. Esther was very interested but, true to her calling, she kept insisting on telling him of the wonderful way of salvation. He was intrigued by her story of Christ. Actually, Ramon was her first convert. (I should tell you that Esther is a graduate of LIFE Bible College, and was known as "Tiny" because she was less than five feet tall.) She was and still is a real soul winner for the Lord (though the years have past and her beloved is gone). She did marry Ramon Blanco, and become a princess to this prince of a man. He did take her to Spain and to his castle, which was a 200-year-old house on the hill. It turned out that the white steed was a white mule. Both of them were wonderful missionaries in Spain for many years. The important part was, by Esther marrying Ramon, doors were opened to ministry in Spain which would have been closed, otherwise. I just had to take time out to tell you this story.

Other of Esther's converts were Antero Acoe and Arturo. I believe both of them are still preaching in Cuba today, though it has been with much duress under Castro.

I am sitting here looking at the names of many of the missionaries we sent to Cuba. I feel I would like to put their names on record for their years of faithful service. I hope I haven't missed any: Maxine and Edward Sorensen, Ralph and Stella Correll, Mary Flynn, Esther Batson De Blanco, Mr. and Mrs. Louis Grossnickel, Norma Stoffl, Virginia Hipple, Arthur and Veda Mae Salyer, Alvin and Olga Fast, Paul and Dorothy Hartford, Louise Stepul, Jess and Irene Nicholson, Luther and Adeline Mieir, Thelma Wagner, Roy and Marg Ackerle, Milton and Betty Dresselhaus, Reverend Adams, Allen Montgomery, and Reverend and Mrs. Paul Hartman.

Some served short terms while others were switched to one of our other fields. One was Mary Flynn, who later went to Africa to assist our son, Sidney Robert. After his death, she spent a lifetime there. Thelma Wagner, our school teacher, went to Bolivia, where she still serves. Alvin and Olga Fast were in Venezuela for years, but these past few years they have been working among the Cubans in Miami, Florida. I wish I could tell the story of each one. I'm glad it is all written down in heaven.

Maxine And Edward Sorensen - 18 Years In Cuba

Let me tell you of the missionaries who spent the longest time in Cuba. It was Sidney's sister, Maxine, and her husband, Eddie. They had pastored a church in Decatur, Illinois, then went to California. Sidney asked them to come to Dayton for our missionary conference in 1942.

Paul Fleming, of New Tribes Mission, was one of the speakers. He gave a very heart stirring message about God's call to a lost world. Should one have a call to go to a mission field? I remember Paul emphasized that **the need** is the call, and that every Christless heart is a mission field, and every Christ-filled heart should be a missionary.

Then Dr. Correll gave a plea for Cuba and the desperate need there. Is there a pastor who will say, "Yes, Lord"? A call for dedication was given, and both Eddie and Maxine answered the call, each not knowing the other was there. They made a deep consecration to the

Lord. Soon they came to Sidney and said they were willing to go. He was surprised but delighted.

They began making preparations to go to Caimito, Cuba, with their four year old son, Larry. Two things concerned them. Were they really missionary material? Later, they conferred with Dr. Oswald Smith, and Maxine confided, "We don't feel like we are the missionary type! We like to dress nice, and I wear a bit of cosmetics, which many missionaries don't. And then Eddie is a born comedian, and wonders if his humor will hinder the ministry?" Dr. Smith assured them it wasn't what was on the outside of the cup, but what was inside that mattered. If they could **love the people** and **love the Lord** enough to give them the message, and had a dedicated heart, that was what was important. As far as humor was concerned, "If a missionary goes to the field and can't see the funny side of things, he better stay home," Dr. Smith said.

Let me add that eighteen years in Cuba testified that they **were** missionary material. They did fall in love with the people. To add a little humor, language didn't come easy for Eddie. He had to really work on it. He had a picture taken of him on his patio, sitting in a chair, with an ice bag on his head. Several Cuban young people fanned him as he wiped his brow with a big cloth. He was reading a book, **"How to Learn Spanish in Six Easy Lessons."** The children and neighbors were around him, laughing and laughing. How they loved him. Everywhere he went, they would shout, "Edwardo!" While Eddie and Maxine learned the language, they gave out Bibles and gospel literature everywhere they went. In August of 1943, their daughter, Sandra, was born. Eddie was made director of the Cuban field. New missionaries came, and many cities were being invaded for Christ

Ralph and Stella Correll (Mom and Dad) went down to see their new granddaughter, Sandra. They thought it was a temporary visit, but they became indispensable as missionaries.

Prayer Hill And Cabanas Bay

Dad and Mother Correll arrived in May of 1943, but the next January, Dad started on a special mission. Sidney realized that one of the most important things they needed to do in Cuba was to establish a **Bible Seminary.** The thing was, where could they find a proper campus? Maybe on a farm, where there would be plenty of room. So Dad, being a former real estate man, was just the one to look for it. He found many areas where they had never had any preaching of the gospel.

Let me quote from one of his letters: "My first night out was very cold. I found a nice grassy spot off the main trail for my horse. I hung up my hammock, and undressed as usual. By midnight, I had to get up and dress, for my Hudson Bay blanket didn't stop the cold. Besides, my horse was lonesome. I was glad when morning came."

He found in the little country stores the very hard round crackers called galletas. He would eat these with a can of tomatoes. He continued, "I had ridden five days through a very wild country. I came to a village with about two or three hundred people, a few stores, and soldiers' quarters. I was not able to speak Spanish, so even though I knew they were very curious, I wasn't able to tell them much. I **did** carry my recommendation from the sergeant in Caimito, my Cuban Carnet, and a letter telling the purpose of my trip. However, the soldiers had made up their minds that I was a spy, and they arrested me and took me back to Havana. I had to leave my horse and saddle. I was delayed five days. I know what it is like to be guarded at night by soldiers, marched along the streets with an armed escort, with rifles held ready. I had a ride in a paddy wagon, but all the time I couldn't help but think how much better off I was than St. Paul, when he was taken prisoner and dragged down the streets while the crowd stoned him. Here I was, riding in a steel cage where nothing could hurt me."

All told, he traveled about four hundred miles. Ralph went back to Caimito and rested awhile. Then he returned to the Cabanas Bay area, for he had been very impressed with this place. One day, he rode to a high hill overlooking the country side. It was a place where he could see hundreds of bohio homes, mountains in one direction and the Gulf of Mexico in the other. He got off his horse, kneeled down and asked the heavenly Father to give us a missionary farm in that community for His glory. In May, my husband went to Cuba and brought with him our very dear friend from Kenosha, Wisconsin, Walter Block. (Remember him from the morning prayer meeting?) In the meantime, Dad had found the farm the Lord wanted us to have and, with the financial help from our friend, the farm was quickly purchased.

Very soon, our Bible School and evangelistic center was developed in one of the most beautiful spots in the world. The young people started coming, both young men and women. The story deserves more time than I can give it here, but during the next twenty years, the Lord gave us a harvest of souls. Only eternity will reveal the labor of love, the seed sowing and the soul winning through the dedicated lives of

170

the missionaries. They not only invaded the country, but they invaded the hearts of thousands of Cubans.

Then came the revolution in Cuba. Baptista fled, Castro came. In the beginning, there was great hope for religious freedom. Unfortunately, this was proven an illusion. Within a year, the missionaries found it was best, for the sake of their people, to leave. What a sad time when one missionary family after another packed their suitcases **(which was all they could take)** and returned to the United States. How often I heard Maxine describe, with tears, how difficult it was to choose what were the most important items to take after eighteen years of calling Cuba home. There were mementos, photographs, gifts and personal effects. "Farewell, dear friends!"

The Legacy They Left

The work was not lost. There were many Bible School graduates who became **pastors,** and when the missionaries left, they put it all into the hands of the national pastors. To the glory of God, they have carried on, through testings and trials. Perhaps every one of the men pastors has been in prison for preaching the gospel, but many were married to wives who also preached, and they held the church together until their spouses were released. It is the amazing story of church under fire, and how it had grown in spite of persecution.

This is when Dr. Correll and I realized the worth of a national pastor. That is why, when we reached **retirement** years, we chose to minister to the nationals, giving them assistance to carry on through Correll Missionary Missions, because you never know when **they will become the lifeline.**

171

Chapter 26

Christmas In July

In the early 1940's, my husband came back to Christian Tabernacle in Dayton, Ohio, from Washington D.C., where he had been holding meetings. He told us about a Baptist church that was having Christmas In July. The reason they stressed it was to protest the commercialism at Christmas time. They carried out the Christmas story, and people attended the services without getting all shook up about rushing around to buy all those last minute gifts, etc. It gave Sidney an idea about how we could use it for missions. He liked having a regular Christmas service to honor the Lord, and the day wasn't important, it was the point that Christ came as a babe in a manger. We would conduct it just like our regular Christmas service, getting the children excited about giving to the baby King. When they brought their gifts to the manger, to the Lord, it would be a missionary offering to send to the missionaries so they could get it before Christmas. What a terrific idea. (You could count on Sidney to work missions into it some way.)

All the staff got together and, in the heat of summer, we had Christmas! We sang carols, the choir sang anthems, and the Sunday School children said their recitations. The church was beautifully decorated with a Christmas tree and other festive trimmings. Then the climax was the Christmas story, enacted by our young people. They portrayed the bringing of the gifts to the manger by the wise men. The shepherds came with their lambs. Then the invitation was given for everyone to bring something for Christ. We always stressed that the most important gift we could give was our hearts.

The financial gifts they laid on the altar were sent to the missionaries all over the world. They were so grateful. Didn't Jesus say, *"In as much as you have done it unto the least of these you have done it unto me"*?

New York Calls

It turned out to be a tremendous blessing, and everyone wanted to do it each year. We hadn't done it to make a big splash with our Christmas in July. But we did have **good coverage** in our local papers. We were really surprised when we got a call from a New York paper, wanting to know what this Christmas in July was all about. Were we trying to change the date and time of Christmas? We answered, "No, we just wanted to have this lovely Christmas season without all the hassle and work that tries to crowd Christ out of Christmas time." We told them we still had our celebration and Christmas music in December. In fact, it made things a lot easier on the choir, because they had already practiced the music.

California Calls

That very same day we heard from a California paper, asking the same questions. We gave the same response, that we were simply sharing the wonderful story of the birth of Christ, without all the commercialism which surrounds it in December. Our people so looked forward to this time that we continued it for several years. The last time I remember us celebrating Christmas in July was in 1952. Life magazine had contacted us and asked if we were going to be celebrating Christmas in the month of July again. If so, they wanted to send down some photographers and a reporter to get the story on it.

The church people were very excited, as you can imagine, and every one worked like beavers preparing for this event, for they had never had such extensive, national publicity before. They really put their hearts into getting the Christmas music ready. Believe me, the church was beautifully decorated both inside and out. Mildred Hannah Laws and other artists in our congregation really put their talents to use. It was a day to be remembered! The music was never better. My husband preached his heart out, that Christ was not only the Christ of the manger, but Christ for a lost world!

Our associate pastor at the time was Lt. Col. Richard Headrick. We mentioned him and his fantastic background earlier in our story. He was in Hollywood movies as a child, and was a boy preacher as a young man. He had a colorful military life in the Air Force, and was in World War II. He even flew Bob Hope to see General Eisenhower once. Dick was at Wright Field at the close of the war, and attended Christian Tabernacle. When he was out of active duty, he joined our staff and became an associate pastor. Just thought you would like to know.

Richard was so clever in so many ways. In fact, he also was an inventor. He made this day (our Christmas in July) an extravaganza. Among other things, he had the brilliant idea of sending confetti down through the ceiling air conditioners to act as snow. It really worked, **and worked, and worked, and worked**, for it continued to snow. The residue would cling to the air ducts and sprinkle down on the audience **for months to come**.

But in the same manner, the gifts that the people gave that were sent around the world continued to work, and work, and work for eternal values.

Update

At this writing, I just contacted Col Headrick (who lives in California), and we talked and laughed about the story I have just told you. He said, "Do you remember, we also got a call from a certain perfume company, and they asked us if there was a copyright on the name 'Christmas in July'?" We told them we certainly didn't know of any. A short while later, a perfume came on the market called "Christmas in July"!

Incidentally, Col. Headrick is writing a book, which is no doubt off the press when you read this. It is called "A Mighty Fortress", with subtitles "Life in the Air Force" and "How I Survived 96 Combat Missions". Believe me, even if you are not interested in planes, you will love this book. It was Dick Headrick who talked Dr. Correll and me into learning to fly, so he is special.

Christmas in July

175

Chapter 27

Radio - A Special Love

If you asked which part of the ministry meant the most to me, I believe I would have to say **radio**. You are no doubt aware that my husband's special love of ministry was **missions.**

My first involvement in radio was in Los Angeles, California, not Dayton, Ohio, though that was the longest period of broadcasting.

The Angeles Temple opened its doors in 1923 to evangelize the world. As I mentioned earlier, I entered LIFE Bible Institute at age 15.

Not long after the opening of LIFE, Aimee Semple McPherson established her own radio station, KFSG. As a student, I had a part from time to time. There was a morning hour from 10 to 11am, which was called The Sunshine Hour. It was dedicated to the sick and the shut-in.

I was writing songs in those days, and I wrote the theme for this ten o'clock hour.

Tune in on your radio and get KFSG.
Set aside your troubles, and bid your sorrow flee.
Forget for one short hour, there's other things to do,
And listen to the message, that our radio brings to you.

Chorus:
In this Sunshine Hour, Sunshine Hour
Coming on the air.
Sunshine Hour, Sunshine Hour
With its word of cheer.
It comes to brighten up the day
To drive the gloom of life away.
This is Radio Sunshine Hour.

Actually, it wasn't until we came to Cleveland, Ohio, that I did a broadcast on a regular basis. It was a morning program, and it was called Radio Revival. We used the same theme that I wrote in 1923, only I used **Radio Revival** instead of Sunshine Hour.

Then the family moved to Dayton, Ohio, in 1937. When Mr. and Mrs. Bert Bruffett called us as pastors of Christian Tabernacle, they had a **Sunday night broadcast**, which we took over as well.

Shortly after my husband and I took over the pastorate, we began "The Happy Family Broadcast." "Come on Roger, Roselyn, Rebecca, Robert, it's time to get up." I can hear Margaret (our girl Friday) as she gave this call each morning around 5:45am. Four sleepy-eyed children would crawl out of bed and prepare for our early morning radio program.

By the time we arrived at station WHIO for our 6:45am broadcast, every one was alert and ready to roll. This was in early 1939.

After our theme Roger, then eight, would say, "Hello everybody. This is your Radio Rog, presenting to you 'The Happy Family'." The four children would sing a snappy song, like "The Hallelujah Train."

Rebecca would sing a solo, Roselyn would read a scripture or poem, and Robert had an item of interest for kids. (He was twelve then.) I played the piano, and Sidney would give the priorities of the Christian home.

We had a motto printed on both sides of a piece of cardboard. On one side it said, "God bless our happy home." On the other side it read, "Lord, help our scrappy home." The game was to see which side won.

We then switched to three afternoon programs of 15 minutes each. The church had been handling the funds of $50 a week. It became a problem, and the board was about to cancel it when I made a plea for it. I said, "Let me have it. All I ask is that I can present the need to the congregation during the service." The board agreed, so now it was up to me and the Lord. Fifty dollars seemed like a mountain. I think the first month or so, we put part of our grocery money into it. But I started a Radio Club through the church and the listeners. Before long we had increased to 15 minute, five days a week.

Later, for many years we had a wonderful spot, 2 to 2:30pm every afternoon. We were the only religious program in that area. Cadle Tabernacle had a 15 minute morning devotional program which originated from Indianapolis, Indiana.

Here's one of our promotional ideas. We had a picture of a dollar bill, and the words "**Let George do it!**" I am afraid you would never run a radio program with George today. But it was exciting, the support that came in. Do you know what? There are **several club members who still** send to our ministry **after 50 years**. Many other members are with the Lord.

178

For some time, we were also on the radio Sunday mornings with our church service. Our radio motto was, "The **Spiritual** Pause That Refreshes **The Heart**". (We go a little beyond Coca-Cola.) It was a time of rest for many shut ins. Mothers could relax with their children in school. Many listened in cars and stores and other places.

Wings Over Dayton

During the war, a song was being sung about "coming in on a wing and a prayer". Bea Wildman suggested that we change the words a bit, and use it as our theme song. Our program took on a whole new dimension. Dayton was the home of the Wright Brothers. The air bases were Wright Field and Patterson Air Base. It was a natural. The letters of the radio station we were now on was WING, so we renamed our program "Wings Over Dayton". Our theme was "Coming In on a Wing and a Prayer". It went like this:

> Coming in on a Wing and a Prayer,
> Coming in on a Wing and a Song.
> Songs of inspiration come to you,
> With a Message good and true,
> Coming in on a Wing and a Prayer. A-ah-men.

Of course, we had the sound of a plane in the background.

The girls who sang the theme and the special songs were called "The Flyerettes". Sometimes they were a trio. Sometimes they were a sextette, in different combinations. Their names were: Marge Acherle, Vivian Baskett, Deed Gardiner, Betty Dearth, Phyllis Miller, Erna Harter, Hazel McConnel, Joyce Hergenrather, Virginia Block and Phyllis Lasher. (Hope I didn't miss someone.)

Sidney was the Missionary Sky Pilot. George Gardener, who was our associate pastor, was the Navigator. Cliff Block played the Hammond organ or piano. I was the Lady Sky Pilot. The Flyerettes wore suits like the airline hostesses used to wear.

You remember, it was around this time that Sidney and I learned to fly and became **real pilots**.

We were so grateful to have Wilbur Botts in our control room each day, putting us on the air. He did work for the radio station, but he was also a member of our church, so that was great. He was a full staff member until we left Dayton in 1960.

To facilitate our whole staff going to the station each day, we built our own studio and control room in the church.

A funny thing happened one day during a broadcast. Our trio was singing, and Cliff Block was at the piano. I was the only other one there that day. I wanted to hear how the song was sounding over the air, so I stepped into the control room, not three steps away. I could look through the glass and see them, and hear them over the control room speaker. When I started back into the studio, the door was locked from the inside. There was no way for me to get back to my desk. I made signs to the girls that I was locked out. It is good thing they were on radio and not on TV, for the girls could hardly control their laughter as they tried to finish their song. When they finished, Cliff played a little extra on the piano while one of the girls quickly came over and opened the door for me. Talk about near panic!

We were so honored for the wonderful support we had from station WING, and for its Vice President, John Pattison Williams, as well as the entire staff. He helped us many times when efforts were made to change our time slot. Pat Williams, himself, gave us the word that Wings Over Dayton had the **highest** Nielson rating of all the daytime programs in the whole area, including network programs.

We tried to meet the needs of the people. Because we were the **only religious broadcast**, we made it a point to invite all the special evangelical speakers who came to Dayton to be on our program, and to invite people to their meetings.

Lady Evangelist Comes To Town

When the lady evangelist, Ethel Willetts, came to Dayton and constructed a temporary tabernacle for a period of special revival, she came to Sidney and asked if our church would take part in the meetings. He said, surely, we would do what we could.

On Sunday mornings they had no service, so it did not interfere with other churches. The afternoon was a rally service. In the Sunday evening or week nights, everyone could take their choice. Our seventy-five voice choir was a real boost, as well as the members of our church. There was a beautiful spiritual move in the city, in salvation and healing. Lives were blessed. It was quite noticeable that not **all** churches were cooperating. But for whatever reason, our people were enthusiastic and refreshed.

After some weeks, the evangelist said to Sidney, "I have to go to another meeting but with the flow of revival blessing here, I don't feel I should close the tabernacle. Will you take over the meetings for several months, or as the Lord leads?" In the natural, this was a crazy thing to do, for our Christian Tabernacle was less than a mile away. It would be like competing with our own ministry. But, after praying about it and realizing that God had enough blessing for all, Sidney agreed.

We would have our Sunday morning service together. Then in the afternoon, we would both go to Willetts Tabernacle. In the evening, I stayed at Christian Tabernacle, and Sidney preached at Willetts. It was almost like the widow in Elijah's day, for as long as we brought the empty vessels, the cruse of oil never ran out. Both places were blessed. We had special speakers which shared in both tabernacles.

On New Years Eve we combined the congregations for a Watch Night Service. We began around eight o'clock with songs, testimonies and special music. Then we had an illustrated sermon, presenting twelve episodes in our life, representing twelve months of the year. When the clock struck twelve, Father Time got up, shouldered his scythe, and took his leave. Then the New Year was dramatically ushered in (which happened to be our three month old baby, Helen), representing the new year.

It had been an exceedingly busy time, pastoring both tabernacles, but there was much regret when it came time to raze the wooden structure. As we took inventory of the results of these past months, we not only rejoiced over hundreds who had found Christ, but Christian Tabernacle had taken in 134 new members as a reward of this ministry.

Wonderful Speakers And Guests

Among the other guests on the radio show was the late Dr. John R. Rice. He was conducting a citywide meeting in the Dayton Memorial Auditorium. We invited him to be with us at 2pm, to give a short talk and invite the listeners to the meeting. As I introduced him and gave his meetings a boost, there was a quizzical smile on his face as he viewed the situation. Here he was, being introduced and encouraged by **the Lady Sky Pilot**, while at his meetings he was offering the book, "Bobbed Hair, Short Skirts and **Women Preachers**".

The Flyerettes were invited to sing in the meeting one night. However, Dr. Rice made them go out and take their **makeup** off before they could sing on his platform. Yes, he had his different ways, but he was a powerful preacher.

So Many Wonderful Guests

What precious guests who spoke and sang on our Wings Over Dayton radio program. They were the cream of the crop. Many of them are still household names today: Dr. W.B. Riley; Dr. Robert Glover; Dr. Harry Stracken and his beloved son, Ken Stracken; the inimitable C.M. Ward (who was with us often); artist Willard Cantalon; G.B. McDowell; Reverend B.R. Lakin; choice singer and preacher Alfred Garr; Loren Fox and Stewart Hamblen (who wrote, "It is No Secret What God Can Do"); the Wheaton College Choir; Dr. Bob Jones (both Senior and Junior); Cowboy Preacher Bill Durban; Cy and Susie Ramseyer (with musical talents too numerous to mention); and Reverend Rex Humbard and his singers. Oh yes, also Jack Holcomb (with that very high, vibrant voice). So many others blessed us at our wonderful church, and also on the radio program, which covered a large area outside of the city.

Truly, Christian Tabernacle was an alive, **evangelical church,** as well as a **missionary** church. That is why it was a great church. My husband's favorite saying was, "**The mission of the church is missions**."

Radio At The County Fair

One of the most exciting diversions was taking our broadcast to the county fair. We borrowed a 50 foot house trailer, built a platform the entire length of it, and installed an awning over it. We had missionary displays outside, and rows and rows of chairs placed like a small amphitheater. For many, this was a welcome rest for weary feet, a break from walking through the fair.

We had a continuous program all through the day. Our staff altered their schedules so that we had music at all times. We had interviews with the audience, usually general chitchat. I remember one man I was interviewing. He mentioned he had just gotten married. So I said to him, "Congratulations! You know, I have just become a mother-in-law, and I would like to be a good mother-in-law. Have you any suggestions?" Without hesitation, he said, "Just keep your big mouth shut." The audience exploded with laughter and applause. Believe me, that was good advice.

At one end of the trailer, the room was made up for a prayer room. It had a small altar with a Bible on it, for any who wished to go in and meditate. The rest of the trailer inside was used by the staff for rest, or waiting between songs, etc. We all loved fair time. What a way to witness!

Radio - Church Away From Church

We ministered many times to those who had not been to church for a long time. I had many funerals from homes whose loved ones had passed on and they had no pastor. Many had been converted over the radio.

I am thinking of one person who wrote to me, even as I am writing this book. She said, "I'll never forget how I came to Christ through your radio ministry and letters. You were always so loving and patient with me as I was getting established in my walk with the Lord. I received a solid foundation from your and Dr. Correll's messages. It has helped me as a Sunday School teacher through the years." This letter was from Ruth Toops in Fairborn, Ohio.

Another time of special blessing on the radio was our communion service. Many could not go to church and didn't have a pastor, so we asked them to get some grape juice and bread (or cracker) right there at home. Then, in some very quiet moments, the staff would sing songs about Calvary, etc. We would read the scriptures, then all would partake at one time. With God, there is no distance.

As a close to this radio ministry which meant so much to me, let me give you the words to our closing theme, which was taken from Isaiah 26:3. Sung by our Flyerettes in that soft, glorious harmony, this was a benediction:

"Thou wilt keep Him in perfect peace
Whose mind is stayed on Thee
When the shadows come and darkness falls
He giveth inward peace.
For He is the only perfect resting place
He giveth perfect peace.
Thou wilt keep him in perfect peace
Whose mind is stayed on Thee."

Our first radio trio: Phillis Miller, Veda Mae Salyer, and Leona Gray. Audrey Mieir at the piano.

Christian Tabernacle staff. Left to right: Helen Correll, Virginia and Cliff Block, Roy and Marg Ackerle, Vivial Baskett, Doris and George Gardiner, Sidney Correll, Kathryn Smith and Doris Smith.

Flyerettes

At the fair

Chapter 28

"I Was In Prison And You Came To Me."
Matthew 25:36

Charles and Berta Korns would do the same thing every Sunday. They would get right up in the middle of church and **walk out**. Sometimes a few others, who were also members of the Christian Tabernacle, would go with them. Of course, my husband and I and most of the congregation knew **why** they left, and we would breathe a prayer in their behalf. They were on their way to the city jail for Sunday Services. This precious couple did this for many years, in fact, until the Lord took them home.

It was no doubt their burden for this work that encouraged Sidney and me to be concerned about those behind bars. At times, we sat in court and listened to the trials of young men and women. Many times, we sponsored boys on our farm. Some of them made good, some did not, but we kept helping. We went to the reformatories, to the "big house" in Columbus, Ohio, the London Prison Farm, and others.

A funny thing happened on one occasion. I was on my way to the Mansfield, Ohio, Reformatory to speak and show one of our missionary films. Sidney was away, so Dad Correll went with me. There had been an ice storm, and the roads were a sheet of ice. We were going at a snail's pace, but cars were slipping and sliding into the ditch or into other cars. Daddy Correll, with a twinkle in his voice, said, "Well, Helen, if you are going to hit something, hit something cheap." About that time we slid this way, and that way, and right into the worst old clunker on the road. We both had a good laugh. No damage was done, and no one was hurt.

We often took our radio staff to these places, for we had heard from a number of inmates who listened to our broadcast each day. We got a letter from the chaplain of the London Prison Farm, asking us to come for a service and bring the radio staff. I wrote back saying we would be glad to come.

Cliff Block, our pianist, the girls trio, Millie Laws, our artist; myself and others arrived for the meeting. We had a terrific service and a large group of the men who had come to listen. They sat in rapt attention. The music was out of this world. Millie did a beautiful chalk drawing. We showed Dr. Correll's film on Africa, "Heathen Rage". Then I preached on "How Shall We Escape!" I don't think they

187

announced the title ahead of time, but it was from Hebrews 2:3; *"How shall we escape if we neglect so great a salvation?"* At the close, we asked for those who wanted prayer to lift their hands, and there was a good response.

The chaplain's secretary, John Borgwardt, had been a real help in assisting the staff to get set up, and taking out all of our equipment.

While they were loading our equipment, the chaplain asked me to come into his office. He said, "I listen to your program when I can, but my secretary, John Borgwardt, would not miss the opportunity to listen to your Wings Over Dayton broadcast. He reads all the material you send out. I have wanted to ask you and your husband whether there was something that could be done for this man. I am frustrated. I know he is here on a murder charge, but there were very unusual circumstances. He has been here fifteen years, and for some reason, there is no consideration to see the parole board."

Then the chaplain went on, "He was born in Germany. His father is a German Baptist minister. He and his wife, two daughters and Johnnie migrated to the U.S.A. when John was thirteen. All went well until the mother died and the father went back to Germany." He went on to tell me Johnnie's story, the incident, his time in prison. Then he added, "I just don't feel John belongs here. It has been twenty years since John has seen his father. As a chaplain, my hands are tied. I just wondered if there was something you folks could do. I know of your compassionate ministries, and that you love people."

After meeting and talking to John, I had a feeling that God was going to do something for him. I told Dr. Correll the story when I returned home. He went to meet the chaplain, and to talk with John. Sidney promised them both he would do what he could.

We got the prayer group together at the church to pray for Johnnie's salvation first, as well as his release from prison, if the Lord was willing.

In the meantime, Dr. Correll had an appointment with the parole board. He met with them, told them about our church, and mentioned that we had been able to assist a number of other boys in making it. He told them we would be willing to sponsor him, give him a place to stay, and find employment for him.

When he came home, he was crestfallen as he told me of the results. He said, "Honey, they just laughed at me and said, 'It will take a whole lot more than your willingness to sponsor him, to get him out.

188

You come back with more evidence than you have now, or don't bother to come back!'"

I said, "Sweetheart, I feel God wants us to do something. There has got to be a way. Do you mind if I go back to the place where it all happened, in the northern part of the state, and just see what I can find out?" I don't know what I thought I could do. I just had that feeling. He assured me he was behind me all the way, and if I found anything at all that would help, he would get an attorney to assist us.

Sidney went back to the prison to talk to John, and to find out all he could. He asked him how he stood with the Lord. John told him of the bitter years until he had finally turned his back on God. He was sure there was **no hope** for him. Sidney told him that with God, all things were possible. John replied, "Well, if your God can do anything, let Him prove it."

Later, I went back and took him a Bible. He assured me that he knew what was in it, as he had read it through once a year when he was a boy in Germany. He just didn't seem to have a future.

But a short while after that, he wrote a letter that sounded urgent. He asked if it was possible that I come to see him right away. I went at my first opportunity, and when he greeted me he said, "Mrs. Correll, I met the Lord in my cell the other night, and accepted Him as my Savior and Lord of my life." He went on, "It seemed like a dream, but I knew He was real. I found myself on the hard cement floor in that dingy cell, pouring out my sordid past to Jesus Christ and begging forgiveness. I had just been reading John 1:12 in the Bible you brought me, *"But as many as received Him to them gave He the right to become the children of God, even to them that believe on His name."* He went on to say that already, things had changed in his life. His language changed, and his twenty-year smoking habit was gone. He no longer had bitterness, but joy in his heart. Now it wasn't as important, whether he got out or not. He knew all was right in his life.

We were overjoyed. Our first prayer had been answered. After John found the Lord, things began to happen. I had never done anything like this before, but I went with a state representative who was willing to help me. We went to the area where the crime was committed. He suggested I go first to the court house where the records were kept, to see if I could read the account of the trial. The Lord must have been with me, for no one can figure how they could possibly let me take **those papers** to the reading room.

I spent a whole day going over the trial records. I got the names of all the jurors. I discovered that there were only six out of the twelve still living after these fifteen years. I had never had any training for anything like this, but I discovered in the margin a note, written by the judge, which said, "**Under no circumstances let this fellow out of prison!**" When this was traced down, we found that the judge had been **bribed** to see that John didn't get out. I had the feeling I had discovered the clue as to why John had not even been able to get an appointment with the parole board. I wasn't too smart about legal things, but I said, "Why do they have juries, when the judge can change any decision they make?"

The Ohio state representative and I made a visit to the jurors that were still living. We explained the situation and asked if they remembered the occasion, and what were their feelings about the case? Without exception, we found **not one** who would be against him having parole. In fact, some were surprised he was still in. They understood the verdict that was given him was seven years. He had already been in 15 years, and he couldn't come up for parole for another ten years, if even then.

We then visited the banker of the town, with whom John lived, and other families in the community. We found them all favorable, and willing to go with us before the parole board in John's behalf.

All of this was tedious work, and took months to accomplish. The Lord just seem to go before us at every step. We got all this material together and my husband hired an attorney. Then Dr. Correll made another appointment with the parole board. This time, **eleven people** walked in with my husband, including the chaplain and a member of the state legislature. Our attorney presented the case. The man who was the head of the parole board smiled and looked at Sidney and said, "Well, I guess you came back with more evidence this time."

After the next meeting of the parole board, John was awarded his parole. It had been a long fifteen years. Let me just add that when Dr. Correll went to pay the attorney, he refused to take a cent. He said, "I just got a joy out of being a part of this. There is no charge."

When the big day came, Dr. Correll and I were there to meet John. Something very important happened next. When John was presented to the congregation at Christian Tabernacle, he was **welcomed with open arms**. I believe many more parolees would be more likely to succeed if they found love and friendly faces when they came out to start over.

190

The next big thing we had was a party for John. His two sisters were there, whom he had not seen for years, and his father came all the way from Germany to be there. All of his former friends that had stood with him from his home town were there. It was a time of praising the Lord.

John had a number of positions around the church. He also became my radio secretary. He had studied hard while he was shut away, and became quite efficient in typing, and he read incessantly. After the first few years of being incarcerated, he was fed up with what he saw, and tried to be by himself as much as possible.

I thought I knew a lot about what went on behind the iron doors, but I can tell you that my education became quite enlarged as I heard the different stories of what actually went on there.

Outside of becoming a Christian, I am sure that the next best thing that happened to John was the lovely lady he married from the church, Geneva Lyon. They were married November 1, 1953. She was a gibraltar of strength to him as he made his new life. He later became a part of our missionary organization, and worked with them until he retired. He and Geneva have been married over 40 years. Praise God from whom all blessings flow.

John has written his own story, calling it "Fifteen Years of Hell on Earth." This is one of the things he wrote: "I was given a parole. I was to be released in 40 days. A psychologist interviewed me and warned me not to expect too much. He said that any person locked up for more than five years can never again become the same, morally, physically or mentally. I am happy Jesus Christ, my Lord, has proven this man's statement incorrect over and over during these last forty years."

What a testimony! There is so much more I would like to say, but let me just add this. Through John's conversion and amazing life afterward, the **former warden of the Ohio State Penitentiary** credited Johnnie as the reason he received Christ before he died. John has spoken in prisons, many times, giving his testimony of the power of Christ.

How many times Geneva has said to me, "Oh, I thank you for getting my Johnnie for me."

John's homecoming

Chapter 29

Let's Talk About Weddings

We have been talking about my life as an ordained minister. I have talked about preaching. But one of the things that you must have if you perform marriages is an Ordination Certificate.

If I were to tell about all of the weddings I conducted or assisted in, that would be a book in itself. I suppose there would be hundreds of them. I have beautiful pictures of many of the weddings, which bring back wonderful memories. But many times as I travel, I have people say to me, "Oh, you married us on such and such a date." I am embarrassed that I don't remember. The best part is how many there are who have been married over fifty years. There is seldom a year goes by but several different couples will call to say that they have just had their 50th or 60th anniversary.

I thought I would just take time to tell you of several which were special or unusual.

My First Wedding Ceremony

I remember the first wedding I had. It was in our first church in Fullerton, California, in June of 1926. The bride and groom were a lovely couple, and members in our church. She was Lila Sarles, and his name was W.E. Cobb, but he was called Ty. They were both 22 years old. A number of their relatives were also in our church. What a beautiful wedding, and even if it was my first, it went quite well. But the most important thing is, the marriage lasted.

Update

I called them in Palmdale California in August of 1993. They were both 90 years old, and still together. They had been married 67 years.

Triple Wedding

Perhaps one of the most unusual weddings was a triple wedding. The following is a portion from the **Dayton Journal**: "Two brothers and a sister participated in a triple marriage ceremony Monday night at the Christian Tabernacle. There were three brides, three grooms, three ministers, and three sets of attendants.

Margaret Terryman, 19, and Earl Wick were united by the Reverend Crawford Jones of Calvary Gospel Church.

Catherine Couser, 17, became the bride of Alfred Wick, with the Reverend Helen Correll officiating.

Priscilla Wick, 18, and Charles Holmes, were united in marriage by the Reverend Sidney Correll.

The Correll's are pastors of the Christian Tabernacle in Dayton. The ring bearers standing in front were Roselyn Correll, Janet Wright and Rebecca Correll.

The couples walked down two aisles to stand before a palm decorated altar. The three brides wore long white satin wedding gowns. The grooms were dressed in dark suits.

They took their places before the three ministers. The first part of the ceremony was conducted by each minister in turn, and the final portion was conducted in unison."

I Shared With A Priest

Perhaps the most unique wedding was that of my grandson, Scott Correll. He said, "Grandmother, Sheri and I are going to be married, and we wondered if you would be willing to assist in the wedding? I want your answer first, then I will go to the priest and ask him."

Sheri is from a fine Catholic family. I knew they had made a real confession of Christ, but it was an unusual request. There was a day when this request would never have been voiced. Now, the ban is lifted on intercommunication. So I said, "Scott, if your priest agrees, I shall be happy to share in your wedding."

Scott contacted his priest and said, "Father, my grandmother is an ordained Protestant minister. I would like to have her participate in our wedding if it would be possible." The priest pondered a bit, then said, "Well, Scott, I see no reason why that would not be all right, but I will have to clear it first."

The answer came back that it would be permissible, but that he would have to make the final statement, "I now pronounce you husband and wife." That was no problem to me.

What Shall I Wear?

Then like a woman, I began to wonder, what I would wear? I did have a black robe, but that didn't seem appropriate. Then I had an idea. Sidney and I had just celebrated our 50th wedding anniversary.

Earlier in the year, Sidney and I had gone to Korea. While there, I had a beautiful long white satin gown made that I would use for our anniversary. It was a gorgeous dress with large peacocks embroidered in gold around the hem. (It's what I'm wearing on the cover of this book.) The sleeves were chiffon, and also had gold designs. I could never have found something like this in the States (that I could afford, anyway). So I asked Scott if he thought that would be okay. He had seen it at the anniversary, and thought it would be great.

On the eve of the rehearsal, I was there to get instructions. Everyone was in street clothes, of course, except the priest, who was in a dark robe. It was amazing, how much he gave me to share. I would read Scriptures from both the Old and New Testament. Scott wanted me to read my poem, "Little Lady at the Altar", but more than that, I would be giving half of the vows. One couldn't ask for more. Not a thing was mentioned about what we would wear.

On the night of the wedding, I was there in my long white satin gown with the border of golden peacocks. My scriptures were ready to read from my red Bible. I wished I had brought my white Bible, as it might look better. When walking into the room where the priest was waiting, I couldn't believe it! There stood the priest in a long white satin robe with a gold designed border on it! And believe it or not, he had a red ceremony book! He asked me to stand beside him the entire ceremony. You could also feel that God was there!

Now for those who might be critical of a Protestant marrying a Catholic, may I say, it was a case of a Christian marrying a Christian.

It has been a joy to be in their home a number of times since their marriage. I found love and gentleness. The blessings are said at the table. There are also discipline and rules. On a recent visit in their home, I went to church with them and their two children. I heard a Christ-inspiring message that was very heart searching. The only difference was communion. It wasn't like we would have done it, but Christ was lifted up. But the thing that impressed me was on the way home, Scott said to the children, "Alright, what two things do you remember that the preacher said in his sermon?" They had an answer.

This they do every Sunday after church. I could wish that all families gave as much attention to the Lord and what the preacher said in church.

Twenty-Fifth Anniversary

While we are talking about weddings, let me tell you about our 25th anniversary. We had been pastors of Christian Tabernacle for thirteen years. I had looked forward to our 25th anniversary, for I had said, "I didn't have a long beautiful dress when I was married, so this is a good time to have it."

Our daughter, Rebecca, had married Bob Cauble a few years before. Why not use her dress again? Rebecca thought it was a good idea. I confess I had to diet a bit to get into it, but I did. What a gorgeous, long, flowing wedding gown and veil it was.

We had the ceremony on the platform of Christian Tabernacle. Our attendants were our six children, three boys and three girls. We had a flower girl and ring bearer. Sidney's father was the minister. We repeated our vows once again. What a festive occasion. The church was packed.

We certainly had a bigger reception than when we were married those twenty five years before. Thank the Lord it was **to the same man**!

Second Honeymoon

The church gave us six months leave of absence and round trip tickets to Europe on the Queen Mary. Our honeymoon also consisted of a missionary mission through Europe and Africa. Also, we were representing Youth for Christ in Germany in a number of campaigns. We were a team along with Alfred Garr, a famous singer with a golden voice, and Dan White, an organist and piano player superb. (This was before either of them were married.) We met many wonderful missionaries and Christian friends. Maybe I can get back to telling of our meetings all over Germany and Italy, as well as The Bible House in Switzerland.

But let me tell you of an interesting experience we had on the Queen Mary. How Sidney and I loved to take our trips by ships. We didn't attend all the activities on board, but we enjoyed being at the Amateur Program. Sidney volunteered us to sing and yodel. Can you believe our surprise, when the evening arrived, to also find on the program the original Von Trapp Family from Austria? They were just returning home after the war. We felt they were special at the time, but never realized **how special**, for the movie, "The Sound of Music" had not been made yet. This might be why I have seen the picture, well, I stopped counting at twenty times after it came out. Especially after Sidney and I had been to Austria, where the Von Trapp story began, I would say to myself, (and anyone else who would listen), I met the real Von Trapps, and I have the passenger list to prove it!

Everybody Loves A Wedding

Even Jesus loves weddings. Isn't it interesting that the very first miracle Jesus did was at a wedding, at Cana of Galilee? Jesus, His mother and the disciples were there and had a part in it.

I have always loved the book of John's Gospel. When I was forty years old, I wrote the Drama of John's Gospel. I called it, "Speak For Yourself John." It's twenty-two chapters long. I gave it as a series on my radio program several times. When I was 80 years old, my son Michael helped to make into a six cassette book (music, sound effects and all). People tell me they have been blessed by it. But what I wanted to say was, I waxed a little poetic as I told about the marriage in Cana of Galilee, in John, the second chapter. I was reminded that God was the author of marriage.

The Very First Wedding

Have you ever tried to picture that first wedding in the Garden of Eden? After God took a rib of Adam, He made a beautiful woman. When Adam first saw her that day, she was the most gorgeous and perfect woman that ever lived, then or now, because she was made before sin entered into the world. She had no blemishes or illnesses. When God finished His creation, He looked it over and said, "It's very good."

I have tried to visualize what the garden looked like, with the fresh, lush green everywhere and the flowers blooming profusely. I have seen orchids in the jungles, blooming where they are seldom seen by man, which convinces me that God loves flowers, whether man sees them or not. So, what kind of flowers did Eve have for the wedding that day? Did you ever stop to think that it was God who gave the first bride away? Read Genesis 2:22. "The rib which the Lord God had taken from man, made He a woman, and brought her unto the man." Isn't that giving the bride away? Alas, sin came into the picture and spoiled a happy marriage, just as it often does today. But Christ came to buy back

197

that first estate, to pay for sin. I believe the Lord gets great joy out of happy marriages, if He can be a part of them.

The Wedding In The Air

Now let us turn our eyes to the future, when every believer will be a part of the bride of Christ. We go from the first book of the Bible to the last, Revelations, Chapter 21. Verse 2: *"And I John saw the Holy City, New Jerusalem, coming down from God out of Heaven prepared as a Bride adorned for her husband. Verse 9: Come hither, I will show you, the Bride, the Lamb's wife."* Please read the whole chapter, and continue to chapter 22. An invitation is sent to you in verse 17: *"the Spirit and the Bride say come, and whosoever will let him come and take of the water of life freely."*

This is one wedding you won't want to miss!

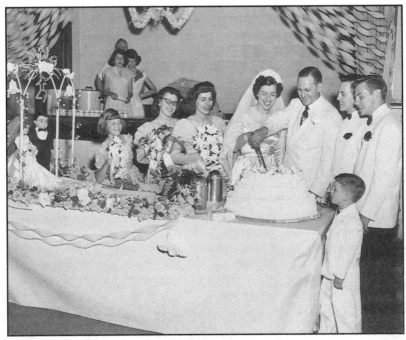

Our 25th anniversary

Chapter 30

All Night Broadcast And
Watch Night Service

Christian Tabernacle - Dayton, Ohio

It was not unusual for us to have a Watch Night Service on New Years Eve. We had done it for years. We would start about 8pm. We would have lots of congregational singing, a number of guests for special music, and a time of testimony of what the Lord had done for us through the year. Then we would have a time of prayer, asking the Lord to forgive the sins and mistakes in our life, and asking for His blessings on the months to come. Maybe we would have a water baptismal service, or a gospel film, short sermon, etc. Time moved quickly, and soon the New Year would be upon us. We would have the exit of Father Time, and the unusual entrance of the New Year. Then we would praise the Lord, put our arms around our neighbor, wish them a blessed New Year, and go home.

One year, I had a new inspiration. The WING station in those days would sign off at 12 midnight. You didn't have all night broadcasts, except maybe from WLW out of Cincinnati. The airways were silent. So, I went to Mr. Pat Williams of station WING and made the suggestion they try something. Let us have the time **from five minutes after midnight to 5am**. I know that was daring. I suggested they would only need one man at the station controls, and think of all the publicity for WING in areas it is impossible to reach when the airwaves are cluttered. It worked! They said they would try it.

Then it came over me like a flood. "Are you crazy? You have already had four or five hours of meetings, those people will want to go home." But we decided to give it a try. We would be broadcasting right from the platform in our auditorium. Preceding New Years Eve service, we wrote letters to everyone on our mailing list. We announced it over our broadcast, and promoted it by every means we had. Oh yes, once we announced we would have **ham and eggs at 5am** for everyone, after our broadcast.

We invited special guests. One of the years, we had Dr. Bob Jones of Bob Jones University. Plus we had many musical guests, such as The Claus Indian Family, Voice of the Hills, the Terrill Family, a singing group from Indonesia, Salvation Army Band, Rose Vegso, formerly from Budapest, Forest Myers and his guitar, and of course, Sidney and I sang.

The building was packed, and strangely enough, it stayed full the entire service. About 11pm, folks began to get up and go to the basement for coffee and donuts. So when they left the church auditorium, you never knew if they were going for coffee or leaving the church. **But the crowd never got smaller.**

New Years Greeting 1957

Let's attend the 1957 New Years Service.

At the stroke of midnight, station WING announces our broadcast coming from the Christian Tabernacle.

The light comes on, and the bells begin to chime. A New Year is here. Six of the Flyerettes begin to sing:

> Time's clock is striking the hour
> Bringing a glad New Year
> Twelve months to work for the Master
> Spreading good hope and cheer.
> Let's make the most of each moment,
> Cherish each week and day.
> The year goes fast, let's be mindful,
> Careful to watch and pray.

The velvet curtains begin to open, revealing a huge white cake, ten feet tall counting the candles. It is decorated with red roses. On the lower layer were twelve red candles. Beside them stood twelve young ladies in white robes and red streamers with the names of the twelve months in gold letters. On the second layer, there were four red candles, and four young men dressed in white with red streamers for spring, summer, fall and winter. On the third layer was the little New Year in his white satin suit and top hat, with a silver streamer for 1957.

The cake was in celebration of eighteen years of broadcasting on WING. At this time, we conveyed our best wishes to Executive Vice President John Pattison Williams and all the wonderful staff of WING.

Then followed a very interesting, meaningful several hours of program. We noticed that after midnight, people began to come in from outside. They were coming from other churches whose services were over. Or, people who were driving and just happened to tune in WING and learn about our special Watch Night service would drive to the church and join us in the auditorium. And most of our early crowd was still there.

Before 2am, or after the illustrated sermon was over, the young folks who were candles went through the audience and served everyone a piece of cake.

It was well after 2am before the crowd began to get smaller.

We had two telephone lines which were kept busy, receiving calls. Some were telling of the blessing of the broadcast, others were requesting songs. We heard from as far south as South Carolina, as far north as Timins, Ontario, Canada, and as far east as Bridgeport, Conneticut. Many said they had been listening all evening. The letters poured in during the next few days from far and near. The farthest was Dunedin, New Zealand, 7,000 miles away. We had announced during the broadcast that we would send a Bible to the one farthest away, so New Zealand was the winner. Remember, this was around forty years ago. We heard from seventeen of our United States. It was so exciting.

Some people, including me, had said, "What in the world will you do all that time? All night?" I am sure everyone who was there was amazed at how quickly the time went, and would say it wasn't long enough. And, would you believe it, we served almost 300 people, ham and eggs at six o'clock in the morning?

It was invaluable to us in the many new friends we made and people who found the Lord or were blessed, and I know the radio station WING was pleased at the far-reaching results. It wasn't long until many stations were broadcasting after midnight. We were on several years, and then I believe some one **bought the time** for another program, but we were thankful for the years of free time we had.

Thank You, Kids, Wherever You Are

I would like to acknowledge the wonderful young people who had a part in this service.

Happy New Year on Top of Cake: Harold (Hal) Simpson. Second layer: Mark Hainline, Sonny Kirk, Sidney Salyer and James Haddix. First layer: Judy Kay Smith, Caroline Sessions, Helen Rowena Correll, Linda Smith, Dona Hile, Delores Blackburn, Carol Suitts, Janet Suitts, Mickey Kirk, Janet Oaks, Avonelle Helton, Ruth Simpson.

Flyerettes: Vivian Baskett, Joyce Hergenrather, Sally Simpson, Betty Dearth, Virginia Block, Hazel McConnell.

Chapter 31

On Itineration

Have you ever played the game where you look at a puzzle picture in a magazine, and you have to see how many **items** you can identify in it? I thought about that when I looked at this picture. This is how it was, whenever I started out on an itinerary. Sometimes I was gone for a number of weeks, to visit churches and hold missionary meetings. Many times, my only companion was the dear Lord himself. I traveled many miles before returning. It was good that I was strong, for sometimes I did most of the lifting and putting equipment up myself.

How Many Items Can You Recognize?

My overnight case; briefcase with my Bible, itinerary, etc.; portable typewriter; case for literature; 16mm film projector; projector stand (legs that screwed out to carry); 16mm films with missionary stories on them; take-up reel; long, heavy electric extension cord; suitcase for personal clothes; large case with promotion material; easel to hold material; large screen to show pictures (notice it is by my right shoulder). Perhaps there were other things, but I can't remember now. You can't see them, but there were always maps near at hand. The most important, though you can't see them either, were the guardian angels. I was very much aware of them.

I loved presenting the challenge of our obligation to carry out the Lord's last command: going into all the world and preaching the good news. In visiting the churches, I reminded them that the **mission of the church is missions**. I not only spoke of winning souls for Christ, but I had special projects. The most important project was raising funds to build the Sidney Robert Memorial Hospital for Kenieba, Africa.

I had two other goals on this particular trip. To get a **Land Rover** for the missionaries in **Mali**, Africa, as well as a much needed **kerosene refrigerator** for the mission station. (They have no electricity.) One church in Ohio got so excited, they had a refrigerator put right on the platform. People gave and donated until we had enough money to send it on the freight ship sailing on October 9. The whole church, children and adults, had so much joy out of seeing God answer the request for funds that they were just bubbling over.

You will notice we also **made the goal** for the Land Rover. I would move the red ribbon up each night until we made it. This, of course, took more than one church. I didn't find the people complaining about asking for money. When they knew where it was going, they felt a thrill to be a part of it. Anyway, it is usually the people **who don't give** that complain!

My work was threefold.

I missed our church in Dayton and my radio program when we left, but now I had a new assignment. Most of my work was to bear the burden and responsibility of Africa, in Mali, where our son was buried, and in Dakar, Senegal, where we had the Christian Academy for all English-speaking children who wished to attend, both missionary as well as business and embassy children. They not only attended from Senegal, but from other countries as well. We also had the Home of Hope children's home. Dot and Moe Moore had a real love for these unfortunate youngsters. They not only gave of their time, but Dorothy, after working tirelessly, became sick and died. Now we had **the second grave** in Africa. Orlando Moore married Barbara, one of the missionary teachers, and they continued there in a tremendous work, along with many other fine workers.

So, my work was part-time in the office, part-time on itineration, and part-time visiting Africa and other fields, and taking 16mm movies and bringing back updated stories. I have been to Africa **seven times**.

204

May I Drop In For A Visit?

In thinking of the years of travel to churches for meetings and conventions, I would like to mention one other thing that was, you might say, a hobby. I loved getting to know people on our mailing list. It was small enough that it wasn't impossible. We never bought a mailing list, but to us, each one was someone special. Even when we pastored churches, I loved meeting people personally—our church members, radio listeners, television friends. That might be why, even when there are many on our mailing list, we have continued to keep in touch.

I think what reminded me of this was a recent trip I took to Dayton, Ohio. I was in the home of Colonel and Mrs. Dewey Jones. They live in Fairborn. They had been members of our church, and Dewey was a board member when my husband and I pastored there. We have been close friends now for many years.

Ruth said to me, "Do you remember how we first became members of Christian Tabernacle? Dewey and I and my sister, Helon, and Vernie Gehron had come to Ohio from the south. Both Dewey and Vernie were working in the engineering department at Wright Paterson Air Force Base. During the day, my sister Helon and I began listening to your afternoon radio program, WINGS Over Dayton. We wouldn't miss it! I wrote to you several times, and always got a personal answer. I became a donor and sent you an offering from time to time. Then I wrote to you that we were moving back to Louisiana, and would miss you. I gave you our address so we would still got your radio mail. We moved to Keatchie, Louisiana, about thirty miles south of Shreveport."

Ruth went on, "Then one day, I got a telephone call. When I answered, a voice said, 'Is this Ruth Jones that did live in Ohio?' 'Yes it is, but who is this?' You said, 'This is Helen Correll, the Lady Sky Pilot from Dayton, Ohio.' I couldn't believe what I was hearing. I said, 'Where are you calling from?' and you said, 'I am here in New Orleans. I was thinking of you when I came into the state. I wanted to touch base with you and ask how you are doing.' We were all just stunned. My sister and I were so surprised, and we so appreciated your call."

Ruth continued, "Some time after that, Wright Field Air Base called Jones and Vernie, and asked if they wanted their jobs back. (It was at the end of the war.) They said yes. You can believe that all four of us could not wait **to come to your church**. We not only listened on the radio, we joined Christian Tabernacle, and we became a part of everything, along with the Gehrons. Vernie taught the Crusader Sunday

School class for years. I have thought many times, if it had not been for your **telephone call**, we might never have come to the church. Believe me, that was so rewarding."

I really could repeat this story many times, and I cherish the wonderful friends we have made. This meant so much more to both Sidney and me than going to a meeting where there had been a large crowd, but there was no further contact. I just wanted to pass this on to you.

Itinerary In 1968

I suppose one of the most interesting years of itineration was in 1968. My husband and I started out on this trip **together**. We had a number of meetings and conventions lined up clear across the country. The car was filled with luggage and equipment as usual, but this time there were **two** suitcases for clothes. We always loved traveling together. As I look over our itinerary, I am not going to bore you with all the stops and meetings we had, because before I returned back to St. Petersburg, Florida, I had been in 29 states. **I did think you might like to follow us on the map to see what an itinerary was like.** I will just give the highlights.

We left St. Petersburg, Florida, for our national tour on **February 25, 1968**. Our first stop was Atlanta, Georgia. We attended a Presbyterian missionary conference. On the 27th, we were at Jefferson, Georgia, at the Faith Baptist church. We showed the Vietnam film, and Sidney preached.

We went on to Columbia, South Carolina, to be at the Columbia Bible College. We had young people who attended there. Sidney spoke to the students. In the evening, we showed two missionary films, then it was on to Charlotte, North Carolina, to be at the Garr Memorial Church for a missionary service.

On to Roanoke, Virginia, for a missionary meeting at the Calvary Memorial Church, pastored by Kitty Gorman and Pearl Adair. The church has supported one of our missionaries for over 40 years. (Little did we realize that one day we would be living in Roanoke.)

Then it was on to Lynchburg, Virginia, to the Thomas Roads Baptist Church. I spoke in the Sunday school to over 1,000 young people. Sidney gave a missionary message in the morning service, and I showed the film, "The Young Doctor Goes Home." In the evening Sidney spoke on **Korea** and our orphanage project. A wonderful offering of $1,345.45 was given for Chung, Ju Orphanage. Sidney made a radio program with Pastor Jerry Falwell.

Hatboro Community Methodist Church was our next stop, in Hatboro, Pennsylvania. This was on March 4. We drove 367 miles. We both spoke. The church gave the "Isolet" that we needed for the babies in the hospital in Africa. Reverend Herman Hildebrand was the pastor. Sidney always said he looked like his Uncle Rich. Bantam, Connecticut, is a very small village near Litchfield. There was lots of history from George Washington's time. We stayed in an old farmhouse from Washington's day. The name of the church was St. Paul's Parish Church. It was a very interesting meeting, and a wonderful place to witness.

From there, it was not far to our next meeting in Boston, Massachusetts. We stayed in the Sheraton Plaza. The missionary conference was in the Ruggles Street Baptist Church. We were in the Boston area for one week. Sidney spoke that night and the next. On the 8th, I went to Peabody, Massachusetts, for a service. I spoke about Africa and showed my film.

Next was Keen, New Hampshire, on March 9, at Sturtevant Chapel. Reverend Kenneth Batchelder was pastor. On Sunday I spoke in the morning, giving the Around the World Report. For the evening service, I drove to Arlington Heights and had a meeting at Arlington Heights Baptist.

On Monday, we drove to Fishdale, Massachusetts, to visit with friends there. Then it was on to Buffalo, New York. Tuesday, Sidney and I went for a walk for about 35 minutes. It was **27 degrees** out, and it started snowing. Sidney was on television. Then he had a wonderful meeting at Metropolitan Chapel of Buffalo. I drove to Lancaster Community Baptist Church, where I spoke and showed the film. Reverend Marsden Sellars was pastor. It was cold and slippery out.

Sidney spoke next in Youngstown, Ohio, at Calvary Temple where Reverend Clem Humbard pastored. We had a precious time with the family.

On Sunday, we were at Pleasant Valley Evangelical Church in Niles, Ohio. This was a real missionary-minded church. Sidney spoke there Sunday night. In the evening, Mr. Wood picked me up and took me for a service in Lucas, Ohio, at First Congregational Church. Sidney came to Lucas on Monday, and spoke at evening service. On Tuesday, we had several meetings there. Thursday, we left Lucas for Cleveland, Ohio. We stayed with our dear friends, Cliff and Floss Hoffman. We had service in Foursquare Gospel Church, and we both spoke. The next day, after one of Floss's famous dinners, she went with me over icy streets to the Negro church for a meeting with The Willing Workers. It was a precious service.

Saturday we drove to Canton, Ohio, to be at the Christian Tabernacle there. Paul and Henrietta Sorensen were the pastors. Sunday morning we were both at Christian Tabernacle. In the afternoon, Sidney drove to Eleryia, Ohio, for a meeting with Reverend Ralph Neighbors. I spoke in the evening service in Canton. We had been on the road one month that day.

On to Dayton, Ohio, for their annual missionary conference. The church was packed. Pat Williams, Vice President of Radio Station WING, and his wife were there. We had meetings all day at Tabernacle. There were a number of missionaries there. I went up Wednesday evening to Sidney, Ohio, for service at the Christian Tabernacle.

On to Fort Wayne, Indiana and Calvary Temple, where Reverend Paul Paino was pastor. This was a great service, and a grand offering was taken for the Vietnam churches.

Next day, on to Oglesby, Illinois, at the Union Church with Pastor Don McClintock. We had supper at the church with missionaries and members. Then followed a good meeting at 7:30.

We had a good breakfast with the McClintocks before driving on to St. Louis, Missouri. We saw Mr. and Mrs. Joe Fields, who were members of our Dayton church for years. Our meeting was at the Assembly of God Church, with Reverend and Mrs. Gene Putnam. In the evening service, Sidney spoke on Vietnam and showed the film. After the service, we listened to the national news. It was ironic. President Johnson was speaking, and made the startling announcement that he was cutting back the bombing of North Vietnam. Then he made the statement that he would not run again for reelection. Our hearts were very heavy about his statement on Vietnam. Sidney always said "The war in Vietnam was lost in America, not in Vietnam." This was March 31, 1968. Incidentally, our son, Michael, was in Vietnam at this time. Sidney visited him twice in the year he was there.

Our next stop was Springfield, Missouri. Sidney was ill with a cold. We didn't have service until Wednesday at the Central Assembly. We both spoke on missions.

In Kingfisher, Oklahoma, we visited with Sidney's double cousin, Theda, and her husband, Les Neeland. They lived on a farm. We saw **the old "Dalton" place** where the Dalton brothers' criminal gangs lived. Even the Dalton mother walked around with a 45 under her apron.

We also walked through the farm and saw where **the old Chism Trail** went through. Our meeting that evening was in The Pentecostal Holiness Church. Sidney spoke, and we showed the film.

Our travels the next day took us over the continental divide. On the other side, we ran into a wind storm. Dust and tumbleweeds swept past us. We arrived in Albuquerque, New Mexico, and stayed in the home of Reverend Mabel Dawes, who is pastor of Faith Chapel. Sidney spoke on Vietnam. In the audience was a captain who had been in Vietnam. He had had 60 men in his unit. He lost 44 of them. He told Sidney, after hearing him speak, that he felt like what he had been through wasn't all in vain.

We left at 5am for Phoenix, Arizona, and drove through the Indian reservation. We had a nice visit with Reverend Max Good and his wife. They drove us around to see the city. We had no service.

Then it was on to Palm Springs, California. It was a lovely drive. We took turns driving, and ate lunch beside the road. Time changed again at the border. Palm Springs was full of hippies - what a sight. We slept all afternoon. The next day, Sidney sat in the sun, but I enjoyed the hot springs. I wished I had a week there.

On Thursday, we drove to Joshua Tree National Forest and Monument. We enjoyed the rock formation as much as the lovely Joshua Trees. We especially enjoyed the Hidden Valley. It is completely surrounded by rocks. It is said that this valley was used by **cattle rustlers** in days gone by. We sat on the ground and ate the lunch we had brought along.

The next day we stayed in our room. Sidney was getting caught up on work. I made it a special day of prayer.

We left Palm Springs on Saturday and drove to Riverside, California. On Sunday morning, we went to the Riverside Union Church for a service. Our dear friends, the Delmar Aldermans, used to pastor the church. (I was scheduled to return there in May for a meeting.) We didn't eat dinner, but rested until 3pm. Then we drove to the San Diego area, to the Spring Valley Church where Reverend Don Tinsley and Rachel are pastors. It was a three-day crusade. Art Chestnut was with us, and he spoke about his work in Okinawa.

We had a couple of days of rest before our next meeting in Duarte, California. We stayed with our good friends, Dick and Peggy Headrick. We went to the Baptist church in Monrovia, pastored by Reverend Wesley Goshorn.

On April 23, the note my diary said "Had Rambler fixed today, new shocks, tune up and complete check up. We have driven 6,788 miles since leaving St. Petersburg."

Our crusade began on the 24th at Bethal Union Church, Duarte, California. Reverend and Mrs. Orlando Moore were there from Africa, and talked about their work in Dakar. I spoke of giving our life in full dedication to God. There were many young people there. I talked about Robert.

Can you believe another month had passed!

Sunday morning the 28th, seven of us were at Toluka Lake Trinity Church in Toluka Lake, for the opening of the crusade there. Reverend Walter Wentworth was the pastor. We all shared in the service. Sidney and Orlando Moore had stayed in Duarte for the morning service. We drove back and had evening service. Sidney and the Moores came to Toluka Lake, closing the crusade there on May 2. I drove to East Glendora for a mission crusade there.

On May 5th, our crusade began at Immanuel Temple in Los Angeles. Reverend and Mrs. A. Earl Lee were pastors. Missionary Art Chestnut also assisted in the crusade. We wove in several more missionary meetings before it was time for Sidney and I **to part once again.**

Hollywood, California, and it was May 10th. We had to be in a studio there, and have the film on Vietnam ready to show. Sidney was interviewed on the program. It was on KHJ, TV. He was on with Sally and Bob Dorman. It was almost 30 minutes, with clips of film and talk. Also, we met the man who received the first Emmy Award, with **Mary Pickford** and **Buddy Rodgers.**

While in Hollywood, we celebrated Mother's Day and Sidney's 61st birthday. They were both on May 12. In the evening, Sidney had a Vietnam rally at Glendora. The church was packed. The Chestnuts and the Moores were there also. Next morning, Sidney and I walked down to have breakfast at VanKamps (with the big windmill on it). We cherished every moment, for this would be our last day together for awhile.

That evening we went to Pasadena, California, to be with Charles and Audrey Mieir, to celebrate three birthdays. Sidney's and Audrey's are on the same day, and Charles' is four days earlier. We always had a lovely time when we got together.

Sunday morning, we had breakfast with old-time friends, Bob and Helen Hammand of China and Asia Missionary Society. We then went to the Glendora meeting. Sidney spoke, and there was a wonderful missionary spirit present.

After the service, Dick and Mable Norris took the missionaries and Sidney and me out for a terrific Mother's Day dinner. When Sidney left for a meeting at the city of Big Bear, I went back for the closing service at Glendora, where there was a wonderful missionary offering. After this I went back to the motel, and **I was alone.**

I have given you a bird's eye view of what ministry is like on **itineration**. What makes a mission grow?

The next day I drove to Banning, California, for a Monday night house meeting. It was a lovely crowd, but what was interesting was that Thelma Ware, one of our members from the Whittier Church, was there. I had not seen her for 40 years. She and her husband had been ministering together for years, until he passed away.

The next morning my host, Juanita Starmer, took me for a hop in their Cessna 175. We flew past March Air Force base, over Oceanside, past San Clemente and New Port, over Disneyland, and back home. Lovely day, but I couldn't keep awake, so I went to bed early.

Wednesday at Riverside, California, once again, for a missionary meeting. Showed my Africa film, "Death in the Valley."

On Thursday, I drove to Northridge, to the Valley Presbyterian Church for a women's meeting from 11am to 1:45pm. The pastors were Ralph Hoops and Georgia Lee. They were both former movie stars. Georgia Lee was in one of Billy Graham's films. I spoke about the baby work in Africa that was so dear to my heart.

Later, I drove down the San Diego Freeway to El Segundo, to the Foursquare Gospel Church. I saw a number of people there I had not seen for years.

On Friday evening, I went with Dick and Peggy Headrick to the home of the Leslie Hromas in Rolling Hills. Audrey Mieir and Sonny Moreno went along. The meeting was arranged by Hanz Sandstrom. This was before he and his wife went into **full-time missionary** ministry. They now head **The Alpine Ministries in Europe**. I showed the Korea film, "G.I. Kids Make Good." I believe we got the money for the washer and dryer we needed.

Sunday, May 19, I was in the mountains at Arrowhead, at the Rim of the World Community Church. George Stanley Johnson was pastor. I hadn't seen him for 30 years. I spoke on Vietnam and "God is Working in Asia." At the evening service, I spoke on Africa.

211

On Wednesday, I drove to Bakersfield, California. I got a motel room, and had some time to catch up on my itinerary. I called my husband in St. Petersburg, Florida. He needed to get back to the office there, as it had been over two months since he'd been there.

Thursday, I had breakfast and wrote to Sidney, bringing him up to date on the meetings. I then drove to Springville, to the Henry Borchardts' new home. It is at the end of the trail, right up in the mountains. What a beautiful, beautiful view!

In the evening, there were 22 there for a house meeting. There were some neighbors who came who never go to church. It was also an open house to show their new home. I showed the Vietnam film, and spoke on "What is New in Mali". All seemed to be impressed. The Borchardts had **given large gifts** for the **Korean orphanages**. (We had five orphanages there.) They had gone on a trip to Asia with my husband.

The next morning, Henry took me in his truck to the top of the mountain, where we could look down on the whole valley. Later, I said my good-byes and headed back down the mountain. It was like going on a roller coaster. I saw hundreds of squirrels and chipmunks. I arrived in Modesto, California, by afternoon. I set up my typewriter and wrote a number of letters. In the evening, I had a meeting in the Prescott Baptist Church. Reverend Ray Kelly was the pastor. There were four Methodist ladies there. I gave my missionary message. I was a guest in the home of the Paul Fulfers. They were old friends, and Paul is a very fine attorney in the city.

God has been so good to let me see so many of His wonderful works. The next morning, the Fulfers took me to the Santa Cruz redwoods, where they have a cabin in the midst of the woods by a lovely stream. This is the place where Audrey Mieir wrote the song, "I Heard God Speak." It is indescribably beautiful. I fell asleep in the chair. Then I went down by the stream, and read the book of Colossians, and prayed.

We drove back to Modesto the next day, and I got my car and headed on. It was Sunday. For the morning service I drove to Lodi, California, to the Neighborhood Foursquare Church. Reverend Earl Opie was the pastor.

After lunch, I drove to Alameda First Assembly Church. After the meeting, another dear friend, Maria Lleverias, who was with the City Women's Club, had made arrangements for a room for me right across from her. She also arranged a garage space for me. She was my hostess, and took care of my meals. I had breakfast with her.

I drove to San Jose, to our cousin, Barbara Adkinson. (She is the one whose mother died in Colorado, and Sidney went back for the funeral.) Barbara's mother was a Correll, and her father was a Gentry, so she was a **double cousin.** I stayed with her. My meeting was in The Church of the Open Bible. Reverend Clyde Johnson was pastor.

Then it was back to Modesto, where I had a service in the Church of the Nazarene. Reverend and Mrs. A. F. Hays pastored. They were most gracious.

I was having breakfast with the Fulfers before leaving on my journey, when the telephone rang. It was Richard Lookeer on the line to say that he had seen the notice in the paper, but it was too late to come to the service. He just wanted me to know that I had led him to Jesus 35 years before. That is always the most thrilling news to hear. Praise the Lord! I drove to Kings Beach at **Lake Tahoe.** This was the home of Bud (Paul) and Betty Schubert. They had a restaurant, and had lived there before they had gone to Africa to build the Memorial Hospital. It was so beautiful there. I went for a long walk along the lake before it was time for dinner.

The next day I spent getting my reports ready to send to the office in St. Petersburg, and also writing letters.

On June 1, I bought two new tires. In the afternoon, Betty took me to the Ponderosa Ranch where they filmed Bonanza. I was quite excited. A man on horseback showed us where to park, then guided us through the house and village.

In the evening, after their restaurant was closed, I had a meeting in the Schubert's home. Our cousin, Ron Gentry, and his wife were there, as well as other guests. The employees from the restaurant were also there. I showed them the film "What is New in the Mali", and got to bed after midnight.

In the morning, after breakfast and a prayer time, I left, but I didn't get far. The car stopped, due to the **altitude.** I sat there for 20 minutes, and then I said to the Lord, "I need your help, Lord. You'll just have to start it." And He did. I praised the Lord all the way up the hill.

I arrived at North Highlands for a meeting in the Hillsdale U.B. Church. Reverend Ramsey was the pastor. In the evening, a Catholic lady was there. She had seen the ad about the meeting in the paper.

The next day as I was headed north, I would finally be out of California. I stopped for lunch at Mt. Shasta. The mountain is breathtaking, and so beautiful.

I stopped for the evening at Roseburg, Oregon. I was very tired. I had driven for eight and a half hours. It was June 4, 1968.

I drove on to Portland, Oregon. I went to Reverend Ulphine Davis' home. They arranged a motel room for me. In the evening, the meeting was held in a bank building auditorium. One of the men who came to the meeting knew us in Kenosha, Wisconsin. My brother Vere's daughter, Pat Richards, was there. We went out for a snack, and when we returned we watched the news on TV. **Robert Kennedy was shot**, 1am eastern standard time.

Land Rover fundraiser

Mt. Rushmore

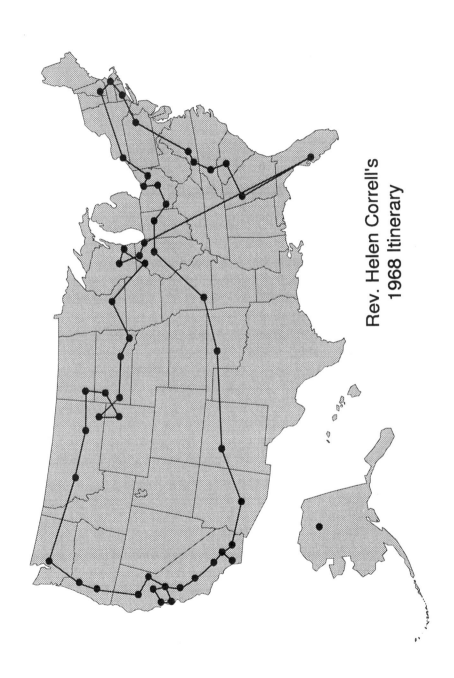

Rev. Helen Correll's
1968 Itinerary

Chapter 32

Alaska

I had one more day in Oregon, and I enjoyed seeing my relatives that I had not seen for some time. One was my cousin Elsie Cox. I had not seen her and Elsie's mother, Annie, since I was ten years old in Vanadium, Colorado. She and her husband were rock hounds. I saw what beautiful things are done with rocks and petrified trees. After a nice visit, I drove through the hills to Longworth, Washington, then on to Interstate I-5. I drove to Seattle, and went directly to the airport to get my ticket for tomorrow morning. I checked in at Imperial 400 Motel, had supper, made phone calls, and packed for Alaska. This had been one of my dreams. I did not know how I was going to do it until I had an invitation to come to Alaska from Mr. and Mrs. Ted Baker in Fairbanks, Alaska. Mrs. Baker was a sister of Clarence Hunt, one of our missionaries. She had several meetings lined up around Fairbanks for me.

At 5:30am, I left my car at the motel. The manager drove another guest and myself to the airport. I was able to fly "clergy" which meant half price in those days. At 7am, I was aboard a jet, headed for Anchorage. Once again, the scenery above the clouds and the Canadian Rockies sticking up through the clouds was a glorious sight.

At Anchorage, I waited only a few minutes for a DC3 to take me to Fairbanks. We flew in the clouds most of the way, but I did get to see part of Mt. McKinley. There was a two hour time change in Alaska. Mr. Ted Baker and his daughter, Mary Ann, were at the airport to meet me. It wasn't far to their place. I met mother Baker who was 83 years old, and son Ted and his wife, Elizabeth. Mrs. Baker (Vivian) didn't get home until supper.

The next morning, Vivian and I went to a Full Gospel Business Meeting for breakfast. Both men and women were there. I spoke on "What God is doing in Asia and Africa".

I spent part of the day trying to rest up.

The next day, June 9th, was Sunday. At 9:30am, I was interviewed by Don Nelson on the radio station KJNP, the gospel station at the top of the nation. It is located at North Pole, Alaska, about 13 miles outside of Fairbanks.

We then went to the Assembly of God church. I gave a few words, and told about my message that I would give that night.

For dinner, I had moose steak.

The evening service was double the regular attendance. A pastor was there from Homer, Alaska, about 300 miles away, who asked me to come for a meeting. Many were quite enthused about the service.

The next day around 9am, a lovely young mother, Mrs. Don Rawlands, picked me up and drove me to a ski lift where we could see both directions. She was so hungry for fellowship. She was a spirit-filled Methodist. I met her pastor. Later, we went to Mrs. Rawlands' home, had lunch there, and met a lovely **Eskimo lady** who was a Christian.

In the evening at 6:30, I went with Reverend Miller and a pilot in a Cessna 170, along with a Reverend and Mrs. Finfrock, to the village of Minto, about fifty miles from Fairbanks. The church was pastored by Reverend and Mrs. Olson. We walked through the village and saw the dogs and the dog sleds, fish nets, animal skins, log cabins, the log church and parsonage. We then had some lemonade. After a visit, we flew back at 9pm, and it was as light as day.

Tuesday, June 11th, I spent the day writing letters. In the evening, I went to North Pole for a service at the Assembly of God church. They said the crowd was larger than usual. There were several servicemen there. After service, I went to the radio station and showed my films to the staff there. Also, I taped a program for the next morning. They graciously gave me a check for the Baby Work in Africa.

Wednesday, Grandma Baker, Mary Ann and I went shopping. We went to the Eskimo Museum. Then we went to **Santa Claus Land, North Pole**, where letters come from all over America, addressed to Santa Claus. It was very interesting to see Santa's Place with all the toys.

In the evening, I had dinner with Mr. and Mrs. Denny. They are members of the Baptist Church. My service was at Hamilton Baptist church. The pastor knew Roy Acherle (one of our UWM missionaries). I showed the Young Doctor film. I also spoke of our Home of Hope in Dakar. I spoke of the need there. The church pledged to send an offering every month for the Home of Hope.

The thing that was so unusual in Alaska was that it never got dark. I wrote letters at night without putting on a light. On the longest day of the year, June 21st, all the sports fans are out in full force and they **play ball all night** with no lights. Frankly, I would not want to be here in the winter for those short days where it **never really gets light**.

218

So much was packed into this week. I couldn't believe it was time to leave again. On June 13th, we left at 5:30 for the airport with the Bakers. We took off by jet at 6:30. At 2700 feet, we passed very close to Mt. McKinley. It is 20,300 feet high, the highest peak in North America.

The plan stopped at Anchorage, but we didn't get off. It was a through flight. We arrived in Seattle at 1pm, their time. I soon discovered **I didn't have a motel reservation** like I thought, so I got in my car and started driving. I drove to Moses Lake, Washington. I stopped at five motels, but all were full. Finally, I got the last room at another motel. I called my beloved, and was so glad for a nice visit by phone. I then took a hot bath and went to bed.

Before I started out the next morning, I made my report. There was a question. Was it really worth my time and the mission to go to Alaska? When I figured up my offerings or honorariums, I more than covered every expense of my trip. Besides that, the one pledge alone made by the Baptist Church of $40 a month for the Home of Hope would have been worth it. They sent it for years. **No one ever** doubted my trip was worth it. Besides, I had a dream come true, and a wonderful time.

The next morning, I left Moses Lake at 9:30. I drove about 20 miles and heard a terrible noise. I thought it was a flat tire. The tire wasn't flat but, with the rough roads, the rubber was coming off of one tire. I drove slowly for 20 miles to Ritzville, and bought a new tire. I ate brunch while it was being fixed.

I Crossed Three States Today

I had left from the state of Washington. I crossed the state of Idaho and into Montana to the capitol, Helena, arriving at 6pm. (Change of time.) Would you believe it, there were **no rooms anywhere**. A convention was on, and Senator McCarthy was in town. The Lord was with me, and **I got the last room** at the **Capitol Motel**, right **near the state capitol**. I went to a shopping mall and ate my supper. I went back to my room and called my sweetie in Florida, and my host of tomorrow at Ismay, Montana. What a day!

Saturday, June 15th, I left at 7am. It was a beautiful sight, surrounded by mountains. I drove to Bozman and ate breakfast. I made a call to someone on our mailing list, and discovered she went to school with our daughter, Penny, at Hampton Du Bose Academy of Florida. She also knew our daughter-in-law, Betty Correll.

I drove on in the afternoon and ran into a real thunderstorm, and hail. It was very tiring driving. I stopped at Miles City for gas and oil. I called the Garbers at Ismay. They met me at the road where they turn in. It was so muddy, we left my car and went in their truck. They went back later and got my car.

We had a service in their home. It was quite a family, with six children, two Catholic Priests, and others.

My Fiftieth State

We left the ranch after breakfast. Mrs. Garber and one of the girls rode with me. Surprisingly, the roads were quite dry. I let them off at Baker, Montana. I drove on into North Dakota, then on down to South Dakota. It was time to blow the bugle, for this was **my fiftieth state. I had now been in every state in the U.S.**

I saw buffalo, antelope and deer, and I thought of the song, "Home on the Range." I stopped at Spearfish, Wyoming to see the sight where the Black Hills Passion Play is given. Then I went on down to New Castle, Wyoming for my meeting with the Assembly of God church, which was pastored by a darling young couple, Reverend and Mrs. Rexroat, and their adopted son. All were so very cordial. I spoke on missions, and showed my films. I stayed in a little apartment in the parsonage.

Monday morning, after breakfast, I was on the road again. I went west and north to Ekalaka, Montana. On the way, I passed the Devil's Tower, a spectacular rock formation, said to be the highest in the states. Then on north, over the worst roads I had been on since Africa. It is impassable when it rains. It was a 200 mile **backtrack** to Ekalaka, Montana, which is just a wide place in the road. Financially, I wondered if it was worth it, but when I saw how very much they needed fellowship, I remembered the Lord was always interested in the individuals. Their church is an independent church called Old Congregational Church. There were people from four different churches there. I spoke, and showed them three films. It meant a great deal to them.

Tuesday at 9:15, it was back over the rough roads, though not as far, to the main highway, and into South Dakota. How could you go through there without going through Deadwood, Wild Bill Hickock and Calamity Jane City? Then on through the Black Hills to Mt. Rushmore, the four faces of presidents. What a tremendous sight. What workmanship.

220

But as I stood there admiring it all, I felt a little sad. I so very much wished that I had someone standing beside me, to help me enjoy it. Then I remembered that the Lord was right with me, and I said, "Oh Lord, I remember. You made the mountain those faces were carved on." I felt better.

I went on through Custer National Park. I saw more herds of buffalo beside the road. Signs were everywhere, marked "Dangerous, Stay in Your Car." Donkeys came and put their noses through the window. It was a narrow winding road through the park.

I arrived in time for dinner with Pastor and Mrs. Richard Tufte, pastor of Assembly of God church. They had three children. We had a lovely roast beef dinner. After the meeting, I stayed in the pastor's home.

June 19th. Today was our 43rd wedding anniversary. I left after breakfast with no special destination. **My meeting was canceled for tonight.** I was so tired, I was about to fall apart. I skirted the Black Hills and came to Rapid City, South Dakota, the second largest city in South Dakota. I took the car to be washed. It was covered with mud. I had my suit and dress cleaned, and my hair washed and set. I checked in at a motel. Rooms were still hard to come by, but I got one.

I went out to eat by myself on my anniversary. I called my husband. He was at our daughter, Roselyn's.

I slept late. I packed the car, got the cleaning, and left at 12 noon. It was good not to rush. I hadn't even had a cup of coffee yet. I drove to Chamberlain, South Dakota, on the Missouri River. I only drove 204 miles, because of the late start. I still had to pay a high price for a room. A storm had passed over during the night.

In the morning, I drove about 60 miles to Mitchell, South Dakota. I was glad I stopped last night when I did. The storm wasn't that bad there, but in Mitchell, trees were all over the streets. Light poles were down all along the way, and were broken like matchsticks. Winds had been 101 miles an hour. God was good to stop me before.

I drove south to Springfield, South Dakota. I was still near the Missouri River, across from Nebraska. The church was Kingsbury Chapel, (interdenominational), the pastor and his wife were Reverend and Mrs. H.J. Locke. There was a very good crowd. I spoke on Africa, and showed films. The battery went dead on my car, but the men took care of it for me. I had breakfast with the pastors. Sweet fellowship.

Hallelujah, We Meet Again

Saturday, June 22nd, I drove about 400 miles to the St. Paul, Minnesota, airport. My beloved husband had arrived ten minutes before I got there. It was so good to be together again. We drove to Paul Bunyan motel near the church (which was the Immanuel Community Church). We both slept several hours, and then went out for dinner. We talked and talked all evening.

Sunday morning, Wayne Boyer came and took us to breakfast. Then I went to Sunday school and taught the high school class. They picked Sidney up for the morning church service. He had a beautiful corsage for me, for our 43rd anniversary. I spoke briefly. Sidney preached on "Must First" (Mark 13:10). We then went to dinner with Pastor and Mrs. Phillip Van Wymer.

We also had the evening meeting. As we were just about to leave the church, Richard Headrick called to say that Luther Mieir had just died. He was one of our UWM missionary board members, and had also been a missionary to Cuba.

We checked out of the motel and drove to Viroqua, Iowa. We arrived about 3pm. I finished my report for June. As I look back now, I remember those long, lonely roads, and all the things that **could have happened, but God**, I thank the Lord, not only for His watchful care, but for allowing me to be unafraid. I do not remember a sense of fear at any time.

On To Moline, Illinois

The next day, we drove to Moline, Illinois, to the home of Dr. and Mrs. Charles Hollis, only it was Charles and Ruth to us. They were like our kids. Ruth was one of our Kenosha girls. However, they were not there, but in Hawaii, on their 25th wedding anniversary.

We had a great crowd in their church, Moline Gospel Temple. So many were there which I could mention, out of our past. It was a real joy to minister there.

The next day, we drove to Kenosha, Wisconsin. We had a service in the Assembly of God church. We met Pastor and Mrs. Wilkerson. What memories, and so many old-timers there from 39 years ago. Sidney and I both spoke on missions. We had a wonderful prayer time and dedication around the altar at the close of service. We stayed at

222

the Walter Blocks' home. The pastor came out to talk to Sidney about how to have a missionary program in church.

Next it was on to Arena, Wisconsin, to the Arena Congregational church. Reverend and Mrs Bernard Norland were the pastors. We both spoke on missions. We had lots of wonderful fellowship and food in the basement auditorium.

Apart Again

After breakfast on June 28th, still 1968, we drove to Wheaton, Illinois. We got to see Betty (Correll) Coughlin, as well as Rich and Steve. After lunch, we drove to **O'Hare airport**. We talked until Sidney got on the plane headed for Europe.

Home Again, July First

I hope you have not become weary following me on just one of my itineraries. After Sidney left, I called my daughter, Penny, who lived in Auburn, Indiana, and asked if she would like to come and drive back to Florida with me. She would and she did.

We arrived in St. Petersburg, Florida on July 1st. **In four full months, we traveled through 23 states.** I didn't register the total miles in my diary, nor the total offering. They were in the report sent in, and both were large numbers.

What Is Missionary Giving?

What has money to do with a missionary program?

There are many different views to this question. Let me tell you a little joke.

One minister was wound up when he told about God's blessing on the church. The scripture had said in Isaiah 40:31, and he read it, *"They shall mount up with wings as eagles; they shall run and not be weary; they shall walk and not faint."* He shouted, "Brothers and sisters, this church is gonna walk!" The congregation answered, "Amen, let her walk." The pastor became more excited, and he said, "That's not all, this church is going to run!" "Amen, pastor, let her run!" Getting more exuberant, he cried, "Hallelujah, this church is going to fly!" "Amen, amen, let her fly!" But, said the pastor, "It's going to take money to make this church fly." A subdued response came back, "Let her walk."

When you think of investment, there is no greater place than in
God's house and above all, in the taking of the gospel to the whole
world. Do you know why? It is an **eternal investment. Did you ever
think of putting money in the bank of heaven for all of eternity?**
When you die and leave this world, you take absolutely nothing, no
matter how much you possessed in this life! There are no pockets in the
shroud. It would be so sad to go into heaven bankrupt. Jesus told us that
whatsoever you do to those in need, you do to Him.

May I close this chapter on itineration by telling you one story?
It didn't happen in this particular year, but I think it will illustrate what I
want to say.

Guest Speaker At An Annual Dinner

I was invited to be the speaker and to show the film of our son,
"The Young Doctor Goes Home," at the annual dinner at a certain
wealthy church. I was always glad to have the opportunity, wherever it
was. The host had heard me on the radio, and invited me.

I arrived and was pleased at such a beautiful church. The people
were very pleasant and gracious. The dinner was delightful, the very
best. At the end of the meal, I was introduced and began to tell a bit of
our work. Then, we went to the auditorium where the projector had been
set up. I showed my film. It had not been too long since it had been
made. It told the story of our son who was a doctor, a surgeon, who went
to the mission field to work with people who had no other medical
contact, etc. Then it told the story of his tragic death. Many times,
people had said to me, "How can you stand to watch the film night after
night?" I had replied, "To get the message out, and to feel the work he
gave his life for was not in vain."

At the close of the film, the pastor got up and, in quite a
nonchalant voice, he said, "We thank Mrs. Correll for coming today. I
am sure you have enjoyed this film. If there is someone who would like
to do something, we will have a plate at the back of the church and **you
can put your pennies in it**." It had never happened like that before, but
can I be honest with you? I was furious! That man had **never heard a
word I said!** I was talking about a young man who was a doctor, a
surgeon, a missionary, who had given his life to a needy people. I, his
mother, was giving my life to tell the story and give an opportunity to
share. And this man said, "put your pennies in the plate!" Now let me
say, I never went with an offering in mind. I **think** they gave me a

speaker's honorarium, I don't even remember. But the whole picture overwhelmed me with his uncaring response. He had one of the wealthiest churches around. Everyone had come in an expensive car. They no doubt lived in lovely homes. They didn't get the dinner for free, and I had been told that they had a large mission fund that they never touched. It wasn't as though it was an impoverished crowd. What a blessing they could have been, if the preacher had **caught the vision** or the picture of **a dedicated life**. It was the word **pennies,** I guess, that set me off. I don't even remember if anyone put pennies in the plate. Though I never said one word, I was devastated.

But isn't that the picture oftentimes? We have money for food, and lovely eating out. We have money for cars, homes, pleasures, cosmetics and gifts for others, but **nothing** for the greatest work in the world, helping others, to say nothing of making **a deposit in heaven.** I have wondered, if I felt like that, **how does God feel?**

I have recorded this in my book, that the Lord might speak to hearts the same message he gave to Malachi 3:8.

If you could only know the thrill of giving to the God who has given so much for us. There is a chorus that goes:

> After all He has done for me
> After all He has done for me
> How can I do less, than give Him my best
> And live for Him completely,
> After all He has done for me!

Chapter 33

Go! Go! Go! Billy Graham Special Train

There was real excitement as we were preparing for the Billy Graham Crusade in New York City. This was our announcement on the radio: "Have you had your vacation yet? Would you like to take a trip which would include pleasure, sightseeing, and spiritual inspiration, all wrapped into one? Then take the last Special Wings Over Dayton excursion to the Billy Graham meetings at Madison Square Gardens in New York City. The date: August 23-26. See the Empire State Building. Take a three-hour yacht cruise around Manhattan Island. You will dock by the famous ship, The Mayflower. Have breakfast in the Terrace Room of the Hotel New Yorker. Stay at New York's largest hotel, then crown your entire trip with reserved seats for the last weekend of the Billy Graham meetings in the Garden. All of this for $56.95. This includes round trip fare from Dayton to New York. Breakfast in the Diner. Call for Reservations - Helen Correll, Tour Director." This was in 1957. **Can you believe those prices?**

The above notice was for our second tour. We had already taken one group in June. There were 100 people on the first tour, and over 200 on the second trip.

To be in Madison Square Gardens, and to see 20,000 people packed in for a gospel service, with another 6,000 outside that couldn't get in, was a sight you would not soon forget. We heard Jerome Heinz (converted opera star), then listened to the stirring message of that God-blessed evangelist. That's a feeling pretty close to heaven. (This was 37 years ago, and he is still preaching.) The great reward is to watch the multitudes go forward from all parts of the auditorium. I wonder if all the converts from Dr. Graham's meetings will have a **reunion in heaven** as they bow down before the Lord in thanksgiving that they heard the call and answered?

Breakfast In The Terrace Room

What a glorious morning as all 200 members of our tour were sitting in the beautiful Terrace Room, awaiting breakfast. Somehow, the blessing from last night was still lingering in their hearts as they laughed and talked, enjoying the fellowship with newfound friends.

The meal was delicious, but the real thrill came as we listened to our special speaker, Mel (Martin) Dibble. He had recently been a famous talkshow host on the network station WLW-TV. His show was called "The Mel Martin Show." What a testimony as he told us of how God had changed his life. Let me give you some of the highlights of his testimony.

Mel was born in Atlanta, where his father was the pastor of the Baptist Tabernacle. Mel was singing and giving Bible verses on the platform at age six. He grew up and had extensive education at such places as Wheaton College, Moody Bible Institute, etc. He even assisted a pastor in Pontiac, Michigan, but there was something lacking, and he resigned to become a salesman. Little by little, he got farther away from God. His father became ill and died. Then in 1950, Mel got into television. His services were frequently sought at banquets and parties, increasing his income to a fancy sum.

He got away from his Bible and prayer. Then he started to drink, until he was on the verge of being an alcoholic. His homelife was near breakup. His wife, Ruth, always prayed that God would bring him back. Several friends wrote to Ruth about Billy Graham coming to Cincinnati, and she desperately made plans.

Mel Dibble Meets Billy Graham

An old friend, Dr. Donald Barnhouse, took Dibble to see Graham at the Gibson Hotel in Cincinnati. Dr. Graham said to him, "Mel, I know you studied for the ministry, and I know a hundred people who have told me that they are praying for you. You are in the wrong business. You ought to get right with God." Conviction came over Dibble. "The Holy Spirit propelled me to the floor," Mel relates. Graham prayed, then Dr. Barnhouse. Mel broke down, sobbing to the Lord how evil he had been. Later, he confessed to his wife what a bad husband he had been. Then he called his mother out of a prayer meeting in Los Angeles to tell her the good news.

The next morning, Mel went on TV at 9am in Cincinnati, beginning **without** his usual theme song and sales patter. He looked straight into the camera lens, and said, "Do you wonder why I am not beginning with my theme song? The fact is, you are looking at a different emcee today. In reality, my name is not Mel Martin, but Mel Dibble. I was born of a godly Baptist minister. I have been out of the will of God for many years. Last night at Taft Auditorium, I heard Billy

228

Graham preach. Afterward, in Graham's hotel, on my knees, I came back to God. In a moment, I am going to walk out of this place and back into the evangelistic field. I know I am giving up a prosperous position to go on with God. Where I'm going, I do not know yet." He broke down with emotion, and he turned to the soloist and asked him to sing "It Is No Secret What God Can Do." The camera men, instead of focusing on the singer, followed Dibble across the stage to the door. His left hand grasped the handle of the door, and his right hand supported him as he leaned against the door post, momentarily bowing his head. Finally, with a strong gesture, he pulled the door open and walked out. The TV screen showed the closing door, a moment of real-life drama.

That night, Dibble gave his testimony at the Taft Auditorium. The door was open for Dibble to conduct evangelistic meetings. What a moving story. Our group was very touched.

Just An Added Word

Sidney and I were there that night in Cincinnati, and my husband went up to Mel afterward and invited him to come to Christian Tabernacle in Dayton, Ohio, for a meeting.

It was a memorable night when he came, and there was a packed church. It was New Year's Eve. Our special guest was Mel Dibble. His wife, son, and mother were there. He stayed with us for five nights in a holiday revival, as our evangelist. But tonight was the grand climax. What a meeting we had!

Back To New York

Now back to New York, where Mel was our special speaker at the breakfast. Now you understand why it was so great to have him.

Many of our group were visiting New York for the first time. I think all enjoyed the ride around Manhattan by boat. Many said, "It was the best trip I ever had."

On the train going to New York, it had been fun getting to know one another. We sang and sang. I went from one end of the cars to the other, meeting everyone. We had two cars all to ourselves. I will confess that, on the way home, there wasn't much singing. Most were sleeping.

Hear are some of the remarks of those who went: "I'll never be the same!" "An experience of a lifetime." "I have never been so close to heaven." " It was worth every cent of it." "I'm going back to be a better Sunday school teacher."

As I am sitting here reminiscing, **I still have all the names** of those who went with me on the train. I notice many of them are already with the Lord. I remember it was my job to check the names on my list to see if all were present. It reminds me that "When the roll is called up yonder," I expect to be there. Will you?

Helen Correll, Tour Director

Chapter 34

1957 - What A Year Of Ecstasy And Agony!

The chimes had struck the midnight hour and ushered in the new year, 1957. It was a glorious Watch Night service.

Sidney To Gaza Strip

Later, my husband went to Germany for missionary services. While there, he received a cable from John Pattison Williams, President of Radio Station WING, requesting him to leave for Jerusalem immediately to cover the involvement of Israel in the Gaza Strip. (Sidney had previously received credentials as a correspondent from the United Nations.) He took the next available plane. He arrived at the new gathering headquarters of the Israeli Army. Upon signing in, they pointed to a bus which was leaving for the area of conflict that moment. He ran out with his cameras and gadgets, and was the last person on the bus.

It was a moving experience, to mingle with these military men and women. He was so impressed with the high caliber and determination of each of them. They fought hard, but as the bus returned, it was heartbreaking to see the disappointment and tears as these fine Israeli soldiers had to withdraw from the Gaza Strip due to a political agreement. When Sidney returned to Christian Tabernacle, he preached on "Will Israel Survive and Israel-Prophecy Fulfilled?" This was May of 1957.

The Young Doctor Goes Home

Little did we know that, less than two months later, in October, we would walk through the valley of the shadow of death and know the darkest hours of our life, when our doctor son was killed.

We told you the story earlier in "My Life as a Mother." Let me give you a portion that was in the 16mm film we made later, giving the father's heart. My husband is speaking: "Can you imagine what it meant to me when my own son finished his long years of training as a doctor and surgeon, and sailed to the African continent as a medical missionary? I felt a tremendous responsibility to this boy, and to all the missionaries of United World Mission. I dreamed dreams of conquest,

231

conquest of this whole western part of Africa. And then, the cruel message from the Western Union operator: 'Sidney Robert went to be with the Lord October 15th, 4am.' In a blinding flash of pain, my world caved in, and the awful question rushed in. 'Why?' All these years of preparation. The work was just begun, and there was not another missionary doctor in a thousand miles. And now our son was so quickly gone."

"Later, as Mrs. Correll and I flew to Africa, we both felt challenged in our hearts. We were not only going to bury our son, but we were going to add our part in carrying on the gospel to these people he loved."

"Arriving in the capital of Mali, Bamako, we went immediately to the government hospital where our son had passed on. Neither Mrs. Correll nor I had any sense of bitterness as we looked at the room where he died. But I was reminded of the high cost of world missions."

"For one entire day, Mrs. Correll and I rode the train from Bamako to Baufulabe, a freight train coming behind us, carrying the body of our son. At the station, the missionaries were there to meet us. From there, we had to travel 96 miles over rough, difficult roads to the Kenieba Valley, where our son and his family had been stationed. Mrs. Correll went in the station wagon with some of the missionaries, but I stayed to ride in the big truck with the body of our son."

"While his casket was being loaded into the truck, there was a blind boy coming along the track and standing by, looking so pitiful. I found myself caught up in a feeling of compassion for this little blind lad, and for every spiritually blind person in this whole circle of Baufulabe."

"As we made our journey, I thought much of David Livingston. He was the very first missionary doctor to open up the heart of Africa. He literally poured out his life. He spent years trekking through the bush, building rafts and passing over the great rivers, ministering to the sick and always preaching. He died on his knees. When the news flashed around the world 'Livingston is dead,' young men and women picked up the challenge and literally rushed into Africa to bring the gospel light throughout the whole continent in an incredibly short time."

"I thought about the Sudan, Senegal, and Mali, much of it still without the gospel. Surely God would raise up young people who would be willing to give their lives for this cause. Even as we rode those many miles, I once again made my commitment to finish as I had started. Nothing would stop me from what Christ put in my heart."

"At long last, our journey was over. It had been a sad journey, but it had been a spiritual experience. The grave had been dug by the boys from our mission station, and upon our arrival, we laid our son's body in the grave, knowing that he himself was with the Lord."

"Later in the day, Pastor George Mabille conducted a simple service at the graveside. Catholic, Protestant, Muslim, and pagan had come to stand by his grave. One chief said to me, 'You lost a son, but we lost a father.' Another said, 'Our whole village wept for three days when we heard the doctor had died.' Others said, 'We have lost our hope.'"

"The very next day, we went to the sight that Sidney Robert had chosen for the hospital. He dreamed of a place that would provide healing for the desperate physical needs of this part of Africa, and stand as a testimony to the power of Christ. The African men began clearing the ground, and Mrs Correll was so eager to get on with the job that she grabbed a rake and joined the African men with their hoes and rakes. It brought much amazement and amusement to these mountain boys. Then came the day when we turned the first shovel full of earth in a ground-breaking ceremony for the Sidney Robert Correll Memorial Hospital."

"We also had the privilege to take part in the dedication of the new chapel on the mission station near the grave and hospital. This building was constructed by the village people who gave their time and labor after Sidney Robert's death as an expression of their love and devotion."

"While there, the heat was very terrible, and the storms were violent. There were wild animals, and especially snakes. We averaged killing a snake a day. Some were deadly snakes, affecting the nervous system; death comes in 24 hours. They were a constant hazard to the little children around the station. (Note: Thank the Lord that in over thirty years we never had a missionary die from snakes or animals.) In this valley, 80% of all babies die before they are two years old. There were villages where one half the people of the village were totally blind."

The above was taken from our film, "The Young Doctor Goes Home." We have it now in video, and it is still being shown.

Let me tell you what happened to me on this trip to Africa. As I stood by the grave that day, something happened. It was as though a mantle fell on my shoulders. I must carry out my son's vision for this area, not as a missionary, but Sidney and I made this movie, which had the challenge for the hospital. Sidney's burden was for the **whole world,** but my ministry would be to travel across the United States speaking in churches, asking for workers and funds for a memorial hospital in Africa.

Quite some time later, while speaking in a church in California, I asked, "Is there a builder in the crowd who will dedicate his life to God for this service?" Among those who knelt were Paul and Betty Schubert. Paul (Bud) was a contractor, building whole sections of houses. To make a long story short, both Paul and Betty went to Africa, taking their two children, Greg and Denise. With the help of the other missionaries and the nationals, they built the hospital. God supplied funds as we visited many churches, and in the years that followed, I had the joy of returning to Africa seven or eight times, taking movie film, and bringing back updated stories of the work. We never got another doctor, which made my heart very sad, but we had a number of nurses through the years who did doctor's work, including operations. Mary Flynn of Barracksville, West Virginia, and Shirley Thomas of Canton, Ohio, were veteran missionary nurses who spent a lifetime there.

Chapter 35

The Big Decision - On The Move

These were good years in Dayton, Ohio. It had been our longest pastorate, almost 25 years. I had felt we would be there a lifetime, but we were facing a big decision. The church had grown so much, and United World Mission had expanded around the world. How could we continue to handle both?

Something happened after the death of Sidney Robert in Africa, which left us at the crossroads. The work and responsibilities of both the church and the mission were more than we could handle. But like a parent trying to decide which child to give up, it was a difficult decision. How could we give up Christian Tabernacle after all these years? We had dedicated, married, and buried so many in the church. Oh, how we loved these wonderful people. How could we resign and leave? The biggest heartrending question for me was, "What about our radio ministry of Wings Over Dayton?"

Then we thought of all the missionaries around the world, and the thrill of the growth in these countries, for this had been Sidney's burden all of his Christian life, to take Christ to the whole world. We had incorporated World Mission in 1940 when we began our work in Cuba. Then in 1946, Sidney called together around 17 pastors of independent churches, and World Mission became United World Mission. From then to 1960, Sidney had been president and director of the mission for 13 years. This was our big decision.

I went to Florida for a few days of rest, thinking we had decided to stay with Dayton and the church. In the meantime, United World Mission had its annual board meeting. The question was presented to them. When I returned, I was not prepared for the results of the meeting. We were to resign Christian Tabernacle, and give ourselves entirely to United World Mission. Sidney went to great lengths to tell me **why** the final suggestion had been made. One of the members had presented this important fact: It will be a lot easier to find a pastor for a church than to find a man with a vision to head a mission.

After the matter had been discussed further, Sidney felt this was from the Lord, and we would be ready to yield to his will. Sidney also felt it was better for the church and the mission to move the U.W.M. headquarters to Florida. Most of our missionaries were from Cuba,

South America, Africa, etc., and coming from a warmer climate, it would be practical to arrive in the homeland where they did not need clothing for cold weather.

The World Is Our Parish!

John Wesley had said it, so now we repeated it: **"The world is our parish."** We would now face another big move in our life. Sidney's heart was always in a world ministry, but now the two of us would stand side by side in reaching out to the lost world.

We Resign Christian Tabernacle

Sunday, October 18, 1959, we resigned from Christian Tabernacle. During the morning service, we had a memorial for Sidney Robert. The church had previously surprised us with a *This Is Your Life* service. Friends from far and near were there. It was a delightful time.

The Board of the church presented Dr. Correll with one of the offering plates of the church, so that he could always take **a second offering** (which my husband loved to do). They also gave us new luggage and a number of other gifts, and were so very gracious and kind to us.

George Gardiner, who had previously been our associate pastor for several years but had been pastoring in Boston, Massachusetts, resigned his church and returned to Christian Tabernacle to become the pastor.

On October 21, Sidney left for South America for special missionary ministries, among others, to be with the Wycliff Bible Translators in their jungle camp, and to make a 16mm film of their work.

For the present time, I continued to live on the farm and conduct the radio programs each afternoon until the following January.

*Helen and Sidney Correll lived out a vision for missions
modeled after John Wesley's words "The World Is our Parish"*

Chapter 36

Africa Bound, 1960

What excitement on the farm as we prepared for our missionary journey. Denise and Greg Schubert, ages 13 and 11, had been with us for six months, while their parents, Paul and Betty, were in France, in language study. The Moore children, Doris (13), Timmy (11), and Janis (7), came from their aunt's home, also in Ohio, to leave with us on this great adventure. Dot and Orlando Moore were also in language study.

It was on the last day of January, 1960, that we made our way by car, driving through bitter ice and snow, to New York, where we stayed in the old Paris Hotel. While in New York, we met with our dear friend, Leona Sagasta. We had known her for years. It was interesting how we first came to know her. Leona went with her father to the Statue of Liberty. Sidney had flown to New York for some meetings. He had taken our daughter Roselyn along with him. He wanted to show her the Statue of Liberty, and while there they met Leona and her father. Sidney told them about his meeting, and Leona said she would be glad to come. Before they parted that day, Leona had offered to take Roselyn around to see the sights while my husband took care of his church business. From that time, on down through the years, Leona was always there to help get our missionaries on their way. We would call her our "New York missionary."

Miss Sagasta had told us how much she had enjoyed the children I had with me that January. She had taken them for a walk down one of the streets. The littlest girl, Janet, looked up and said, "Oh, look up there." When Lee looked up she saw a replica of the Statue of Liberty on top of one of the buildings. She was amazed and said, "I have lived here most of my life, and I never noticed that before." The next day we went to the 33rd Street Pier in Brooklyn where we boarded The African Grove freight ship. Believe me, it was no small task, getting the children and all the luggage on board.

There were only eleven passengers on board, and **we were six of them**. For the next couple of weeks I was to be their "boat mother".

The Voyage

The first part of the voyage was not the most pleasant, as there had been a lot of storms brewing on the rough and frigid January seas.

We sailed to Nova Scotia first, but we could not leave the ship, due to the howling winds and ice. We were fortunate, though, as we had just missed the worst storm in forty years by one day. We left Nova Scotia that evening and headed for Dakar, Africa. We still had rough seas, and I can remember Timmy's cot sliding up and down the deck as the ship rolled and tossed. Needless to say, a few meals were missed those first days.

As we had calmer seas, life became much more active. Believe me, we were well fed. Because this was not a passenger ship, there were no play areas, so we had to invent our own games We played follow the leader, and other games. We asked one of the crew for a long piece of rope, and tying one end of it to a pole on deck, we invented our own version of jump rope. Even the captain of the ship joined in jumping. The crew took the children on a tour from the top of the pilot house to the bottom of the engine room. On dreary days we read, painted, and made scrap books. We had daily devotions, and a missionary lady from Monrovia, Liberia, worshipped with us. I could not have asked for better children, both in their conduct and Christian testimony. We were one happy family aboard. Oh yes, we celebrated two birthdays, and the chef made a special cake for the occasion.

Dakar, Africa

It didn't seem like two weeks, but at 8am Sunday, February 14, the S.S. African Grove pulled into port at our destination, Dakar, Africa.

As the ship was being moored into its berth, we could see the excited parents, Dot and Moe Moore and Bud and Betty Schubert, down on the pier. The children were hanging over the railing, shouting a multitude of questions. "Did you get my Christmas card, Mommie?" "See, I got the watch you sent me." "Hey dad, the captain jumped rope with us." "Mom, is that a new dress?" Then there would come squeals of "Oh, I'm so glad to see you! Are you glad to see us?" You couldn't hear what was being said on dock, but you could see them wiping away tears, and feel the emotions of the great moment. Four happy parents had survived the first of many absences from their children. That was one of the prices of being a missionary.

As soon as the gangplank was down, they were allowed to board ship, and greetings were completed with hugs and kisses and more tears. The missionaries engaged one of the African men and his crew to take the **baggage from our cabins**. This consisted of 12 suitcases, 6 overnight cases, several canvas bags, 2 black boards, and 5 large cardboard boxes. With all this coming from our cabins, you might wonder where we slept.

The African customs officer came to the foot of the gangplank, took one look, marked a big "A" on every bag, and waived them through. How we wish it had all been that simple. Everything was piled into and onto a dilapidated taxi, and then we waited for our clearance from immigration. The African immigration officer came on board. He shook hands with the captain, then sat down to clear us for debarkation. There were two gentlemen with him. One was a harbor policeman, and the other was an **interpreter**. The officer checked our passports and gave us a form to fill out with name, occupation, reason for being in the country, when and where were you born, what were the names of your father and mother, etc.

The Schuberts and the Moores had filled out forms for the children, but the immigration officer pointed out that I had not written down the names of the children on my sheet. I said, "They are not my children. I was just their guardian." The interpreter explained it, the policeman explained it, the captain explained it, but he could not understand it. Why was I bringing them when they were not my children, and who were these other people? He shook his head, but said the names are not on my paper. The captain of the ship picked up the passports and showed him that they were different ones with different names. He still shook his head. You would have to experience it to understand it. You could only smile, never loose your patience, be courteous and start all over again. There were more details, but finally we were given our release papers. These children had been my charges for this voyage, and now we had safely arrived. Mission accomplished!

Do you want to hear more?

We went to the mission house in Dakar. All the baggage was carried up the steps to the third floor. The missionaries had two rooms for their families, and the use of the back porch. All ten of us were sitting on books, trunks and two chairs. Some had to stand, but we enjoyed our stew, fruit salad, and french bread.

That evening, we had a wonderful time of fellowship with Reverend and Mrs. Talmage Butler, a missionary pilot and his wife. The next day, we went to the docks to get **48 pieces of baggage** that had been taken **from the hold**. The ordeal showed us another reason why missionaries must be endued with patience and money. The missionaries had much to do to prepare for us to go interior to our Kenieba station. It was 800 miles by train. There were kerosene stoves and refrigerators to buy. Purchasing them in Africa saves shipping and customs costs. Finally, we were ready for the trip. The long, hot, dusty ride on an African train alone can remove all illusions that missionary work is just a **romantic adventure**. The African trains are similar to the European ones. The isle is down one side, and there are compartments with seats facing each other. At night, the seats slide out and make beds. You have to provide your own sheets, and bring your own food and drinking water for the 18 hour journey. Can you imagine no air conditioning, windows open, with dust and cinders flying in?

Kenieba Station - Home For Four Years

After the 18 hour train ride, we arrived at the railroad station in Kayes. They loaded everything into the big mission truck, and rode miles over very rugged road to the mission station. As we arrived, the missionaries came running out to greet us. The African natives came from the nearby grass-roofed huts, as well as neighboring villages. All wanted to meet the new missionaries, and they welcomed me back as well. Then, striding across the compound came a tall distinguished black man in flowing robes. He was **the commander** of the village. With a smile, he held out his hand to give us a warm welcome. It was almost as though the trials of the journey were forgotten in the joy of the moment.

It was interesting to watch the African young people come with such curiosity to meet the newcomers. I was touched by the love and understanding of our missionary children as they made the effort to try to exchange words in the Africa language, to learn to sing songs in Menika, and to learn some of the African games. They, in turn, taught the African children American games. I wondered what the next four years would mean in the life of these five lovely American young folks.

Mounds And Mountains

In Kenieba Mali, Africa, there are many mounds and mountains. On our mission station was a very high **mound** known as Termite Hill. It was located close to the mud huts with the grass roof where our new missionaries lived. Yes, they lived in a large hut made from mud bricks, with a tall grass roof. The children found Termite Hill fascinating to explore.

The ground where you see this large mound was once level, but a swarm, or colony, of termites began to work. The dictionary says, "a termite is a wood-loving worm." Here in the United States, they may attack your home foundation, but in Africa, these white soft-bodied creatures, which look like an ant, began their work in the dirt. During the dry season, they bore into the earth, inch by inch, making miles of tunnels back and forth. They bring the earth to the top, much like an ant hill, and begin to build a tower. Their saliva, or the juice they secrete from their mouth, cements or glues the dirt and gravel together as they build higher and higher. They do have a problem, though, for should they appear in the open, the birds, the cats, the dogs or even the African people love to eat them. The people do roast them first, though.

When the rainy season comes and these underground tunnels begin to fill with water, the termites then resort to their high tower. After the rainy season is over, a very curious thing happens. The mating time begins, and these earthbound creatures develop, or sprout, wings. They soar and mate. This lasts a very short while, and then, alas, the wings fall off, they are earthbound once more, and now the process starts all over again.

There is a benefit to these mounds which helps the African people. They break these hills down, pulverize them, and because of the glue-like substance the termites have put in it, they use it as mortar in building the mud bricks for their huts. It is actually waterproof.

I might add, the termites also devour any wood in buildings, so that only the very impossibly hard wood like mahogany can be used. That is why it is necessary to use cement block and steel frames for houses or buildings.

I hope you liked the story of the mounds. Kenieba village itself is in a valley, completely surrounded by mountains.

From The Bush To The Jungle

At the end of my five weeks in Mali, it was with reluctance that I prepared to leave. Once again, I was leaving part of my heart in this valley, Missionary pilot Talmage Butler came out from Dakar to transport me in his lovely 4-seat Bonanza on my journey.

We went to the little airstrip near the mission. I never took off from here without thinking, "If only this airstrip had been here when our son was hurt, he might have survived." But that is in God's hands.

243

We took off and waved good-bye to all the precious missionaries, plus many loving African friends. We flew south, nonstop to Monrovia, Liberia. Being a small plane, we flew low enough to see the rivers, villages, and things of interest quite clearly. Several times Talmage would do a tight turn, making a circle so I could see something of special interest. Then we climbed to the altitude ceiling as we crossed miles and miles of rain forest and jungle below. My pilot informed me that there were large areas filled with snakes and wild animals which had never been penetrated by the outside world. Then, to inspire my faith, he said "If anything should happen and we had to land, we would never be found." (Thanks a lot, friend!) In spite of these thoughts, I did enjoy the beautiful flight, and we landed safely at Monrovia, Liberia. I said good-bye to my gracious friend and pilot, and met some missionary friends there.

I must hurry on. Thursday, I took the DC3 airplane on what is laughingly called "the milk run." The airplane leaves from Dakar, but I got on at Monrovia. It touched down at the coastal capitals, Ivory Coast, Ghana, Nigeria, Cameroons. Many people back home were surprised that I would make this trip alone, but I was not afraid. Actually, I wasn't alone, for my heavenly Father was with me. The journey was really uneventful, until we came to Douala of the Cameroons. A local war was going on, so the captain said, "You will be taken by airline vans to the hotel, and we urge you that no one go out of the building at night. You will be picked up and returned to the airport in the morning." You can be sure that I had no desire to sightsee. On the way to the airport the next morning, we saw vehicles peppered with bullet holes.

Sheer Panic

I understood that we were to leave at 9am. I had supposed we would take the same plane we got off of last night. As I looked out the windows of the waiting room, I saw my plane moving out. I had been a pretty good traveler even when alone, but I confess I experienced sheer panic. All the signs were in French, so I could read no directions on the board. No one would listen to me, for no one spoke English. I got out my ticket, even showing it to the flight attendant. They would only say something in French and walk on. It gives you a feeling of what it is like to be a **minority**. When I saw the plane move out, I was near tears. I sent up a prayer with a desperate groan. Then a man who was also a passenger saw my plight, and said, "I am on your flight also. I believe we leave from the gate over there." What a relief!

This flight took me to Bangui, in central Africa. By now, I was very much aware that Africa is a big continent.

Imfondo, Africa

Once again, I was in a fine missionary home in Bangui until I could catch a military plane that went to Imfondo, where our mission station was. Now that was a ride! The seats were just benches along one side of the plane, and baggage and mail bags were piled high on the other side. It wasn't the most comfortable ride, but I was grateful, for it only took an hour to fly there. It would have taken two days by river boat.

Little did I realize that I would stand beside another grave while in Africa. I had received a telegram in Bangui, saying that our veteran missionary Verna Sigler had just passed away in the hospital in Brazzaville. I knew Verna had been ill, but I had so looked forward to visiting with her. It had been ten years since Sidney and I had been there last. The mission headquarters at home had felt she should return for medical help, but they allowed her her heart's desire: "Please let me die in Africa where my heart is." This was God's time for her.

What a joy to be with the other missionaries, Gene and Sandy Thomas and their two children, and Wes and Joy Daniels and their four children, just to see the work these young people were doing, and to know the hazards they faced each day for Christ. Their tireless and consecrated efforts would shame many of us in the homeland.

The station was located on the Ubangui River. In the front of the station was the river, and just behind the buildings was a fence. On the other side of the fence was the jungle. Wild animals were not only close, but went right through the yard. I remember well one evening when I was there before. I heard a gun shot. Shortly afterward, Gene came in and just nonchalantly announced that he had just shot a wild animal in the front yard. No big deal.

There is just one road in the village, and it runs north and south. Transportation was bicycle, motor scooter, or dugout canoe with an outboard motor. What amazing stories I could tell.

245

Easter And Verna Sigler's Homecoming

Easter morning, I spoke in the chapel for a memorial for their "Mama". I told of her consecration, her love for the Lord and for them, and her glorious hope of the resurrection. That afternoon, the riverboat came from Brazzaville, bringing Verna's body back to her beloved Imfondo.

Evidently the jungle drums had been broadcasting the message, for along the river banks were tiers and tiers of Africans, standing in mute sorrow and respect. For miles up and down the river, praises were sung of her devotions to the black man. Never a weary heart or a sick body had been turned away.

The funeral was held the next day. The chapel was packed, with scores standing outside. Every white (French) official in the area was there. The African commander of Imfondo was there, as well as the commander and family from the Congo Belge. (This was in 1960.) Many had walked for miles. The service was in three languages: English, French, and Lingala. Thirteen Bible students carried her body from the chapel to the grave, and knelt in consecration to the Lord.

Space will not allow me to tell of the many experiences I had while there at our jungle station. What a lighthouse!

Update

Gene and Sandy Thomas are still there. This year of 1994, they celebrate 40 years of faithful service to the Lord, and they are still ministering. However, they are now in Brazzerville, the capital city.

All too soon, I boarded the military plane back to Bangui. From there, by the big super G plane, I went to Paris, France where I visited for two days with two of our missionary nurses. Then I went on to Berlin, Germany, and back to the good old U.S.A. During the 3 months I was in Africa and Europe, I visited 23 of our adult missionaries and 20 children, which included Ken and Judy Durst and their 4 children who were in language study, preparing for their work in Mali.

"Go ye into all the world and preach the gospel to every creature."

Aboard ship

In Africa

Finding a friend

Termite Hill

Chapter 37

A New Home , A New State

Shortly after I left for Africa with the missionary children, the farm sold. This was the last link in going on to our new ministry. So, while I was in Africa (after the farm had sold), Sidney went to St. Petersburg, Florida, and bought a place for us at 130 Pinellas Way. He felt like a new groom getting a home for his bride, who would soon be coming to occupy it. Sidney then came to Boston to meet me. I was returning from Europe, and he would meet me there.

He had arranged an extensive itinerary for us. Instead of going directly to Florida, we had one month of meetings beginning in Park Street Church of Boston, Massachusetts, as well as other cities in the state. Then it was on to New York state, New Jersey, New Hampshire, and Connecticut. It was wonderful to share the missionary vision with both pastors and people.

It wasn't easy on us, coming back to the states and realizing we would never get to go back to the farm we loved so much, and to know we were no longer pastors of the church we gave our life to for 23 years. The radio program, Wings over Dayton, which had been such a part of me, was now gone.

I was reminded again that you dare not cling too closely to the things of this life. Even the good things, sometimes, you are called upon to turn your back on, to go forward for God. Maybe that is why the Lord said in Mark 10:29-30, *"There is no man that hath left houses or brethren or sisters or fathers or mothers or wife or children or lands for my sake and the gospel, but he shall receive an hundred fold now in this time, houses, brethren, sisters, mothers and children and lands with persecutions and in the world to come life everlasting."*

At Home In St. Petersburg, Florida

After the intensive weeks of meetings Sidney and I had ministered in, we arrived in St. Petersburg, Florida. He was all excited to show me the new place. It was lovely, a beautiful but simple typical Florida one-story home, and it had a lovely Florida room and an adjoining swimming pool, all enclosed like a room with a green netting. This was not only a luxury, but for Florida, a necessity. We all enjoyed it. Incidentally, our grandchildren learned to swim in it, as well as a number of missionaries' children. Some of the grandchildren were there all summer each year. They used to say, "We want to go to Grandma's place with the swimming pool in her front room."

Well, when we arrived, my husband didn't carry me over the threshold as I was too big for that, but he was beaming. He so wanted to please. I really was delighted with it. Once again, it was not only home to us, but it was home for many people. At times there were sleeping bags all over the Florida room floor for the children.

Setting Up Housekeeping

When Sidney bought the house in St. Petersburg, he was advised that it was better to just sell your furniture up north and get regular Florida furniture. (If any one ever tells you that, forget it!) So, my husband told his father to have a sale and sell everything. When I heard about it in Africa, I sent word home, "Please don't sell my silverware or linens or dishes. And, of course, bring all our personal things as well as our files and office things to Florida." I won't go into detail, but Dad Correll took Sidney at his word; **he sold everything**, which included my contour chair which I loved, and a rocker the church had given us for Christmas. But, do you know what I think was the hardest to replace? All of my gadgets from the kitchen, things that take years to collect: knives, measuring cups and spoons, can opener, toaster, etc. At the sale, these things went for 25 cents a basketful. My dear husband felt so badly and promised, "I never really realized, and I wasn't there when it happened, but we will never do that again. One consolation, when we go to heaven we won't have to worry about taking anything. Hallelujah!" I will admit, I felt badly for a while, and Daddy Correll said, "Well Sidney said, 'Sell everything,' and I took him at his word." I am glad for one thing. My daughter Roselyn, who lived not too far away, was at the sale, and bought the cookie jar for the children! Oh yes, being a lady preacher isn't all spiritual. As I think back on this experience, it doesn't even compare to the loss of those who have lost everything, sometimes even a loved one, in an earthquake, flood, fire or some other disaster. Then you realize what really matters.

Getting On With It

Michael, age 14, and Kenny, age 12, stayed in Dayton till school was out. Then our son-in-law, Bob Cauble, drove them down to Florida.

It had been hard to leave the farm, because this was all Michael ever knew. Kenny became part of our family when he was eleven. However, I don't think they minded the move too much, because we had a pool, and it was not far to the beach.

It was one thing to get settled as a family, but it was a much bigger job to locate office space and a place for the mission. The reason for moving the mission to Florida was that the church really needed the space that United World Mission occupied for Sunday school rooms. Second, Florida was chosen because most of our missionaries at that time were in Cuba, South America, and Africa. It was good to have a warm climate to come home to on furlough.

Both Sidney and I had meetings lined up for the rest of the year, but I had a job to do first, editing my 16mm film. Whenever we had gone on trips together, I would take the still pictures and Sidney took the movie pictures. He had filmed "The Young Doctor Goes Home," but before I left for Africa with the missionary children, he put the K100 movie camera with the turret head in my hands and said, "Now it is up to you to bring back your story by movies." He also told me I must not take pictures without the tripod unless it was impossible to use it. He put me through a small teaching course, and then I was on my own. We had "The Young Doctor" film edited with sound, professionally. Now we would edit our own film and write the script, then have the sound put on.

So, now I had these hundreds of feet of film to edit. Do you know what is the hardest part? Having to let so much of the film on the cutting room floor. Oh, how I hated to not put in every good scene. I would say, "But we have to use this!" So we had the rolls of film developed, and we were both thrilled at the story I had.

Let me just tell you some of the things I shot. The missionaries had prepared for the third mission conference. Those who were there were Joe and Olga Elles; Mary Fynn, Ada Yarnall, and Alberta Fannin, our three nurses; Don and Jean Schultz, Paul and Betty Schubert. Paul was the builder and Betty helped in the dispensary. Dot and "Moe" Moore were only there temporarily until they could get back to Dakar, Senegal, to start a school for **missionary children**. In the meantime, Mrs. Moore was holding classes in one of the native huts. Mr. Moore was helping by driving the truck and helping the building program which was moving ahead.

For the five weeks I was in Kenieba, I was photographing: the different mission buildings, riding in the truck to other villages, visiting the lines and lines of sick folk who came to the dispensary, climbing the mountain to the villages - each one had a story. I took a picture of the first cement block at the hospital site. I could tell you how I almost fainted one day while watching the nurses perform an eye operation. Just like the cutting room floor, I wish I could tell you all of these things. I did tell of our trip to the river 16 miles away to get sand and gravel to make the cement block. We saw a crocodile swimming by, also the imprints of a hippo and her baby. One early morning, when we came to the river, there were foot prints of a lion, made the night before in the pile of sand which the Africans had brought up from the river the previous day.

I so enjoyed watching the native men and women as they were planting peanuts. That is one of their biggest financial crops. From morning to night, there was always something for me to see. But in the mornings, I would go to the chapel for my devotions. Then I would go and sit by the grave of our son, Sidney Robert, not to weep (though I did some), but to read God's Word. I read John 12:24, *"Except a corn of wheat fall into the ground and die, it abideth alone; but if it die it bringeth forth much fruit."* I saw this as a reality. The Lord worked day by day in the hearts of many. While there, I received the inspiration to call my film "Fruit from my Kenieba Valley!"

June 19th of that year, my husband and I celebrated our 35th wedding anniversary.

Making movies

Chapter 38

Our Christian Heritage

"Are you crazy?" Anyone who would take a group of teenagers on a trip to Europe is either crazy or just asking for it! But that was an inspiration my husband and I had.

Sidney had the wonderful experience of taking adults on tours, mainly to the mission fields. He found out that if he could get people to see the need, they would respond much more than they would to him trying to describe it. There were those who, after visiting an orphanage (Europe in the 1940's, later the Philippines, Korea, Vietnam, etc.), would give thousands of dollars toward the orphanage, buy clothing, build a church, give a truck or other transportation, where they would never be touched in a church service.

Youth Tour

This youth tour dream was something different. We wanted to have the blessing of traveling with Christian youth or their peers. What would be their goal? So few really knew that so much of their Christian roots had come from Europe. So we called the tour "Our Christian Heritage."

Sidney contacted missionaries or Christian leaders in the different countries to get a group of young people together to meet teens. The plan was to discuss the way they could share their Christian faith or testimony. We sent out promotion to our contacts. We were looking for youth or teens who would like to go. We would take a limited number.

Finally, all arrangements were made. We were to meet in **New York**. In the meantime, we contacted Reverend Tom Murphy of Pinkerton, Michigan, asking if he would like to go as our tour pastor? He was to give daily Bible studies. Sidney and I had been in his church and were very impressed with him. He responded that he would be glad to go.

The day of our glorious adventure had come. It was December 5, 1962. We would sail on the beautiful S. S. France. Our journey would be 36 days. It would cover the Christmas holidays, plus a few extra.

The weather was dull and dreary, but our young folk were bubbling with excitement as they met their travel mates. We introduced them to Pastor Murphy from Michigan. Janet McNutt and Cheryl Feeback from Covina, California, had come the farthest. Lynn Rae Farris arrived from Kenosha, Wisconsin. Ed Vandermolen and his sister Ginger were from Wheaton, Illinois. Leny Guenzler was from Rockford, Illinois. Don Foos was from Bradford, Pennsylvania.

What a lot of chattering was going on. Now meet Jim Smith from Detroit, Michigan, who was the youth leader there. Then came the kids from Ohio: Ruth Buser from Amherst, Ruth Ann Jones and Barbera Hecker from Dayton, Lynda Siehl and Jill Eshelman from Covington, and our granddaughter, Pamela Cauble, from Reynoldburg. Pam was the youngest at 14 years old.

Then, of course, came Helen and Sidney Correll from St. Petersburg, Florida. I was the mother of the group, and Sidney was the tour director and Dad to the kids.

I don't believe any of them had traveled abroad before, so there was so much to see and explore. That gorgeous dining room had food that was out of this world. There were so many decks to walk. What an exciting moment as they all crowded along the rail. The ship's whistle sounded its deep booming blast, and we could feel the movement of the ship as it eased out into the waters and began the journey. It was night, and there was a chill breeze. Out in the waters you could get a faint glimpse of "the lady with the torch." Everyone felt the thrill that millions have felt, looking at the monument of freedom.

The first order given after the evening meal was to meet in **our stateroom**. At nine o'clock, they were all there. Needless to say, for 17 people it was a bit crowded. They didn't seem to mind. They sat on the beds, the floor, any place there was a space. My husband had his guitar, and we had a songfest. We ended up singing, "Do Lord, Do Lord, Do Remember Me," the old Negro spiritual. That stateroom hummed, believe me. Pastor Tom read a scripture, then my husband gave a briefing for the trip. What a master of every situation he was. He said, "You know, they said we were crazy to take a group of teenagers to Europe. Fathers and mothers were somewhat worried about you. But I am not worried. You will be the ladies and gentlemen I believe you are. Mrs. Correll and I have the fullest of confidence in you. So just let me give you just a few ground rules."

"Number one: I expect you to be examples on this ship of what Christ would have you to be. Frankly, some of the officers were a little worried to see this many youth in one group. Prove them wrong."

"Number two: There will be many historic adventures to see as we go from place to place. I want you to make the most of it. You will see other cultures. You will hear other languages. It will be an education in itself. Make mental notes of them. It will also be dangerous at times."

"Number three: I want you girls to come back safely, so that we don't get in trouble with your parents. Boys, you can help me do that. There are twice as many girls as there are boys, so I want **each of you fellows** to be **responsible for two girls**. I want you to see that they are safely in their rooms at night. This is not my responsibility, but yours. It is like the buddy system." (These boys took it to heart and, though they were teens and not angels, we had no problems on the entire trip.)

"Number four: There will be devotions and Bible study each day on the ship, and we would appreciate each one of you being present. We will meet in a large room assigned to us for the occasion, at 10am. Bring your Bibles. Reverend Murphy will bless us."

May I report that Pastor Murphy was a blessing with his touching Bible studies. Some of the kids said, "You can tell by his well worn Bible that he is not a stranger to God's Holy Word."

Sunday, on the high seas, we were asked to conduct the divine services. Janet McNutt sang "Amazing Grace." Lynn Rae was at the piano, and Reverend Murphy spoke.

One of the interesting things the kids were able to do on the ship was when some of the crew took the whole group on a tour of the beautiful vessel, from the engine room to the bridge. The whole voyage was a wonderful experience.

When we left the S. S. France, we heard nothing but praise from the entire staff, from the captain down.

Arrival In England

Our Atlantic journey was over. We entered our first new country. We arrived at the port city of South Hampton. Going through customs was easy. Because we were a student tour, we were passed without inspection. We took the boat train to the city of London.

What a tour! Buckingham Palace, home of Her Majesty the Queen, and the colorful band that parades each morning. We looked, hoping to see some of the royal family. On past the Victoria monument. We walked through St. James park, which was a sanctuary for the birds. What singing!

255

Ruby Clarke, our missionary to Africa, was studying French in Paris, but she met us in England and joined the grand tour. Now there were 18 of us. On with the tour. We passed the Houses of Parliament along the Thames river. Overhead towered the celebrated clock, Big Ben, 320 feet high.

Nearby was the West Minster Abbey, the nations premier church and memorial. We were standing on ground consecrated since the seventh century. It is not only the scene of the coronation of monarchs, but also the resting place of David Livingston, who contributed much to our Christian heritage.

Then Trafalgar Square and Lord Nelson's Monument. Unforgettable, the British Museum. Who can forget the British Museum, the largest library in the world, 16 million books in one room. We saw sculptures representing classic art 500 years before Christ. What fun it was to visit the Dickens House where Charles Dickens lived and wrote.

Our First Group Of European Youth

Russell and Betty Mills brought some high school and university students to our hotel to meet our young people. They were our guests for dinner at the hotel, then we retired to a room arranged for us.

They had a great time of fellowship as they discussed what young people in the 1960's could do to keep their testimonies, like John Wesley, founder of Methodism, whose spiritual impact on England had saved the nation from a bloody revolution, by revival.

We closed our evening get-together by having a question and answer period. Sidney had asked our missionary, Ruby Clarke, to conduct it. Ruby Clarke is black. She was, and is, a wonderful lady whom we knew a long while before she went as a UWM missionary. She had worked at Wright Field in Dayton as a secretary to a colonel stationed there. She was a very dear friend of ours as well as of our church.

Questions were being asked and answered. Then one young man asked, "Do you mind if I ask a personal question? **How does it feel to be black?**" We all wanted to crawl under our seats. We were so embarrassed. What would she answer? Ruby kept her cool and just smiled as she said, "I will be glad to give you an answer, if you will answer one for me first. **How does it feel to be pink?**" You see, many of the people in the cooler countries have very pink cheeks. I don't know if it is the climate or what. Well, that whole group broke up. They howled with laughter. The young man's classmates slapped him on the back shouting, "Yeah, how does it feel to be pink?" Before this, everyone was quite British and standoffish, but that broke the ice, and they were just a bunch of school kids together. They became friends.

Hello, Paris

Some people think Paris is the most beautiful city in the world. Other writers have said that it is a city of dissipation, pleasure, luxury, extravagance and sin. They are very worldly wise, but have **no place for God**.

The Eiffel Tower reaches 984 feet into the blue sky. Built in 1887 for the Paris Exposition, it has become a symbol of Paris. Church of the Madelane was constructed by Napoleon. Chopin was buried there. The Arch of Triumph stands in the center of a star where 12 boulevards meet. It was built to commemorate Napoleon's victory, but we were more concerned about it being the street through which our G.I.s marched, pursuing the German army to the north.

Under the arch itself was the grave of the unknown soldier. A fire is burning that is never allowed to go out. But as we looked, we wondered, where was the fire that burned in the heart of **John Calvin**? He was a lawyer who became dissatisfied with his church, and allied himself with the reformation. The fire isn't altogether dead. Though the nation is more or less pagan, the gospel is going forth.

We met some fine French young people and shared a time of fellowship with them. They sang the same songs, gave the same testimonies, but alas, we discovered **the language barrier** for the first time. There was an impact which our young people felt, the **loneliness of being a foreigner**.

Through East Germany

The midnight ride through East Germany to the isolated city of West Berlin, over 110 miles through **red communist territory**, was an experience I am sure was never forgotten. I cannot take time to describe the sinister, evil atmosphere that accompanied every mile of that night train to Berlin. We could understand why most people flew. We breathed easier as our train crossed the border into West Berlin, a place of freedom and hope in the midst of a red sea.

West Berlin

Down through the center of this great city stood **the wall**. Paul Haueter was there at the station to rescue us. With him was a representative of the West Berlin government. He informed us we were their official guests. They had a beautiful sightseeing bus which was at our disposal, including Miss Rice our interpreter. We passed the Brandenburg Gate. The Bronze Chariot of Victory was no symbol of victory now.

Our young people were impressed as they walked along this wall that divided brother from brother. There was the Church of the Atonement right on the dividing line behind the wall. Before being ejected by the Red Guards, the congregation set the hands of the clock at one minute to midnight. Buildings once alive with business were blocked out. The tops of high walls were covered with broken slivers of glass, embedded in concrete. In spite of this, many dared to leap for freedom. Some made it, some did not. Their broken bodies were picked up, and one could almost hear the cry "Give me liberty or give me death." Our young people stood around the cross that stands in memory of Peter, the teenager who was shot down on the east side of the wall as he was climbing to freedom and was left to die until his murderers carried away his dead body.

Checkpoint Charley

At the official U.S Army Checkpoint Charley, we walked with our young people past the gate and down the streets of **East Berlin**. On down Main Street, rubble was still lying everywhere. Everything was so grim and cold, no smiles, no good will. We had no desire to stay long. As we came back through the Soviet customs and then crossed at Checkpoint Charley again, some of the girls wept with the emotion of it. Our hearts bled for those who never had this privilege.

The Wall Is Gone

As I am writing this and remembering, the wall is gone! So is Communism! But how soon will they, will we all, forget!

Innsbrook, Austria

After a long train ride, we arrived at Innsbrook, Austria. It was the city of the 1954 Olympics. Just before we arrived, they had had the biggest snow storm in 11 years. It looked like a fairyland. Our California girls **had never seen snow** before. What fun they had throwing snow balls at one another.

It was Christmas time, and the chimes and bells were ringing. We were among the Tyrolean Alps. Magnificence and splendor at 6,600 ft. We couldn't help but exclaim *"My help cometh from the Lord which made heaven and earth."* We took the teleferic and cable car, making four changes, to the summit. As far as the eye could see, there were peaks and more peaks, magnificently beautiful. Then going down by funicular, over the tops of the fir trees, we could look down the slopes and watch the skiers gliding by.

Christmas Eve

On Christmas Eve, we had our own special party. We had an exchange of inexpensive gifts. Everyone was a bit pensive, as most of the kids had never been away from home on Christmas before. But they were sweet and wonderful. Christmas day, we went by bus to the picturesque village of Sefeld. All the way, we sang and sang and sang.

Rome, Italy

From the moment we arrived in Rome, we were carried back in history to the Apostle Paul. We visited the Coliseum, built in 80 A.D. by the Emperor's son. The inauguration lasted one hundred days. During this celebration, 5,000 animals were killed for the pleasure of the people. Then they wanted **human blood**. The most likely to satisfy their evil hearts were **the Christians**. We saw the rooms where these godly people were kept as prisoners. Each day, a few were brought to the center of the arena. The hungry lions were allowed to enter. We could almost hear the raucous laughter of 50,000 people who watched with glee. What did it matter if these were human beings? Life was cheap. Heaven alone knows the number of martyrs for Christ.

The Vatican

On Saturday we went to the Vatican, residence of the Pope. We enjoyed seeing St. Peters Basilica, and the magnificent ceiling of the Sistine Chapel, with the art work of Michelangelo. What dedication of workmanship! What a masterpiece! We stood with a tear in our eye and heart as we looked at the **pieta**, or the sculpture, showing Mary, the mother of Christ, holding the body of her Son after He had been crucified on the cross and taken down. She was holding Him with a grieving heart. Every mother who has grieved for a son can appreciate that scene. But how many, as they see this amazing scene, realize **He died for us**! The best part was that it was not the end. Three days later, Christ was alive! And because He arose from the dead, we shall never die. What a hope!

December 30th

We were in Rome five days. We saw many interesting sights. Now it was time to move on. Our gracious hosts at the Condoti Hotel came out to the taxi to wish us a fond farewell. It literally poured rain as we got into the taxis and left for the railroad station. Baggage was a big part of our trip. Can you imagine, 2 suitcases apiece, for 17 people? That was a lot of bags.

I could tell you some funny stories (and some not so funny stories) about train rides. Like the time we got on the wrong coach, and the fellows had to carry all the luggage through the cars to the right coach. God bless our boys. They were not only gentlemen, they were lifesavers. Many times there were no porters, so they would grab a cart and start loading or unloading baggage. No one used **the doors** for baggage; you should have seen those suitcases going through the **windows**. I might say, the girls did help too.

En Route To Naples, Italy

We were on our way to Naples, where we would board the American export line named Independence. It was December 30th, and we arrived at 5pm. The U.S. Navy ship was docked next to our ship. Our kids had a lot of fun, talking to the sailors who were on the wharf below. At 9pm, we were on our way. We would have one more stop on our way to New York. We would visit with young folks of Spain.

The Mediterranean

As we steamed through the Mediterranean, it was a good time to reflect and remember our Christian heritage. We learned what one dedicated life can do. We recalled that John Wesley not only made an impact on England, but because he became the father of Methodism, we share that life with the Methodist churches of America who become soul winners for Christ.

Martin Luther had so utterly changed a nation with his reformation in Germany, that his influence spilled over into our own country through the Lutheran Church. John Calvin of France joined the Protestant Reformation and was very influential with many followers. In France, they were called Huguenots. In England, they were called the Puritans, and Calvin's form of government was called Presbyterian.

All of these men had one purpose in mind, and that was changed lives through God's son, Jesus Christ! We are indebted to these and other courageous men who dared to take their stand through persecution and trial, not forgetting David Livingston, who was the inspiration for hundreds of young people to be missionaries around the world.

New Year's Day

On New Year's day, we were at the Riviera at Cannes, France. The day was beautiful. We went ashore and visited some of the shops, especially the flower shops. The kids enjoyed sitting in the **outside cafes** having French pastry, but mostly we sat by the seashore and watched the people go by. Of course, some of the young people wandered through the streets to see what they could see. They saw people with money trying to find happiness, but they didn't look happy.

We were back on the ship for dinner. Then we went back to the deck along the rail as we moved out into the sea, leaving France.

Barcelona, Spain

It was a very cloudy day as we came into port at Barcelona, Spain. The Statue of Columbus was pointing toward a new land. We were met by Samuel Villa, a protestant pastor of Spain. At this time, they did not have the religious freedom they now have. Pastor Villa secured a bus, and brought with him a number of his young people. This man reminded us of St. Paul. He was small, fearless, dynamic, energetic, and daring. He had been persecuted, put in jail, and suffered for Christ in many ways. His church had been padlocked, but he would take the locks off and hold church. His young people had also suffered for Christ. They worked at various lesser paying jobs and received about $6 a week, but they took time out to come visit with us. There are many other ways I could relate their suffering, but I won't take the space.

We went to the church which was a building without a name on the outside. How they sang, so loudly and joyfully. What testimonies these Spanish youth had showing their faithfulness to Christ. Our youth group got a real appreciation of the freedom we enjoy in America.

We arrived back at the ship at 7pm, in time for dinner. Someone was heard to say, "I've got to stop eating like this!"

Homeward Bound

What would an ocean voyage be like if there were no boat drills? Down to your cabin, find your life preserver, up the steps to the deck where your head steward is waiting for you. Hear the instructions for what you would do "if." Wait for the ship's whistle. Take your life preserver back.

For over a month, our wonderful group had been together. It was so rewarding to read what they said.

One wrote: "I came on this trip to learn more about people and see the different ways of life. Also, I was interested where Christian culture had its start. I cannot put in words how this trip has affected me. I can say I am glad that I am a Christian, and glad I am an American."

Another said: "I thought this might be a 'once in a lifetime' chance to see Europe. I am happy I could do so with a Christian group. I felt it would round out my educational experiences. I plan to marry this summer. God has shown me through these experiences that I will make a better wife and mother because of it."

Another said: "This has been a wonderful journey, and I feel the spiritual impact was tremendous."

All of them touched our hearts and made us know we were on track with God, to undertake **what could have been a headache**.

New York City, U.S.A.

We docked in New York January 11, 1963, at 10:15. We went through immigration. After that was over, we all met together with

Reverend Dan Buser, Ruth's father, who was there to meet her at the ship. He had prayers with everyone, then through tears and hugs and last minute reminders to write, we said our good-byes.

Update

That was over thirty years ago as I am writing this. Our whole group loved Pastor Tom Murphy and his wonderful Bible studies. We had heard he had gone to the mission field. We had gotten his newsletters. We contacted him and he wrote us in 1990. Here is a portion of what he said: "We became interested in missions when you and Dr. Correll came to our church to hold missionary conferences. We received some of the greatest challenges of our lives. After going with you and the wonderful young people of the group, my heart became burdened with the needs of Europe. In 1966, my wife and I and our four children sailed out of New York bound for Holland. For 17 years, we established an evangelical church in Maastricht. We built a lovely building, then turned it over to other workers and moved on to start a new work in needy **Ireland**." At the time he wrote, they had been there seven years. He also told us that two of their sons are also in missionary work.

This is just one report. Jim Smith from Michigan has been involved in Zaire Africa and I believe is the **head of a mission** there. Lenny Guenzler of Rockford, Illinois, is very much involved in his church. Our granddaughter, Pam, went to Senegal, Africa, after graduation, and taught French in our Christian academy there for two years.

I am not sure where all the rest are, but the influence of that trip still goes on. God help us to never lose the inheritance that has been our Christian heritage.

Aboard ship

Chapter 39

Journey To Asia In 1978

As our 747 jet left the continental United States, Sidney and I flew over the vast expanse of the Pacific Ocean. In spite of the miles and difference in time, we landed not in Asia, but our 50th state, **Hawaii**. How we loved to go to the big island of Hawaii. Come with us to the shore of Kealakekua Bay (just a short distance from Kailua Kone). I want to tell you a fascinating story you may not be aware of.

These islands, eight in number, had never been discovered by the merchant ships which plied the waters between China and the Americas. Then one day, Captain James Cook wrote in his log, "Suddenly an island made its appearance." This was on January 18, 1778, just **two years after our independence**. So this British exploring vessel made its way into these virgin harbors. It soon became a favorite and convenient port of call for all ships crossing these endless oceans. Since the islands didn't have a name, Captain Cook honored the Earl of Sandwich by calling them "The Sandwich Islands". I don't know when they were first called Hawaiian islands.

I won't take time to tell you about the diseases, the drinking and corruption, and the evil these first merchant men brought to these lovely gentle people, nor of the sad ending of this fine Captain Cook, who not only discovered the islands, but met his death there by the hands of the natives. As you are standing with us along this bay, you will see a monument where Captain Cook died. This is one of the tourist sights.

Now we want you to look to your left and see another monument not far away, which bears the name of Henry Opukahaia. This is an amazing story. His name wasn't Henry yet, just Opukahaia. He was a bitter young man who had seen his father and mother killed before his eyes in one of the last wars among the island people. The enemy had mercy on this lad and raised him. They wanted him to be a tribal priest, but he wanted none of it. He wanted to get away from it all. As he was standing by the bay, he looked at a merchant vessel that was anchored there. Diving into the waters and swimming through those great waves (as so many of the boys did), he swam out to the ship. He was taken on board when the captain was convinced he had no parents who could give him permission to sail with them. It was a long voyage from there to China, and eventually to the new England states.

He had many varied experiences in this new country, but he had not realized how unprepared he was with no education. He was found on the steps of Yale University, weeping. When he made known his desire to learn, they took him under their wing and taught him to read and write. He was then introduced to the Christians in the area, and was soon led to Christ. They called him Henry Opukahaia. After experiencing the joy of the Lord through this wonderful salvation, he became very burdened for his people whom he had left behind. The merchant men had told him nothing of this good news. So everywhere he went, he asked for prayers for his country, and would someone please go and tell them. All this time, he was learning to read God's word. He told it everywhere, and he would say, "Who will go with me to tell this wonderful story?"

It is another of those happenings that causes one to ask, "Why?" It was something you cannot understand, but have to trust that God knows best. This young man, with such a burden on his heart, was not to be the one to go on this mission. The cold weather that he was not accustomed to took its toll. He became ill and, with the plea still on his lips for his people, he died.

John 12:24 says *"Except a corn of wheat fall into the ground and die it abideth alone; but if it die, it bringeth forth much fruit."*

His burden did not fall on deaf ears, for soon volunteers for this far away country were assembled in Park Street Church in Boston, Massachusetts. I believe there were 17 who made the commitment, and just 42 years after Captain Cook discovered these islands, help was on the way. The Thaddius merchant ship sailed out of the Boston Harbor on October 23, 1819. Little did these missionaries know the testings, seasickness, trials, harrowing experiences, and hazardous journey that would be theirs for **six months**.

James Michener's account of sailing around Cape Horn is quite descriptive of things they must have experienced. They didn't realize that many of the taboos and superstitions of the island people had already been broken. It was as though God had prepared the soil for their planting time. They sailed into the bay, **very close to where Henry had swam to the ship**. They had to wait for permission to land, as authorities had banned the white man with his evil habits. The Queen was convinced that these people were different. So Reverend and Mrs. Asa Thurston and Reverend and Mrs. Bengham came ashore at what is now known as Kaila Kona. They were to establish the **very first church in the islands**. The Thaddius sailed on, and delivered the other missionaries to other islands of the Sandwich group. Later, the Benghams went to Honolulu.

But now come with us and see the miracle of this church. The first building was very large with a thick thatched roof, similar to their dwellings. The non-Christian governor had ordered the building of the first church, and it surpassed anything they had ever seen before. It was erected on heathen ground where human sacrifices had recently been offered. It was dedicated on December 10, 1823, and Reverend Thurston noted, "This is our place of worship, dignified with nothing but simplicity and neatness." All the chiefs and people of Kailua assembled for service, and a few months later the congregation averaged 600 to 1,000. It was not only used for church, but for the general education of the people as well.

In 1826, the early missionaries reported having a service just north of Kona, where they preached to 10,000 on a Sunday morning. When the people couldn't get into the building, the governor requested a larger one built.

An interesting story is told in connection with the 1826 meeting. When a number of missionaries from Oahu and Maui met with many of the principal chiefs of the islands, and the church was dedicated to the service of the almighty God, there were 6,000 people present, including scholars and teachers from 40 schools. Within a year, after the construction of the second building, the congregation at Kailua consisted of about 3,000. Two years later, it was filled to overflowing, and people traveled great distances to attend. All the canoes belonging to people who lived in adjacent villages were requisitioned on Sundays to take people to church. On one Sunday, over 200 canoes were counted, and each one had from 3-15 people who traveled 12-14 miles from their homes. But alas, this second church was destroyed by fire at the hands of an arsonist in 1835.

Now, let us go to the building as it is now. The cornerstone of the Mokuaikaua Church was laid January 1, 1836. The pillars and beams you see today are the original ones put up in that year. It's dimensions are 120 by 48 by 27 feet. The actual construction took a little over a year. The posts and beams are of Hawaiian trees called Ohia, very hard and growing only in the higher elevations. The pews and pulpit are made from another tree, Koa (called the mahogany of Hawaii). The walls are made of lava rock, some so huge you wonder how they got them in place. They were cemented together by mortar made from burnt coal. All the materials were from the islands. **There wasn't a nail** in the whole structure, but it was put together with wooden pegs. It was made entirely by the native people who had never seen a building like this, but their pastor, Reverend Thurston, must have been with God on the mount and gotten the pattern from Him, as Moses did. It was an amazing wonder to the whole countryside. This building has stood solid through many earthquakes, tidal waves, storms, and is just as strong today as it was when built over 150 years ago.

Sidney and I always loved to make this our church home when in Kaulua Kona. (His double cousin, Lois Camp, has lived in Kona for many years, and it is always a joy to be together.) Dr. Henry Boshard, a Hawaiian, was pastor of the church. He was a graduate from the University of Hawaii, as well as Fuller Theological Seminary in Pasadena, California. His lovely wife was Iris, and we had many meals and times of fellowship together. We were always welcomed with the Hawaiian leis and the love of the dear people of the church. Reverend Boshard preached a real evangelical message. It was such a joy to share with them.

It is always the custom at the end of the service to tell the story of the coming of the first missionaries. As I sat and looked at the replica of the ship, it left me dazed with amazement at God's working. I could picture in my mind the scenes I have just told you. I thought of the dedication of those missionaries who were willing to leave their home, loved ones, and comforts, to go to a far off land, to a people who had no knowledge of God. They were willing to go at the risk of their lives.

If you can find a map, follow that ship down the east coast of the Americas, from Boston on down past South America, around the treacherous Cape Horn, through the most hazardous water in the world. Arriving at the islands, think how God used them to change a completely illiterate people into God loving, God fearing, gracious, well educated Christian people. **Could these dear missionaries, in their wildest dreams, ever have imagined that this mission field to which they had been sent would one day be the 50th state of their so recently formed United States of America?** It blows my mind. Doesn't it yours?

If you think of Hawaii as a heavenly vacation land, remember it was the product of missionaries. We have found that the Hawaiian people loved and **still love the missionaries**. It is said that one of the greatest achievements of missionary work was accomplished in Hawaii in an incredibly short time.

Another place which is very close to us in Hawaii is on the island of Oahu. It is Kings Bible Church, pastored by Reverend and

Mrs. Stanley Kaneshiro. We were there a number of times. We were also welcomed by the most gorgeous carnation lei around our necks with the customary kiss. One of the times I remember especially was the year we had a **missionary convention** there. A banner reached across the entire platform with the words, "Untold millions still untold."

Audrey Mieir and her choir were with us. Audrey was so moved by the banner that she wrote the very challenging song, "Untold Millions Still Untold."

Do You Know This Story?

We think of later history that was made in our 50th state as we pass Pearl Harbor to see the battle ship Arizona. It is a silent reminder of that black day, December 7, 1941. Reverend Kaneshiro pointed Koli Koli Pass out to us, where the Japanese Air Force slipped through the radar device and struck the fatal blow. There is also a tremendous illustration of God's forgiving grace. The very leader of this attack on Pearl Harbor was Mitsuo Puchido. Some time later he was **converted to Christ** through an American who flew in the first bombing raid on Japan. He was captured, and put in a Japanese jail. The American, Jake DeShazer, found Christ in that jail in an hour of despair, as he was reading a Bible. He became an evangelist to the Japanese people after the war, and Fuchida was one who found Christ through his ministry. "Amazing grace, how sweet the sound, that saved a wretch like me." Incidentally, we knew this Jake DeShazer as he came to our Christian Tabernacle in Dayton, Ohio, and told this story to our people. Jake DeShazer and Fuchida gave their personal testimony in a Christian service together in Honolulu.

There is so much more I would love to tell you about Hawaii, but we must be traveling on.

269

First Christian Church of Hawaii

Chapter 40

On To The Philippines

We were overwhelmed with love as we arrived at the Loaog Airport and were met by our missionary pastors, the Tuzons, and the national pastors, the Morales, and the student body, as well as others. They sang "There's a Welcome Here." The love continued until that last day when they all gathered at the church and sang "God Be With You Till We Meet Again", amidst tears and cries of, "We will miss you. Please come back."

Our Bible Crusade

We had a ten day crusade in the beautiful Bethany Community Church. It is one of the finest and solidly built structures in that area (thanks to the gift of the Walter Blocks of Kenosha Wisconsin).

There were banners that reached across the street, handbills with our pictures everywhere, radio announcements, word of mouth, and even provisions for transportation for those who needed it. Best of all, many prayers had gone up in an air of expectancy.

Before each service started, we noticed a very interesting procedure. The front seats were occupied by children. They sang songs with gusto and lots of motions. As more people arrived, they were ushered to the seats **among the young people**. As the seats filled up to the back, the students and children were **gradually and quietly moved** to the balcony, and the newcomers took their places. **Many visitors were now in front seats!** (Usually, visitors end up sitting in the back.) As jeeps, jeepneys, tricycles and buses arrived, the building was packed to the street.

Each night, there were musical groups from one of the sister churches as well as the Bethany Singers. Sidney and I sang with his ukelele. Our messages ranged from salvation and Bible teaching, to missionary challenges.

One night, Sidney was speaking on one of his favorite messages about the Moravians, who sent one out of every ten members to the mission field. I can hear him yet as he challenged the audience with their responsibility "to win the Asians to Christ. Why should the Americans do the job that **they** could do?" It is reported that the Philippines is a Christian nation because it was not encumbered with a background of

Hinduism, Buddhism, or Moslem heritage, but has been open to the gospel. There are thousands of Christians in the islands. **"Why not** send your converts to Indonesia, India, Singapore, etc.? **Why don't you go? Why not? Why not?"** repeated the interpreter. **"Why not?"** replied the young people, in both Ilocano and English. As the meeting closed, they knelt with tears and said, "Here am I, Lord. Send me." Indeed, they do have wonderful workers among the graduate students who could go, but there was one factor, and that was **finances.** That is why we have had a burden to help the **national** pastor.

Bible Marathon

II Timothy 3:16 says, *"All scripture is given by inspiration of God, and is profitable for doctrine, for reproof, for correction, for instruction in righteousness."*

One of the many highlights of the crusade was the Bible Marathon. The idea of **reading the Bible through without stopping** excited everyone. They had never heard of it before. A chart was made for people to sign which hour they would like to read. We had done this before in the United States, and sometimes during the night hours, the reader would have to go an extra hour or so because someone didn't show, **but not so here**. There was never a lack of readers. In fact, the next one was eagerly waiting his turn.

We began after the Thursday night service. The meeting was never dismissed. People just slipped out as they had to leave. Reverend Josue Morales began with his deep resonant voice, *"In the beginning God created the heavens and the earth."* He read in English, and the people read along silently. The loudspeaker was on, and he could be heard outside. Because he had begun at 9:30pm, he read until 11pm. What about the night hours? No problem, the students brought a pillow and a blanket and would be right there when their hour came. Someone always sat beside the reader, checking the clock, the chapter and verse, and alerting the next reader. They had switched to the Ilocano language, but as Sidney and I went to bed in the parsonage next door, with the windows open we could hear their voices, and it was a comforting feeling. Sure enough, they were still reading in the morning.

Several pastors of other churches signed up. They got such a blessing that they said, "We want to do this with our young people in our church." A man who was just passing by came in and sat awhile, asking what was going on. "Could I read for an hour?" Reluctantly, a Bible student gave way for the visitor. A blackboard was on the platform, and the place of the scripture was registered on the blackboard.

An example of how the people felt was illustrated by one of the young men who had read, who spoke to Sidney, saying, "I feel such an elation when reading the Bible - even the 'begets and begats'." One very educated lady with several degrees, who is a principal of schools, asked to read at 7am Sunday morning. This is what she wrote in my guest book: "I enjoyed being involved in the Bible Marathon and it was a marvelous experience, conversing with the Lord through His Word." Ruth Morales, who supervised all of this, was pleased that she could read the last chapter of the old Testament, as her husband had begun in Genesis.

Monday evening during the meeting, curiosity ran high, wondering when they would reach the last chapter. The audience read silently along with the readers. Josue took over again at Revelation chapter 15. At 8pm, he reached chapter 22. He stopped and **every reader** who had shared in the Marathon **came to the platform**. Then, with the audience, they all read as one voice, some in English, some in Ilocano, the last chapter. It was like the rumbling of many waters. From Genesis to Revelation in 96 hours.

Besides the crusade in the main church, we had some very busy day and evening services, jail meetings, radio broadcasts, and daily Chapel services with the students. Sidney spoke at the Kiwanis and the Northern Christian College.

We Visit The Outlying Churches

Our farthest trip was to Claveria, located at the very top of Luzon. You look north over the South China Sea. We drove 5 or 6 hours over dusty, bumpy roads, riding in a **jeepney**. (That's a Jeep with a longer body, parallel seats, open sides.) There were nine of us crowded in. What a beautiful drive, past rice fields and small gardens, following the shore for many miles, sometimes going through jungle growth that looked to be in the South Seas area. There were whole valleys of coconut palms. Then we went on the mountainside. We learned that there had been a landslide. Traffic was now going through, but it was difficult. There was a bad area one half mile or more, which was a narrow **one lane road**. To the left was a **sheer drop** of 2,000 feet to the sea, and on the right was a high mountain where the rain had caused the slide and brought down tons of earth and large trees. Some were still perched in precarious positions, ready at any time to slide, and some rocks were still rolling down. The road was somewhat slushy, even though the road equipment had cleared a one-lane passage. The bus ahead of us unloaded its passengers to walk to safety, then the driver, after several attempts, succeeded in passing the dangerous area. Believe me, **we prayed!** And with the Jeepney in low gear, we ground through the mud and sighed a grateful "Praise the Lord" when we were again on solid ground. When we returned four days later, even though it was dry, tons of earth had slid down and we had to wait for the one-lane to be cleared.

What splendor and beauty as we came into Claveria. It was not a small town, yet there were no paved roads and no electricity; but when there is, it will be a real center.

We were honored to stay in the home of an attorney. The floors downstairs were of tile, and reminded us of Cuba. Our bedroom was upstairs, and the bed was of fine wood, the bottom made of woven bamboo. We did not have a choice of soft or hard mattress - there was none. I'll admit our pampered American bones rebelled, but one could get used to it. Our hosts were so gracious, and allowed us every courtesy.

The shower was out the back door in a cement cubicle, with a partial wall going across the front. Unfortunately, we are taller than they, and the privacy leaves something to be desired. The procedure is not a shower, but a big wooden tub full of water just drawn from the well. You use a container with a small amount of water, and you soap yourself well. (You can sit on a little stool like the Japanese do, except the water is cold - and I do mean cold.)

After you are scrubbed, you use the smaller pan and pour water over you from the big tub, to rinse. Of course, in hot weather it can be very refreshing. As for the toilet, it was in the yard also. But alas, it too was made for smaller people. But, we were still so grateful to our hosts for their big hearts and hospitality.

When we came from our room and walked through the dusty streets, I felt like the Pied Piper. You could hear everywhere, "The Americans, the Americans." Wherever we went, we had a following. When we went to church, these children were on the front seats, and we discovered that they had been well trained in singing with as much fervor as we had seen in Laoag. What precious pastors. Two young ladies, one very tall, one very short, but what dedication! We noticed, as the meeting progressed, that the percentage was 1/3 children, 1/3 young people and 1/3 adults. The church was filled as far out into the darkness as you could see. How they prayed for a permanent church.

The next day, we walked several blocks to a lovely corner lot 100 x 110 feet, with many coconut and citrus trees on it. This was the dream of Santos Tuzon, to have a large church here for a center like in Loaog City. We marched around the lot, prayed the prayer of faith, and I am glad to report that, through loving gifts of many people, they do have a large permanent church there which is a fine center.

We walked the two blocks to the beautiful China sea. We stood on the beach and watched fishermen pulling in their nets. That night, I preached on Luke 5:1-11, Jesus by the sea, *"Let down your nets,"* and they forsook all and followed Jesus.

Churches South Of Loaog

No way could I tell you of their thirty churches, including one area which we did not get to. It takes several days on foot to reach them - or you can go in a helicopter. It is in the mountains where the former head hunters lived (past tense). We had pastors ministering to these people. There are terrific stories, but our limited time didn't allow us to go.

Let us take you to one more church. It is south of Loaog, in a fishing village named Puro. The unique story of this place is that it is an island (Philippines has 7,000), but we **drove** to the island. We could only come and go at **low tide**. At high tide, you were on an island and there was no way to get off. Once again, the Jeepney used low gear to get through the wet sand. There was a lovely, well-built church there. A sweet couple and a single man were the pastors. The church was packed to the street outside. **What a great meeting!** We stayed at the pastor's home, which was a "nipa" hut with a grass roof and bamboo floors, but we slept on the only mattress in town. It had never been slept on before. They managed to get it somewhere for this very special occasion. Bless them. The fisherman's family with eight children lived next door. They were all in church, and the husband had a special position. But it wasn't always so. Their only support was what they caught from the sea. We ate in their home, and they told us this incredible story. The wife had been a Christian for years and **had prayed for her husband** to find Christ. She was on her knees every time he left.

A Real Fish Story

One day as this man went out in his small fishing boat, a large commercial ship passed, and capsized his boat. For some reason, he couldn't get to his boat, so he headed toward shore, about 20 miles away. Hour after hour passed, and as he swam, he became exhausted. He could not go on, so he sank down in the water and was losing consciousness. He became aware of something tap - tap - tapping him on the side. He found himself kicking and coming to the surface. He looked, and saw it was a fish who had touched him. It would swim ahead and come back, so he followed, and he declares that that fish swam beside him until he almost reached the shore. Before leaving him, the fish came up and nipped him and swam away as though to say, "Good-bye." He rolled onto the shore and fell unconscious. Some fishermen found him and took him home. Now that is not just a fish story, but if you don't believe in Jonah and the whale, then you may not believe this. But it really has to be true, for that man was **so shook up** that the first thing he did was give his heart to Christ and join his family in the church. Thank God for a praying wife.

> "Only one life will soon be past;
> Only what's done for Christ will last."

Chapter 41

India

"I have but one candle of light to burn. I would rather burn it out where men are dying in darkness, than in a land that is flooded with light."

We Take Our Journey

After our fast-moving evangelistic efforts in the Philippines, we were glad for several days of rest in Hong Kong. This is a famous shopping center, but our shopping consisted of buying groceries to take to India. We purchased coffee, cheese, flour, canned meats and other items. Sylvia Rassman had said, "Please bring me a can of peaches. I'm so hungry for them."

We had emptied out our suitcases in the Philippines. Now we refilled them, and they were bulging. We were glowing with the joy it would bring to these isolated missionaries. Well, we glowed until we checked in at the airport and they weighed our luggage. We were stunned when the man said, "That will be $44 for excess baggage." This had never dawned on us. He comforted us by saying he had already given us an extra 17 pounds free. We paid the fee, and then we began to glow again when we thought, "What is $44 when it will bring joy to our co-workers in Bahraich?" Then we began to wonder, "Wow, what about customs?" But to the credit of the Indian government, groceries were welcome items.

We bypassed the city of Calcutta and stayed all night at the airport. The next day, we flew on to Lucknow where our missionary, Dr. Shama Rassmann, and his son met us. Sylvia was at home, preparing for us. Home, or Bahraich, is 80 miles away. Now hold onto your hat, as we are going to take a trip that will surpass all roller coaster rides.

That Ride To Baraich

You haven't seen crowds until you see Asia. There are masses and masses of people. My husband and I have had many hair-raising rides in vehicles racing like mad in many cities and countries. The city here was much the same, except through the busy streets there are the "holy cows" that meander through traffic without a care that they might be hit. They seemed to know the driver would fare much better to hit a man than a cow. But the real thrill comes when you go outside the city limits. Cars are fewer, but the highway is filled with the multitudes who travel this road.

First, let's get the picture. We are outside of town, and the paved strip down the center of the highway is a little more than the width of two cars. Then, there is a drop-off of two inches or more on either side of the strip, to a large gravel shoulder. Who wants to walk on the gravel when there is a smooth road? (There are no sidewalks) The road is filled with bicycles, which are usually carrying several persons. Or, there could be four or five bicycles abreast, some going your direction, others coming towards you. There are dogs without number, and motorcycles racing their motors instead of blowing their horns. Then there are the cute little burros, about 30 inches high, with a pack of laundry across their backs, led by a laundry man headed to the river to do the washing. In between all of this are bleating goats, and those skinny, scrawny horses which look like they are on their last legs, pulling a cart with from 10 to 15 people in it. You just would not believe it! There are droves of those "holy cows", who dare you to hit them. Our closest call came when one of the holy cows ran into the road and stopped. When the driver started to edge around the cow, it darted in front.

Can you get the picture? Not only is there all the above, but there are also masses of people walking in the road rather than on the graveled area. Our horn sounded constantly all the way, in order to move the slower traffic to the sides.

It is getting dark now, and it's time for the bullock carts to head home with great loads of wheat which has just been harvested. Even though it is evening, the carts have no taillights. You can see the carts coming **toward you** by the light in the bullock's eyes. I forgot to say that it doesn't help your nerves when your mental reflexes pull you to the right, but you are driving on the left, the British way. I had heard the young men at home talking about playing chicken on the highway, and now I knew what they meant. Most of the walking traffic was off the highway now, but there were those big trucks and buses. They would come toward you, right in the middle of this one-strip highway. Just before a collision was about to take place, someone had to give. It was usually us. I was in the front seat with the driver. Several times, Sidney would reach over and pat my shoulder, saying, "Honey, I am proud of you. You never even winced." I replied, "I just closed my eyes, knowing the guardian angel was with us." I would like to add that our driver was a really good driver (along with our angel), or we might not have been able to tell this story.

Light From The Lighthouse

How good it was to turn into the mission house or compound. The light had been burning brightly here for years. As we drove up, the sign said, "Welcome". After happy greetings, a delicious meal was waiting for us. It was good to see Shama, Sylvia, and the Rassmann sons, and families who are so dedicated to the work there. It had been thirteen years since I had been there, and there were so many changes. This big house, with its high ceilings and walls made of mud, has stood for half a century. One difference now was a metal roof put on under the tile, to keep out the many snakes that would come in (mainly Cobras). We were given the guest chamber and our own bathroom, which we really appreciated.

Modern Mission School

The first item on our agenda was to visit the Modern Mission School. When I was there in 1965, this school consisted of just a few children, meeting on the veranda of the church. They had dreams and visions of their future, and there were great heaps of bricks ready to be used in building that dream. We had participated in laying the cornerstone. Now, we approached a beautiful, large building where 465 children were enrolled. What a thrill! They were lined up in two rows to greet us. First they had red, white and blue leis for around our necks, and then the children had baskets of flower petals which they threw on us as we walked between the rows, just like we were bride and groom.

Then the children stood in rows and sang choruses in English. One chorus reminded us of summer camp days. They sang with motions, "If you're saved and you know it, say amen, clap your hands," etc. They did it with vigor. Then they recited a scripture verse, and all bowed their heads and repeated the Lord's Prayer. You might say that that doesn't sound so unusual. In the first place, you couldn't do this in America in a public school. Secondly, most of these children do not come from Christian homes. They are Hindu and Moslem. These are the children of doctors, lawyers, bankers, and businessmen, and pay a tuition which is used to pay the teachers. There were 15 qualified teachers, and the only reason there weren't more children was because there was no more room.

Each teacher has 30 students. The school begins with kindergarten, and ends with fifth grade. "Do the parents know they are having Bible teaching, Christian stories, gospel songs, prayer to one God in Jesus' name?" They do, and if they complain, the school administrator says, "If you object, you can take your child home, as we have a waiting list of others who wish to attend this school." The child usually stays, because it is the most efficient school in the province. Even the government is so impressed by the scholastic level that they would like to give funds to expand the school. But the Rassmann's say, "No, this is a mission school. We will not lose our right to say or teach what we wish."

We were so thankful for the gift sent by Reverend Albert Oyer, which made possible the Oyer Hall. Seven years before this, Sidney had told the Rassmanns, "You must build it twice as large as your plans call for." They did, but it was still too small.

The Village School

This school is on the mission compound, but the children come from many surrounding villages. There is no tuition charged for them, and without this school, these children would have no education. There were 81 children there when we visited it. Some of them walk for several miles, and usually have nothing to eat in the morning, for they come from very poor homes. The teachers give them Bible stories and scriptures to learn. They also sing the Christian choruses, and were so proud to step forward and repeat their scripture verse in their native language.

We had the joy of seeing them on "milk day". Once a week or more, they give the children a cup of fortified powdered milk (when they can get it). Our goal since then was to be able to give them milk more than once a week. We visited one village where several of the children lived. It would break your heart. Someone said, "This is the real India." This particular village was wiped out of existence by a flood several years before. About 100 of them stayed on the mission station at the village school, bringing their cooking utensils and what few belongings they could grab. They brought their bullocks and bed rolls, and stayed until the waters went down, and then they went back to start over again.

The Dispensary

"I was sick and ye came to me." At the time of this trip we made to India, Dr. Shama Rassmann was still living. What a quiet, unassuming doctor he was. What tender compassion, love and medical aid he gave to many who came day by day. He treated many ailments and many skin diseases. He worked from early morning until late at night to meet the needs of the people, never turning anyone away.

Update

It was a sad day when we got the word that Dr. Shama had died of a heart attack. My husband went out to see Sylvia and the family, to give them guidance for the future. Sylvia said, with tears streaming down her face, "Doctor Correll, what can I do? Without a doctor here, the government will close down the clinic, and the people will have no place to go." My husband prayed with them, and with faith he said, "Sylvia, this is God's work. He will supply the doctor, and the work will go on." How right he was, for very shortly they had Dr. Afaque, who came to minister there. One miracle happened after another until, at the time of this writing, they have six doctors working there. It is no longer just a clinic, but is now a hospital where inpatients can come and surgeries are performed. Amazing things are accomplished there. Hundreds are served every day, through the outpatient ministry and the hospital. We are still looking toward building a three-story building there.

The Church

There was a new church there since we last visited. The old one had collapsed during an earthquake. This one is solidly built to last. Sidney and I both had the joy of speaking there. People are really gracious, and as I have said, we love the people. There are some Hindus and Moslem who attend church besides Christians, but this is a very difficult area which I will mention later. They love to hear the Word, but it is a law that you cannot make a convert or baptize them in water unless they sign an affidavit saying they did it on their own and were not coerced. We did have a water baptismal service while there, and two persons were baptized. One of them was a former Hindu. The pastor is a former Hindu, but gave his life to Christ and became a pastor under the

281

Methodist church. He is very good at visitation in the homes, but also gives out literature to those who come to the clinic and hospital.

Many times, there are Christian persons or groups who come to the mission from the United States or Europe. They have meetings in the church, but also do visitation in the villages.

Feeding Of The Poor

We always look forward to the feeding of the poor when we visit India. It is an annual event. Many of our mission families in the U.S. make it possible with their gifts. It is a time when the doors are thrown open for whosoever will, to eat as much as they want. That is so common here at home, to go where they advertise **all you can eat**. But in this part of India, this is the only time of the year they can have a full stomach. However, they only send the word out to the villages. If the invitation would be given in the city, they would be deluged.

I had not realized how much work is involved for the occasion. The preparation begins the night before. Piles of wood are brought to the outside kitchen area. They hire a regular caterer for these times, and he brings his huge copper kettles. It would cost thousands of dollars to buy those kettles. At 5am on the day of the feast, a man comes and kills the goats they are to use, and he dresses them for the big pots, which are already filled with water and have been placed over a burning wood fire. A group of women are there to prepare the vegetables to go into the pots with the goat. They use tomatoes, potatoes, parsley, onions, garlic, mustard seed oil, cloves, curry, spices and pepper. I never dreamed all of this went into it. It takes all morning to prepare. Kettles and kettles of rice were cooked, some with saffron in it to make it yellow.

At 11:30am, the mission compound gate is opened to the hundreds of people who have been waiting. Each has his own tin plate (or a banana leaf), and a can or container to drink from. They don't need a knife or fork as they use their fingers.

As they came streaming through the gate, I remember among the first were the blind, being led by children or older men. Old and young lepers came from the villages. Several old men with long beards were sitting together, and we named them Abraham, Isaac and Jacob. There were both Moslem and Hindus, and if they were not **very** hungry, they would not come to eat together, for it is against their religion. One dear old man had walked 15 miles to get one good meal. The workers around the mission served as waiters, and after the people were seated on the

282

ground in an orderly manner (as the Lord did with the 5,000), the workers came with huge wicker baskets, lined with banana leaves and filled with steaming rice. A large portion of yellow and white rice was served to each person. A second man followed with a bucket and a ladle. He covered the rice well with the curried meat and vegetables. Best of all, they could have seconds, or more if they wished, and most did. Water from a nearby well was supplied. For some of these people, this would be the only full, healthy meal they would have, maybe in a lifetime, unless they could come to the next year's meal.

"In as much as ye have done it unto the least of these, ye have done it unto Me."

Surrounding Darkness

Outside of this circle of light where the poor are fed, there is darkness so thick it can be felt. (Exodus 10:21) Temples and mosques are everywhere. During a Hindu celebration, we would hear the gongs, clatter, and loudspeakers blaring with chants and endless noise, so that we could not sleep.

Have you ever asked, as I have in the past, "**What** do they worship in these Hindu Temples? **Who** do they worship?" Worship! They have 300 million gods! That is right, 300 million gods. And they say it with pride. Some of the gods are snakes and rats and peacocks, and all have a temple built for them. How can you possibly count 300 million gods, including the holy cow?

I have pondered these tremendous statements of 300 million gods. I wonder which one they go to when they need help for a problem that is to big for them? The snake? Or who can they lean on when they lose a loved one, and they wonder if there is any eternal hope? Is there any comfort in the fact that, if you are not careful, you might come back in another life as an undesirable creature? When your heart is full of sin, and you want to find forgiveness, where do you go, to the monkey? They say he is a god, too. I can hear Moses thundering out the first commandment, "Thou shalt have no other Gods before Me!"

Has God given them up? As the book of Romans says, let us pray that He has not. That is why we send missionaries. That is why it is so important to take the message to all of those in darkness. **The light of the world is Jesus!**

God bless our mission house, dear Sylvia Rassmann, and the three Rassmann sons: Mark and his family, Albert and his family, and Frank and his family, who are so ably giving compassionate love, help, light, and caring in a place of darkness.

Chapter 42

Portugal, Spain and Romania

Journey of Three Lady Ambassadors

Our journey to Portugal, Spain, Romania and Czechoslovakia began in September, 1981. Three ordained lady ministers met for a farewell service in Staten Island, New York, at the Gateway Cathedral, pastored by Reverend Daniel Mercaldo.

Sidney Correll was there to assist in the special dedication and commissioning of Helen Correll, Mrs. Paul Sorensen (Henrietta) of Canton, Ohio, and Isabelle Helmle of Pasadena, California. All three had been friends for fifty years.

At the airport, we faced a challenge. We not only had our own luggage, which was packed with things to distribute along the way, but huge suitcases and two large duffel bags stuffed with clothes for the refugees in Portugal. What if we had to pay excess baggage? Thanks to the TWA Airline, after presenting a letter from the pastor as to the purpose of the contents, it was taken free of charge.

After a lovely flight, we arrived in Lisbon, Portugal. We got our baggage on three carts. The duffel bags were so heavy, we had to **roll** them onto the carts. Then, what a surprise, no customs! We went right through the passport check and into the waiting room. There we met our refugee missionary, Georgina Moiteiro. She was overjoyed to see us, and delighted with all the things we had brought. It took two taxis to get us to Georgina's home. As we drove through the city in the rain, we felt God's showers of blessing.

Portugal

The next several days were spent visiting many of the million refugees who had to flee from Angola, Africa, when the communists took over. What are refugees? They are not necessarily poor, deprived people, or emaciated people from a famine area. They can be anyone who is forced to flee under pressure to another area. Sometimes, they take with them only the possessions they can carry in a suitcase or carton, or maybe just what is on their back.

Some of these Portuguese, when they lived in Angola, had come from lovely, well-kept homes. They were respected citizens, some white and some black. Now they were cooped up in tiny areas, with whole families living in a single room.

Georgina took us in her car, given to her by the Correll Missionary Ministries, to the ancient city of Leira. On top of the mountain is the old Moorish Castle, and at the foot of it were blocks of long, old army barracks, where soldiers and horses used to stay. We visited some of the families living within the cold, damp, timeworn walls. There was **no** heat or light, as very little sunlight penetrates this ancient building. In some places, it was so dark going through passageways that you had to use a flashlight to guide your steps. In the rooms, we saw beds piled one over another like bunk beds. Clothes hung along the wall on homemade racks. The floors were made of stone, and were **so cold**. Later, as we spoke to a large group that had gathered, we sensed the loss of many of these people who lost everything. I was impelled to turn to John 14:1-2, and read the words the Lord gave when he said, *"Let not your hearts be troubled, ye believe in God, believe also in me. In my fathers house there are many mansions, I go to prepare a place for you."* What a wonderful opportunity to tell them that there was a hope for a better place in the future, and to tell them of the One who cared for them.

We also visited Esteril, where the refugees had made a little city of lean-to huts made out of tin, cardboard, or any material they could scrounge. What a delight to see the children sitting on a rock wall, repeating scripture and singing choruses. They looked well-dressed in the clothes the Americans had sent. Everywhere, we met people grateful to those who had made it possible for them to have their staple foods of rice and macaroni.

Spain

We rushed on to the next stop in Madrid, Spain. We were there only **three days**, but we spoke two nights in the churches there. The first night, Esther and Ramon Blanco led the meeting. The second night, Carlos and Yolando Gomez, missionaries of United World Mission, were in charge of the services. I was so amazed at the religious freedom they now had, compared to 1950 when I was there. We had a wonderful dinner together, talking about old times.

Madrid To Bucharest

Our first crisis occurred. Carlos took us from the hotel to the airport and helped us check our baggage (which now was considerably less). We waited one hour and a half at gate 11, where we were told to wait. We became uneasy when there seemed to be no activity. It was only twenty minutes until flight time, so while Isabelle watched our hand luggage, Henrietta went one way and I went the other to get information. We both rushed back, saying we were to leave at gate twelve. We hurriedly grabbed our things and went through the line into the final waiting room. The flight was called and we moved with the crowd to the stairs descending to the ground level to board the plane. Suddenly Isabelle cried out, "My purse, I don't have it!" Henrietta went with the crowd to hold the plane, and Isabelle and I rushed back to the waiting room. It was nowhere in sight. Then an airline employee, who insisted that we must get on the plane, finally went back into the area and came back with it. Praise the Lord, nothing was missing, but you can appreciate the panic. Not only money but passport, visa, everything involved with the trip was in Isabelle's purse. We were three relieved ladies when we finally settled back in the Romanian plane and became airborne.

It wasn't a pleasant trip as we were surrounded with loud talk and volumes of smoke. I almost choked on a small **cigar** an airline employee was smoking. Oh, how I wished for a **no smoking section**. We made one stop in Luzanne, Switzerland, then on to Bucharest, Romania. We arrived at 8:30pm, after a five and one half hour flight.

Remember, Romania was still under communism. We had gone through security check before we got on the plane, but we had to go through it again before we could enter the building. Then, it took another hour and a half to go through passport check. **My feet were aching!** At 10pm, it was time for customs inspection. Perhaps because we were near the end of the line, we sailed right through with no problems. We were very grateful, because we each had a large Thompson Chain Reference Bible for English reading pastors, besides our own Bible.

Reverend and Mrs. John Tunea, our hosts, were there to meet us and take us to the Nord Hotel. The government required us to stay in the hotel instead of private homes, at our expense, of course.

Romania

My husband had gotten us invitations to speak in the Baptist churches in Romania. We received the answer back that they would be glad to welcome us. But, some time later, we got an **urgent** letter saying we would be welcome to speak, **but we must wear hats**. What would we do? None of us ever wore hats inside church or outside. Isabelle, from California, said she would not buy one, but she would borrow one. Henrietta and I bought hats.

When we arrived in Bucharest, we spoke many times, and without exception they said we were **the first women to ever speak in their church**. The pastors were most gracious, and we could have spoken many more times if we could have postponed our leaving.

We did make an interesting discovery. The ladies there **did not wear hats!** They wore **babuskas**, or scarves, to cover their heads. They were fascinated by our hats, and wanted to know where they could buy one!

My husband was so right about visiting Romania. We did feel honored and humbled on our visit, as we traveled by train, by plane, and by car through the entire western half of Romania, speaking in sixteen different places. We were very touched by the beautiful reception we received.

From the moment we entered the platform at the great church in Bucharest, Golgata, something gripped our hearts. As we looked out over the sea of 1,200 to 1,400 faces, we felt the amazing wonder of God's moving hand in a nation which disclaimed His very existence. Then, when the choir began to sing an anthem or a grand old song of the church with such beautiful harmony and well-rounded sound, we were overwhelmed! We felt lifted into heavenly places. And when the entire congregation picked up on the song "How Great Thou Art," we had the feeling that every voice in the auditorium was giving every ounce of energy they had. Everyone participated like a great symphony of music.

If you looked around the congregation, you would see that the women sat on one side of the aisle, and the married ladies had a scarf on their heads. Their faces were not made up with outward beauty, but there was an inner glow that radiated Christ within. Sitting on the other side of the aisle were men of every age. Isabelle said, "I have never seen so many men in church at one time." The choirs and the bands, as well as the audience, were filled with **young people**, contrary to the efforts of the state to keep the church a place for the aged.

What a privilege to speak when you feel every eye on you, and every ear intent on what you are saying. I said I felt humbled. It was because I felt unworthy to stand before these precious people who had known so much of suffering, pain and persecution. What determination they had, to go God's way no matter what the cost. What stories they had to tell. Hebrews 11:38: *"the world was not worthy of them."*

It wasn't just the crowds. We have seen large audiences at home, and we have good choirs. What was this phenomenon? I began to realize that **it was the church!** It was a haven, a refuge and an escape! Christian fellowship was literally shelter under the wings of the Almighty!

How we felt the warmth as the women would hold us tight and kiss us on each cheek, sometimes again and again. They were so grateful for the Christian friendship we had shared with them. Both men and women urged us to come back the next year. Outsiders would be brought to the meetings, not because of an advertising campaign, but because they could feel the warmth and love in their empty, cold hearts.

I realized why it was **so special** to experience this heavenly atmosphere in the church. You would then walk out into a cold, unsmiling, suspicious, regimented, unloving world that had denied the existence of a God who is the source of beauty and glory. These Christians do not stay home to watch the electronic church, as there were no Christian television programs there. There were no Christian bumper stickers and no Christian bookstores. They did have gospel radio programs, only because the message penetrated behind the Iron Curtain.

Neither could the authorities restrain the moving of the Spirit of God over the hungry hearts of the people, and like magnets, they are drawn to Christ, and the church unity, and fellowship. No wonder the churches were full wherever we went. Even choir practice and band practice gave a chance for them to be together.

Romanians do believe in ERA (Equal Rights for Women) because we saw women sweeping the streets, digging ditches, carrying building material and working in the fields. **We never saw smiles of joy,** but only troubled countenances. We watched as lines of people waited at the market to get milk, sugar, flour, meat, etc. The chances were good that, after waiting in line, they would be disappointed and go home empty-handed.

It is said, "You can't stamp out the Word of God or the message of Christ, any more than you can take a broom and sweep back the waves of the sea from the beach." But in these countries, they try. There are those trying even in our country. I don't think **anyone** would really like to have our country be like that.

There are so many things I could tell about the spooky feelings of our every move being watched. The wife of one of the pastors was our interpreter. She accompanied us to the different places, but was not allowed to be in our room with us. We **paid** for her room when she could have stayed with one of us, as there were just three of us. The pastors told us to **discuss nothing** of our plans or mention any pastor's name, as you never knew when your room was bugged.

When we would eat in the hotel, often one or two pastors would come and fellowship with us but, when we went to the elevator, someone from the desk was right there to see that no one went to our room with us. This is just a little of the other side of the coin. It made us understand why the people so enjoyed church. I would love to go back to Romania and experience what it is like with religious freedom.

In spite of these things, we three ladies had a rewarding time in Romania. I wish I could share much more with you. Each night, all three of us preached in the church service. We had many more invitations from pastors to come to their churches, but our time ran out.

My theme verse for Romania was Philippians 3:10: *"That I may know Him and the power of His resurrection, and the fellowship of His suffering, being made comfortable unto His death."*

Romania still needs your love and prayers.

Arriving in Vietnam

Laura Smith, Helen and Sidney board helicopter

Chapter 43

Vietnam

In 1967, my husband and I were on a trip around the world. We flew from Hawaii to Tokyo, Japan; to Seoul Korea, to see our five orphanages there; on to Taipei, Taiwan, to be a part of an International Christian Leaders Conference; and from there to Hong Kong.

From Hong Kong, we went to Manilla, Philippines, where we had meetings with Greg Tingson. He had a tremendous work, not only in Manilla, but he was also known as the "Billy Graham" of Asia.

From there, it was on to Saigon in Vietnam.

Gordon and Laura Smith had spent over 38 years as missionaries in Vietnam. For the last few years, they had been a part of United World Missions. Because of this, Sidney had been to Vietnam eleven times. His heart ached for these wonderful Vietnamese pastors who had suffered so much in ministering to these people. Most all of them had been in prison, and some had become martyrs.

My first visit to Vietnam was in October of 1967. We stayed at the Caravelle Hotel in Saigon. We met with many of the missionaries at the Christian Missionary Alliance Headquarters. All missionaries were still working there, in spite of the war.

I learned about so many things which Sidney had known before. For instance, you can never tell who is beside you, friend or foe. The Vietcong infiltrated everywhere, and our military men found it hard to know where the battle lines were.

Then we flew to Da Nang via Air America Airlines. Da Nang is in the central part of Vietnam. There were san pans, river boats and fishing ships. To many people, these boats were the only home they would ever know.

As we arrived at the airport, Gordon and Laura Smith were there to meet us. They took us through the busy downtown streets to the United World Mission Headquarters. One of the first things to shock me as we drove through the city was the many amputees among the Vietnamese people. These were the results of the war.

At the Smith's home, one of the first to greet us was Chi Na, the maid, holding Bobo, the Gibbon ape. He was quite an entertainer, and a beloved member of the family.

One of the next impressions I had was of the close relationships between the missionaries and the American servicemen. It was almost like home away from home. Laura was always baking good old American apple pie to have whenever the "boys" dropped by. It seemed that was quite often.

Marble Mountain

We made a trip along the well-guarded road leading to the Marble Mountain and the New Medical Center there. Along the way, we passed the barbed wire enclosure where about 1500 Vietcong were imprisoned.

I am sure many of the servicemen will remember this imposing mountain of **solid marble**. There was also a Refugee Center there. The missionaries ministered to them as well as to the people of the village at the foot of the mountain. On the other side was the lovely property which had been given to the mission for a new Leprosarium Rehabilitation Center.

I can only touch on the highlights of our trip. There is still so much to tell.

Kontum

We flew with the military for about an hour over enemy-held territory to Kontum, where the Smith's son, Stan, and his wife, Ginny, and their children lived. They had a church which was really at the gateway to the tribespeople. This had been Stan's special ministry for quite some time. Stan loved working with these Vietnamese pastors.

We had an opportunity to listen to their heartrending stories of persecution. Many had worked there for ten years, and the Vietcong would come in and, not only destroy their churches, but wipe out whole villages. Many were killed because they were Christians. We felt humbled to even be in the presence of these precious pastors who had hazarded their lives for Christ. One had even been buried alive.

They had an elementary school there, with about 200 children. Many of the children were from soldiers fighting in the war. Some were from Buddhist families. What an opportunity it was, to minister to them through the Christian teachers in the school.

It was quite an experience to be in Stan and Ginny's home, also, for you were close enough to the action to hear the sound of the **outgoing rockets** toward the enemy territory. They lived in constant danger, but their **trust** was in the Lord. The missionaries learned to live with it, and didn't seem that much concerned. Stan took us just outside their bedroom door to what they called a bunker, which was quite a large hole in the ground that was covered with sandbags. He said, "What you hear now is outgoing rockets, but should we get **incoming fire**, we run to this bunker and jump in until the attack is over." There had been some devastating shells dropped not too far away. Believe me, it was an experience I wouldn't soon forget.

Headed for Chu Lai and Ly-Son

Back in Da Nang, Chaplain L.W. Robinson, at the Marine Air Base in Chu Lai, phoned Gordon Smith. He asked if Gordon was available to go with them to the Ly-Son Island for the dedication of a church that had been built there **by the marines**. Gordon asked us if we would like to go along. We certainly would.

So early in the morning, Gordon, Laura, Sidney and I went to the military air base and got onboard a huge Chanook 53 helicopter, along with thirty servicemen. We all put on Mae West life vests. There were no seats in the craft, so they let me stand by the gunner and look out as we flew. Everyone else sat on the floor.

We flew south about 100 miles along the coast, which was along Vietcong-held territory. We came to the helicopter base at Chu Lai. It was near where the muddy jungle river empties into the China Sea. Here we were met by Chaplain James Robinson and Major Richard G. Courtney, the commanding officer of Headquarters and Maintenance, Squadron 36 Mag. We visited for awhile in the chapel there at Chu Lai.

Then we boarded a Sikorski 34 helicopter to fly us to the Island of Ly-Son. There was another helicopter flying beside us for our protection. We were off again across the China Sea. On the way, the chaplain told Sidney and me the story about how this church was built. The chaplain had talked to missionary Gordon Smith, saying, "So many of my men want to do something constructive on their **off-time**. What could they do?" Gordon told them that the pastor on Ly-Son Island very much wanted a church building for his congregation.

When the chaplain relayed this to his marines, they jumped at the opportunity. They just took over. They talked to the pastor about what he had in mind, drew up the plans, scrounged for the materials, and then bought concrete and steel. Then privates, captains and colonels alike gave their manual labor, side by side, until the job was done. In the different chapels, thousands of dollars were given by the men, so that all had a share. I should add that Vietnamese Christians of the Island of Ly-Son, both men and women, shared in the manual labor.

We were landing on the beach. Crowds were moving as one, down the banks to greet us. There was much laughing, talking (though we didn't understand it), and handshaking.

It was a beautiful church. The people waited outside until we all went in. Then, every available space was taken. Laura Smith went to the little portable organ and began to play "Open the Gates of the Temple." What a terrific service. As the dedication service proceeded, we watched the chaplain and the commanding officer. It seemed **they were as proud of building this church** as they were of doing their tough job in the military field. I remember after the church service, the major said, "I believe this has been the happiest day I have had in Vietnam."

The weather was hot, and I do mean **hot**. I remember my husband's shirt was ringing wet with perspiration, but it was worth every moment of a very emotionally filled day.

When it was time to go, we got into a Huey helicopter to fly home. We had been in three different types of helicopters that day. I will never forget the ride home. A gunship flew alongside again as our protection. Suddenly, as we were flying, we looked below us and saw smoke and flames in two different directions. It was an actual **air strike**. It was as though we had a ringside seat, up in the air, watching it all. We arrived back in Da Nang safely, after a very full day. We never ceased to have the highest respect and praise for our **men in uniform** who were doing their job for their country, as well as for the Lord.

Even I cannot begin to tell all the things I witnessed in my one trip to Vietnam. How I wish my dear husband, who was there eleven different times, had written a book of the things that touched his heart. I might add that our youngest son, Michael, was in Vietnam for a year in 1967, and served with the Support Command of the 1st Cavalry Division during the TET Offensive. Later, he was assigned to Cam Rhan Bay, in charge of Special Services at the 6th Convalescent Center, where the less seriously wounded troops recuperated before returning to their units. My husband visited him twice while he was in Vietnam.

Dedicated to Our Vietnam Servicemen

(I would like to dedicate this section to those brave men who fought in Vietnam.)

My husband, Dr. Sidney Correll, not only went to Vietnam as a missionary executive, but also as an **accredited journalist** and **war correspondent**. He had the rank of a Full Bird Colonel, which he carried both in Korea during the war, and in Vietnam. This gave him access to wherever he wished to go, so he saw things from the inside out.

Let me quote one of the paragraphs he wrote: "If there is one thing that has characterized our half million men in Vietnam in 1967, it has been the involvement of thousands of them feeding the hungry, caring for children by finding homes or an orphanage for them, bringing gallons of milk and tubs of ice cream to the orphanages, working with the lepers, building churches, bulldozing locations for buildings, and putting in electric lights. This is just a part of what they have done. I am wondering if there ever has been an army like this one. There was more involvement by our men with the Vietnamese people in the year 1967 than ever before. I want to say, 'God bless them for having a heart for the people around them.'"

He went on to say, "After spending twelve to thirteen months in Vietnam, they returned to the United States. What did they return to? They returned to the sound of **no brass bands, no parades and no hero's welcome**. They were **rejected by their former employers, ignored by their neighbors, sneered at by their friends,** and much more. These men have endured long periods of loneliness, constant threat of danger, the awful threat of the steaming jungles, and death that awaits. Over one hundred thousand soldiers were wounded in Vietnam, and many died. Although these men did not talk much about their experiences, it will be true in the future that politicians, the American society and even some of our Christian churches are going to have to answer to these men for our actions in these years in Vietnam."

Another thing Sidney said was, "It has been pointed out to me that **seventy-five percent** of the missionaries in Japan were **former servicemen**."

Another statement was from a lieutenant colonel, who was a chaplain. He said he had extended his time in Vietnam because he found what he had been looking for all of his life, **the privilege of leading hundreds of men to Christ.**

When my husband would return to the United States and talk about not only his missionary work, but that of our servicemen, I heard him say many times, "If the war in Vietnam is lost, it will be lost, not in Vietnam, but in Washington!" Perhaps it was a mistake to get into the war, but it was a **greater mistake** to not let them win it after they were there!

Among other things my husband would do, would be to ride with the military men in the Med-a-vac, or the men who went out to rescue soldiers in battle (and many times the dead). He went with them and saw firsthand the times when our men **saw** groups of Vietcong in the area. They reported them, but were told, "No, let them alone." They would have to come back, angry in their hearts that, here they had the enemy right in their grasp, and were not allowed to take them.

Sidney also visited the tent hospitals that were set up in the fields to take care of the wounded, before they were taken to hospitals at a greater distance. He talked to the men, wept with them and prayed with them. It was on one of these visits that **Sidney and Bob Pierce**, of World Vision, met at the bedside of the servicemen. They met many times around the world. They had been friends every since Bob had made his missionary commitment in one of Sidney's missionary meetings in Los Angeles. They both loved the servicemen, and the people of the country and the children (who were so often the victims of war).

I dare not go on, but can you see why he returned again and again?

China Beach Orphanage

I must tell you of the great joy we had as we went to Gordon Smith's China Beach Orphanage, along the beautiful beach of the China Sea, which was two miles down the beach from their headquarters.

In 1962 the Smiths knew they had to do something to help the many Orphans that were everywhere. They gathered up thirty-four of the children and made a place for them in their backyard. The mayor of Da Nang, however, stepped in and gave them a property along the beach.

Then the marines hit the beach! They had become acquainted with the Smiths and saw their dilemma. Here they came with bulldozers, trucks and all manner of equipment. They began receiving money from the marines, the chapels, the Social Service and every available place. Materials were brought in and, much the same way as I told you of the church in Ly-Son, they came from everywhere saying, "What can we do?" One building after another went up as the funds became available. The marines gave the manpower needed to erect this haven for children there in Da Nang. They called it the China Beach Orphanage.

They were all waiting for us when we arrived. The gates opened as we were walking up, and there was a burst of laughter and jostling as two or three hundred children came running toward us. What happy sounds we heard.

It broke our hearts as the Smiths told us stories of how some of the children came. They told how the Vietnamese of the plains and the mountains were warned of an attack. Wherever possible, the people fled to the cities. In the refugee camps they were living in hovels, dispirited. Among them were many children whose parents didn't make it.

One of the saddest stories was the story of little Nang. She had lived in one of the mountain villages that was overtaken by the Vietcong. The inevitable came when the American Special Forces approached the village. The Vietcong opened fire, and when the fighting ended, it was mostly the simple people who were caught in the crossfire. The greatest tragedy was thirteen hysterical, weeping children, who were standing near their dead parents. Terror seized them when the servicemen picked them up and took them to their helicopters. The children would jump off, and the soldiers would have to chase them. Finally the "big bird" took them away from their village. They took them to the Special Forces camp. Here they were fed, and the men dressed them up in their T-shirts. They took care of them for several weeks, and they became like family.

Then the marines brought the children to the China Beach Orphanage. Little Nang clung to her serviceman, and was terrified that he was going to leave her. She was a special child. She only had half of a foot; the other part had been shot off. Finally my husband coaxed her to come and sit on his lap. What a God's blessing, that there was a place like this.

We saw the school they had there for them, the long tables set up on the veranda where the children ate, the huge bowls of rice and kimchi and vegetables and meat to fill their stomachs. Do we get hardened to these sights? I hope not. One of the large new buildings was several stories high. It was built by the marines as a **memorial to General Hocmuth**, the only general killed in the war. Men of high rank often came to the orphanage. My husband had met several of them. They, too, found a solace in sitting and holding the children. One very touching sight was to see a colonel, outside near one of the buildings, holding one of the children. He handed her a little gift, then with his arms around her, his head dropped low and, if you looked close, you could detect tears coming down his cheeks. It was almost a sacred moment. What memories did it bring back? Did it remind him of home?

I remember two young marines that came one day. One was really tall, and the other was short. They were playing touch tag, or something similar, and other games. We took a picture of the tall marine with two little guys, one on his back and one on his neck.

Does this sound like all the servicemen were spending their time in the brothels, or drinking, or shooting dope? Some of them even talked to the children about the Lord, because we heard the kids singing, "Jesus loves me this I know, for the G.I.'s tell us so."

This was my memory of Vietnam. God bless you, marines and missionaries!

Chapter 44

The Warrior Takes His Last Journey

A warrior, a missionary statesman, a man with a vision, a heart of compassion, a faithful witness, a gentle spirit, a servant of Christ, a teammate, a husband - how can one man be all this?

Paul said, *"I can do all things through Christ who strengthens me."* Phillipians 4:13

Then follow the admonition in I Timothy 6:12: *"Fight the good fight of faith, lay hold on eternal life, to which you were called . . ."*

Before I leave you in this story of my life, I must tell you again about my beloved husband.

His was a life of trips and journeys. How many times in the course of the years did I see him off on a train, a plane, a bus or a car, going out to minister to the world? Everywhere he went, he brought the love of Christ. Several times I was with him on an "around the world" trip. We would stop at mission stations along the way. I don't know how many trips **he** made. I only know he had been in ninety-two countries of the world. Eternity alone with reveal the fruit!

He was a man who knew physical suffering and pain. He had experienced broken bones (one time, both heels at once), two or three heart attacks, diabetes, four serious kidney stone attacks, and angina pectoralis for twenty-three years. He often preached with a "nitro" under his tongue. Oh yes, he also had pneumonia and **a stroke**. I found this written in a letter on his **seventy-second birthday**: "The pain in the night is not physical. My struggle lies in the area of, how shall we, Helen and I, carry out our missionary responsibilities?"

He had been in hospitals around the world so many times, for different reasons. The nurses always testified how kind and uncomplaining he was. Could he have known something special that Paul talked about in Philippians 3:10: *"That I may know Him, and the power of His resurrection, and the fellowship of His sufferings"*?

In July, 1983, he had a stroke that paralyzed him on his right side. His leg was helpless from the hip down. He was hospitalized for two weeks. Then, through **prayer** and **hard work** in daily physical therapy, and Sidney's determined spirit, he was soon using a walker and then, a while later, a cane.

Can you believe that, the next January, he was on a Pan American plane with our missionary, Sylvia Rassmann, headed for India once again? He was there five weeks, and shared his love with eight different villages. He had taken money for **one thousand blankets**. Albert Rassmann went all over town to buy that many. But when they got to the place they were to distribute them, lo and behold, two thousand men had waited all night to get a blanket.

While there he took deathly sick with gastroenteritis. For five days and nights, he vomited and had diarrhea. In his half-conscious state, he heard the Indian doctor say, "He is going to live." Sylvia had been bending over him and saying, "Dr. Correll, please don't die!"

As he became stronger, the doctor said to him, "Dr. Correll, you should really go right home." But this man, who was a fighter, said, "No way. I must go to the Philippines, as I have a job to do there." He went by himself in a plane which stopped at Bangkok. He had a short layover, so he phoned me in Charlotte, North Carolina. "Hi honey, did you know I have been sick?" "No, I didn't know," I replied, "What happened?" "Well, I was very sick for about five days. But I can't tell you about it now, for they are calling my plane. I will be in the Philippines in three hours. Bye, I love you." Sometimes a little news is worse than **no** news. After Sidney hung up, I called Greg Tingson of Manilla, and told Greg what I had just heard. Greg was there to meet Sidney when he arrived. He took him home with him, and his good wife, Egla, who is a nurse, took care of him for three days. Then he took a small plane to Laoag City, and close to one hundred of the Christian workers and friends were there to meet him, giving him a big welcome and putting leis around his neck. God just seemed to give him supernatural strength, for in the next few days he conducted workers conferences and preached every morning. He interviewed fifty-two national workers, and made a photograph of each one of them.

Then he went back to Manila and our dear friends, Greg and Egla Tingson. While there, the doctor told Sidney that, due to the importance of his pro-time tests, which were associated with his stroke and the taking of Cumidin, he suggested Sidney leave for the Straub Clinic in Honolulu, Hawaii.

Needless to say, when it was suggested that I fly to Hawaii and be with him, I was ready to go. I did not catch the plane there in Charlotte, but when I was packed, I loaded my little Toyota Corolla and headed west. This was on February 26, 1984. Some folks were concerned about my driving alone to California, but I assured them I was not alone. The Lord was with me. My daughter, Penny, made a sign for me that I kept, along with my Bible, on the front seat of my car, that said,

"God is my copilot". I had the car completely checked. My driver's license was renewed on my seventy-sixth birthday, and I was ready to go. I did promise that I would not travel at night. Our daughter, Rebecca, took over the missionary mail while I was gone.

I had a wonderful time all the way from Charlotte, North Carolina, to California. I stopped mostly with friends and relatives. I arrived at my daughter, Roselyn's, house in La Habra, California. I had just one day to repack, leave my car there, take a flight from Los Angeles, and leave for Hawaii and my beloved husband. Needless to say, it was a wonderful reunion. Sidney had to take tests every few days at the clinic, so for several weeks, we took a much needed rest. We both slept and slept.

I felt the picture would not be complete if I did not include these last years in my story. I so wanted you to catch his indomitable spirit. In spite of all this, the very next year he made plans to return to India, and hopefully visit some of the Eastern Bloc countries as well. So the day after Christmas, we once again packed the Toyota, and this time we headed south to Florida. We stopped along the way, visiting with friends and loved ones. The last visit was with Dr. and Mrs. Peter Trutza of the Romanian Missionary Society. My husband had lost his heart to Romania, also. I did the last-minute packing, and filled one entire suitcase with things for the missionaries in India. I packed groceries, medications, candy, clothes, and a Moody science film. He took two suitcases over, and he brought one back. It was almost empty.

Just Sidney and I were at the airport in Miami, Florida, that day, which was February 11, 1985. He was in a wheelchair, and I wheeled him to the Pan American Airline area. His bags were checked all the way to New Deli, India, where the missionaries would meet him. He had his carry-on case containing his medications, camera, film and sundry items.

We waited. My heart was like lead. How could I let this seventy-seven year old man with heart problems, diabetes, having suffered a stroke and using a cane, go off by himself? It was crazy, but I had never put a thing in his way when he felt God wanted him to do something. By faith, he still had the burden for the hopeless people of India. **How could he not go?**

We had those few special words to say to each other, and then the flight attendant came and said, "I can take you on board now if you wish." We kissed once more and he was wheeled away. As I stood there watching, such a lump came in my throat. He really wasn't that well, and I thought, "What if he doesn't come back?" I remembered a story he had told in his sermons about a young man who felt called to go to a distant mission field. His mother was weeping as he was about to leave, and she cried, "But son, what if you don't come back?" Then he put his arm around her and said with compassion, "Mother, I have to go, but I don't have to come back." When Sidney was asked what if he got sick and died over there, his answer was, "It is just as close to heaven from India as it is from here." I lifted up a prayer and said, "He is yours, Lord." He did come back.

That was February, 1985. In January, 1986, I was packing again. This time I was packing Michael's van. He was our youngest son. The Lord had gloriously brought him back into the fold, and Sidney had insisted Michael should have a gospel concert tour. He had spent most of his adult life playing for "the world." Sidney also said I should go with him, as this ministry was all new to Michael. So we had an itinerary for California and churches on the way, going west. Though Sidney hadn't felt well, he insisted we go. We had given Rebecca our schedule, including where we would be the first night, in Atlanta. We said our good-byes, and left.

Sidney loved being outside, so after we left, he took his pruning sheers to the backyard to trim some of the bushes. He had forgotten about a little stream that ran along the yard. He slipped and fell down, hitting his head on the steel part of the sheers. He wandered over to the next-door neighbor and she knew, by the way he was walking, that something was wrong. He wasn't making sense with his talking either. She called Rebecca, and she and her husband, Bob, took him to the hospital. They were there all day. Sidney had a massive blood clot, and he would have to have brain surgery. The doctor advised Rebecca that he thought it would be best if Michael and I come back. She reached us in Atlanta and told us the news. Early the next morning, we retraced our steps. When we got back, Sidney was in a coma. It was so sad. It seemed his life was really in the balance.

We would visit as often as we could, but the doctor gave us **no hope**. On what must have been the fourth day, we came in and were scrubbing our hands before going in to see him. We looked over, and he was awake and watching us. We talked to him, rejoicing that he was awake. He replied, "I didn't remember anything until in the middle of the night. God came to me and we had a revival for a long time. I feel great!" Then he said, "Were you not supposed to be out in meetings? What are you doing here?"

302

(This is just a little note. Remember, I have talked about packing my little Toyota for trips? Well, you might be interested to know that a young lady we had gotten to help take care of Sidney while we were gone, (she was no one we knew before) had asked Sidney if she could borrow my Toyota to go about forty miles away to visit someone. He gave her permission. She **totaled the car.** Thank the Lord, she wasn't hurt, but that was the end of her as a helper, as well as the end of the car. This happened while Michael and I were in California. We did get other help, and we did go on our planned itinerary. We cut the trip short so we could get back as soon as possible to be with Sidney.)

That year was a difficult year for all of us. Sidney was bedfast for the first part of the year. The recovery seemed slow. Many times, he would fall out of bed. I couldn't pick him up, so I would call either Bob or Mike to come and help. We had a dear friend, Jirka Turnska, from Czechoslovakia, who came to be with us. She was an excellent nurse. Sidney was soon able to use a walker. Then, when it had been about six months, he learned to walk with a cane.

The very first time he was strong enough to go out was when Michael had a gospel concert at the Garr Memorial Church in Charlotte. Sidney even stood in the pulpit with Michael and introduced him. Someone took a picture of them. **This would be the only picture ever taken of them in the ministry together.** Sidney was so happy to know that not only his oldest son, Sidney Robert, served the Lord, but now his son, Michael, did also.

After church that night, Sidney was back home, sitting in the living room. He got up to go to bed and he fell, this time breaking his hip. That year he was in the hospital five times.

He did get better as far as knowing people when they came to visit, but he was no longer able to carry on the duties of the Correll Missionary Ministries. **I stepped in as president of the mission** and, with the help of family and others, we carried on.

In 1989, Michael moved to Roanoke, Virginia. He and his wife, Karen, were able to find a house that was really two homes in one. He always said, even when he was young, "Mom and Dad, I will always take care of you when you are older." And he has.

We were in Roanoke almost two years before the Lord took Sidney home. How he loved the mountains that surrounded our Roanoke Valley. He was also very grateful that he could stay at home, because he always said, "Please don't send me to a home where I am not near you."

The sad part was, he never got over the **desire to preach**. How many times did he say, "Mommie, where do I preach tonight?" How could I remind him that he couldn't preach any longer? I would reply, "Oh, this is Tuesday, you don't preach tonight." Many nights, he would dream he was preaching, and the next day he could almost word for word tell me what he had preached. If it could have only been in a pulpit.

All in all, he was always kind, and he would still say with love in his eyes, "Mama, you're beautiful. I love you." Or when Michael would come in all dressed up to go sing, he would say, "You're a handsome man, do you know that, son?" When anyone came to see him, he would thank them.

In October of 1991, we had our annual Correll Missionary Ministry board meeting. We took Sidney. Though he was not able to participate, he did attend the banquet. That night, Roanoke's Mayor Noel Taylor was our special speaker. In the midst of the meeting, he presented Sidney with the "Key to the City of Roanoke". Sidney was so proud of it. The mayor said that, though he did not know Dr. Correll personally, he certainly knew of his dedicated life for the Lord in worldwide missions. Mike and Karen had the key mounted in a frame and placed in front of where Sidney sat in his chair, looking out over his deck and the beautiful backyard.

As he grew progressively worse physically, we knew it would be difficult for him to stay at home. But, praise the Lord, our daughter, Roselyn, who is a registered nurse, came from California to be with us and take care of all his medications, etc. There were times they talked and talked for long periods about those years when she was young. He remembered the past better than the present.

Towards the end he still ate well, and, to try to get a bit more fat on him, we would give him all the gloriously fattening things, like half-and-half on his fruit or cereal instead of skim milk. He did not seem to have any pain, for which we were grateful, but he was just getting away from us.

The last couple of days, he didn't know us. He did seem to have some pain then, but he couldn't tell us where it was.

One evening, he had eaten his meal, but he wasn't himself. I had gone out for awhile, but Roselyn and Margareta, our Guatamalan girl, were with him. Then, almost without warning, he turned a bluish color and found it difficult to breath. Karen came running over from her side of the house, and the three of them were praying and holding his hand, assuring him of their love. Then he gave a little sigh, and he was gone.

My daughter told me afterward, "Mother, I don't know how to tell you this. When Daddy took his last breath, I didn't see anything, but I **felt** a wonderful presence there that I have never experienced before. **I am a nurse**. I have held a hand before, but it wasn't like that."

Could it be that, during the time he didn't know us so well, he was reaffirming his faith in the words of Paul? In II Timothy 4: 6-8, Paul said, *"I am now ready to be offered and the time of my departure is at hand. I have fought a good fight, I have finished my course, I have kept the faith: Henceforth there is laid up for me a crown of righteousness, which the righteous judge shall give me at that day: and not to me only but unto all them that love his appearing."*

By the time I had gotten there, the paramedics were there, but my beloved was gone. There were several times during these last years when he was sick that I thought he was almost ready to enter heaven. I held his hand, read the twenty-third Psalm, and sang to him. It seemed God's presence was there. Then he would get better.

I wasn't there when the moment came but, looking up, I almost sensed I could see his entrance into glory, and I thought:

Just Think
Of stepping on shore
And finding it Heaven;
Of taking hold of a hand,
And finding it God's hand;
Of breathing a new air
And finding it Celestial air;
Of feeling invigorated
And finding it immortality:
Of passing from storm and tempest
To an unbroken calm;
Of waking up...
Finding it home.

Man of compassion

Sixty-six years together

Chapter 45

Visions And Dreams

Joel 2:28

Today is August 5, 1994. Three years ago today, my beloved went home. Every day, I have missed his loving presence, but I know where he is and I would not wish him back for more suffering.

As I sit here at my word processor, where I have been for many hours at a time during this last year, I feel this is a good day to bring this book to a close. There has been a prayer on my heart that each chapter will be meaningful to someone who needs the message. We used to sing, "I want my life to tell for Jesus." That is my desire.

The title says "Visions And Dreams". Vision is what drove my husband and me to adventure for Christ, no matter what the cost! It was a consuming passion. Dreams are what I am doing as I write these memories of a lifetime. I grieve as I think of all the stories I haven't written, and the dear friends I did not get to mention. But I have come to the conclusion that I will have to do just what I have done sometimes when going to preach at a church. The pastor would say to me, looking at his watch, "Now, can you be **through** by such and such a time?" I have answered him, "Pastor, I am never through, but I can always quit." And I would.

Maybe I will keep on putting down stories I have left out, and if I'm alive at 105, I just might write the next volume.

But what have I left out of my story that you might especially want to know?

My Grandmother

I have had people say to me, "whatever became of . . . ?" So let's begin there. What about my dear grandmother, who took me to raise when I was age 3 and she was 60 years old? I realize now, more than ever, what a task that was. I was very young when I had my first four children, and I was in my 30's when the last two came. I don't think I would want to do it at 60.

What a great lady she was. After Sidney and I were married, she lived with us until we went East. Grammie said she did not want to go into the cold winters, so we got her a little cottage in Fullerton,

California, where she lived until she was almost 90 years old. She lived by herself, but her neighbors helped her and shopped for her. She was always busy. In her eighties, she made a prize-winning quilt from inch-square pieces of cloth, most of it sewn by hand. She lived for the radio programs she listened to, which were mainly well-known preachers. Taking notes, she would write pages and pages from their sermons, and send them on to me. She was my inspiration for writing diaries, for which I am grateful. It has surely been an example to me, how to remember the past.

My Father

Whatever happened to my father? The last time I mentioned him in my story was at my wedding, when he didn't come to give me away. It was because he was so disappointed to think I would go ahead and get married, when he wanted me to live **my whole life** for the Lord as a single missionary.

In the days that followed, however, he adored Sidney, and said that if I was going to be married, he didn't know anyone he would rather see me marry than Sidney. Also, he felt a great love for our oldest child, Sidney Robert. He didn't have a chance to know the other children very well, for he, too, preferred to stay in California. My father was a very brilliant and good man, and I am glad he was my father. He was a fantastic mathematician, even inventing one of the very first adding machines.

But the thing I am most thankful for is that he taught me to know my Bible. He taught me not only where to find the scriptures, but the worth of the Word of God itself. Like the man said, "I believe the Bible from cover to cover, and I believe the cover also, because it says Holy Bible." Thanks, Dad.

Parade Of Bibles

I think this would be a good place to tell you another story. When I was in Bible School, we often went out with some of the pastors and evangelists when they had special revival meetings. So one night, I went with several other students and the Reverend Billy Black. I was to play the piano. This particular night we had gone to Riverside, California. I cannot tell you much about the service, nor could I tell you much that happened afterward, if it were not for this story.

On the way back to Los Angeles, we stopped, as we often did, for a snack. We stopped at what would have been called today a fast food place, but it was called "Andy Gumps Dump." We all went in and sat at the long counter and ordered, no doubt, hamburgers and fries. What is so unusual about that? Nothing. However, sometime later when I was in Pasadena, visiting friends, there was a man whom I did not know, who kept staring at me. I was a bit uncomfortable, when all of a sudden he said, "Now I know where I have seen you. It was in that parade of Bibles that night!" When we asked him what he meant, he said, "I was pretty near my wits' end this one night, and I had a bottle with me when I stopped in at 'Andy Gumps Dump.' I was sitting there after ordering a sandwich, and would sneak a drink now and then, when all of a sudden the door opened and here came a parade of Bibles." (That was us, but we were not aware of it. We always took our Bibles wherever we went, so we more than likely just walked in and laid our Bibles on the counter.) The young man went on, "I got so nervous when I saw those Bibles staring at me, I almost dropped my bottle. I slid off my seat and edged my way to the door, got in my car and somehow got home. I looked in the old trunk my mother had given me years before, and found the Bible she had given me. I sat on the floor, much more sober than I had been. I read it for the rest of the night. I made promises to the Lord, sitting there on the floor, that I would come back to Him and follow Him." What a story! I saw this young man in church many times after that. The Word of God is so powerful. Do you realize the weapon that we have?

My Mother

What ever became of my mother?

I saw her only a few times for years. After her second husband left her, she came to visit us in Kenosha, Wisconsin, after I had four children. It was my privilege to lead her back to the Lord she knew when she married my father. She would try to fit in with all of our activities. When I would be ministering at the church, she kept following me around as I would greet the different people. If I would forgot to introduce her, she would say, "I'm Mrs. Correll's mother." My heart hurt, for I realized she was feeling **such a loss** of not being with me through the years, of really being my mother.

If mothers who leave their children for a momentary love of another man could only realize the cost. Mother went on out to

California and went to Bible School, but later she became ill. Of all things, my father went to assist her in getting settled, but I didn't see her again before she died.

Around The World At Age 82

I thought you would be interested to know that in 1990, at age 82, I went around the world once more, to visit our national pastors under Correll Missionary Ministries. I went at my husband's request. He would say, "Honey, we are a team. If I can't go, then you need to."

Correll Missionary Ministries

If I didn't tell you before, Correll Missionary Ministries was a ministry we began after my husband retired as President of United World Mission. With his heart condition, the strain was too much to carry on the responsibility of many American missionaries and thousands of dollars involved. Anyway, he felt the Vice President should have the opportunity to lead the mission. Sidney could never just quit, for this was his life. So we took on the special care of helping the national workers in a number of the places where we had ministered. It is much less pressure to be responsible for $30 a month for a pastor, than several thousand dollars for an American missionary. Besides support, we raised money for cars, Jeeps, Bibles, schools, medical help and special needs, among other things.

Bound For India With Betty Mills

Now, let's get back to my trip around the world. Dear Betty Terrill Mills, one of the girls from our Dayton church, accompanied me to our mission station in India. It is located in Bahraich, just a few miles south of the Nepal border.

We spent an entire month there, ministering in the church, the hospital and the clinic on the mission compound. There are five doctors who serve, from delivering babies to some of the most amazing surgeries that are performed there daily. What a ministry, to be able to help the hundreds of people who come each day, not only for physical needs, but also for love, caring and spiritual help. Besides, there are three different schools that are part of the mission ministry. But I believe I told you all this in my India chapter, when Sidney and I were there together.

Betty gave a gospel concert one of the nights, and she gave a heartwarming message between songs. She also got to witness the annual feeding of the poor.

Saying Good-Bye

There is so much I would like to tell you, but our time for India was up and, after a farewell dinner, Betty and I left the mission compound, drove back to Lucknow, then flew back to New Delhi. We arrived at the airport and, after checking in at our different counters, we met again in the waiting room for a time of remembering. We had prayer together, and a few tears. At 12 midnight, it was time to part. Betty got up and went to gate 10 where she would catch a plane going to London. I went the other direction, to gate 6. I was headed for Hong Kong.

As I sat near gate 6, I had time to wait. In fact, I waited four hours. I was alone, and yet not alone, for once more I remembered the promise He had given me before I left. Joshua 1:9 says, *"Have I not commanded you, be strong and of good courage. Be not afraid, neither be thou dismayed for I the Lord thy God am with thee wither so ever thou goest."* What more security could I want than that? So I wrote and meditated.

After my trip had been arranged and confirmed with the travel agent, I had talked with missionary Kenny Joseph in Japan. He asked about my trip, and when I mentioned I would be in Hong Kong, he said, "How would you like to take some Bibles into Red China?" I said, "I would love to. How do I do it?" I had given money in the past to Bibles for China, and had been thrilled with the news of revival that was going on in that communist country. In spite of the persecution, thousands of Chinese had become Christians. He gave me the information I needed for when I would get to Hong Kong. So I meditated on this mysterious adventure I was going to have. I regretted I didn't know about this before my ticket was confirmed, for I really needed more time to take this trip to China.

Hong Kong

Finally, at 4am, my plane was called, and I made my way to the gate and onto the Air India Plane. I slept for several hours. We had an hour delay in Bangkok, but then we were off again to Hong Kong.

I was being met by the pastors of the Foursquare Gospel Church in Hong Kong, Gary & Carolyn Cooper. I had never met them, so I wondered how we would ever get together? I had given them my flight number and time of arrival, and said I would be wearing a white tam.

It seemed an eternity before the baggage arrived. I had no trouble getting through customs. I found a baggage cart, stopped at money exchange, and got a travelers check cashed into Hong Kong money. Then I looked down the long wide ramp, where hundreds of people were waiting for friends. I think I gave a gasp, and thought, **"How will I find them?"** I scanned the crowd closely as I rolled my cart down the ramp. Then I saw two smiling white faces and a hand waving. Oh yes, I remembered, I had a white tam on. Sure enough, it was the Coopers, and we had a joyful meeting. We went by taxi to the Park Hotel, where they had reserved a room for me.

It was Saturday afternoon, and I asked their help in contacting those who would tell me about Bibles for China. I got an appointment for Monday.

The Coopers had six services on Sunday. I was invited to go to their English-speaking service and speak for them. In the evening, we had dinner together at the YMCA, and some precious fellowship.

Bibles For China

Monday morning, Carolyn went with me to the church where the Bible sending program was carried on. They usually have counseling classes for the volunteers on what to do, but due to my shortness of time, they waived that and just gave me a few pointers. I was given two small bags (suitcases) filled with 32 Bibles, with used clothing surrounding them. They paid for my train ticket, but it was necessary to get a Visa for Red China. I had to have photos made, and then the folks at the Bible headquarters would get the Visa for me. But, and this was the scary part, I had to turn over **my passport** to them to be able to get it. (Gasp!) I wasn't able to return that afternoon, so I would have to wait and meet the courier in the morning at the train station at 8am. She would have my ticket and my passport. This meant I would have to be **all night without my passport!** If you have ever traveled outside of the United States, you know what that means. It is a chance to practice faith.

Tuesday morning, after breakfast in the hotel coffee shop, I took a taxi to the train station to meet **someone I had never seen who had my passport**! But the courier was there, and three other girls were with her. All four of the girls were in their thirties, and I was 82. It was good to have my passport back, and at 8:30, we started through the checkpoints, signing papers, showing visas and passports. I couldn't get over the fact that our courier, Michelle, did this all the time. She looked like one of the thousands of college girls who visit China daily.

The seats on the train were not too bad, and there were curtains at the windows. Two or three times I filled out slips with name, address, passport number, etc. It was a two and a half hour ride. It had been a long time since I had been on a train. I saw so many interesting things along the way, but I dare not take the time to tell it. Ever since we had crossed the border and were checked again, suddenly, I realized, I am in Red China. This was my first time in China. Sidney was here in 1935.

We arrived in Canton China (now called Guangzhori). We would now go through customs. The girls and I went through the line by ourselves. I mean, **we didn't know each other**. But we would all meet out front by a certain taxi. I confess that I had butterflies in my stomach. All the questions again, "How long will you be here? How much money do we have? Do you have a camera?" and on and on. Because China wants American dollars, and because there were lots of tourists, the customs officials do not check too carefully. When my bags went through the scanner, I don't believe anyone was looking. What a relief. I was out free!

Four of us were at the meeting area, but one girl was missing. We waited and waited. Finally, here she came. Her luggage carrier looked so funny. There was one suitcase which had her personal things in it, for she and two of the other girls were staying a few days. But all the used clothing that had been in the other suitcase with the Bibles, was strapped onto her carrier. She was the only one searched. They proceeded to give her a good lecture for bringing unwanted material (Bibles) into the country. They kept the suitcase with the Bibles, and gave her the clothes.

We were then all taken by a courier to a place where Bibles were prepared to be taken to those Christians hungering for God's Word. If you only knew what it means to those who have yearned for a Bible, to finally be able to get one. It was an amazing experience. I would loved to have stayed a few days, but my plane was leaving the next day. So after we had handed over our Bibles, Michelle and I took the return train to Hong Kong.

What About Smuggling?

Some have asked if it's right to smuggle Bibles like that. I thought back several hundred years, to how Bibles had been smuggled into unwanted areas. Some even baked them into loaves of bread, or put them in bails of hay, or stashed them in bags of wheat. Like the slogan of the postal service, "The mail must get through," so God's Word must penetrate the whole world.

It had been a long day. Here I was in the shopping center of the world, but I was so busy, all I bought were some color postcards.

Wednesday morning, I had breakfast, paid my bill and was ready when the dear Coopers were there to take me back to the airport. I boarded my plane, the "Cathy Pacific," and headed for Manilla, Philippines.

The Philippines

Strangely enough, it had been cool in Hong Kong, so I left in the morning with my leather boots, my sweater, coat, and white tam. It was a two hour flight, and when I got off the plane, it was 90 degrees. Wow! I went through customs, and the man said, "Do you have over $3,000 in currency on you?" I laughed and said, "I wish I did." I wheeled the cart out to the waiting crowd. Then I heard a voice, "Aunt Helen, over here," and there were Ruth and Josue Morales, and Nathan and Opie Tuzon waiting for me. Their van had no air conditioning, so you can understand how hot I was. The next morning, Ruth and I took an **air-conditioned bus** eight to ten hours to the city of Laoag. The others drove in the van that was not air-conditioned. At the bus station, there were crowds of students and pastors waiting for us. They sang and put leis around our neck. It was so good to see them. It had been eleven years since we had been there. I was to be there in the Philippines for 22 days. Ruth Morales handed me a schedule. I was to speak or take part in something every day but one. It was marked as a rest day.

What fantastic days those were, filled with God's blessing. During 22 days, I had visited 17 of the 20 preaching places. I had personally met 33 of the 38 pastors. It would be a joy to sit down and tell you of each place, but they were days of God's blessing. He has been so good to have let me have a share in their ministry.

On With The Reverie

Did you know we will still remember in eternity? This is awesome. Read Luke 16:25. Abraham, God's spokesman, said to the rich man in hell, "Son, remember that in your lifetime . . ." Jesus gave us this story. But think how wonderful it will be when the redeemed of the Lord meet on the other side. We will know each other, and remember our friends and loved ones. And we will meet those who have come to the Lord because of your testimony and mine. Won't we have a wonderful time?

Count Your Blessings

Could we, as we look into the past, count our blessings? I will think of some of mine, and you share some of yours. I think we will have to count them ton by ton, instead of one by one.

When I think that the Great Creator who made heaven and earth is my personal Friend, I am overwhelmed.

This is the same God that was with Daniel in the lion's den, and the Christ who was with the three Hebrew children in the fiery furnace, and the God who was with David when he met the giant Goliath, and the God of Abraham, Isaac and Jacob, that led the children of Israel through the wilderness. **This same God** has been with me, and will be with you also if you will let Him.

He has answered my **every prayer. Sometimes He said no**, but He answered. Sometimes we have been on the mountain tops, but He has also gone with me through deep valleys. The latest, very difficult time was very recent, when my middle daughter, I called her my Rose Bud, the nurse, my "giggling girl", went home to be with Jesus. It happened so quickly. I knew where she was, but it hurt so deeply. My suffering Christ was right there with me.

A Word For Old Age

The Psalmist gives us encouragement when he says in Psalms 37:25, *"I have been young, and now am old. Yet I have not seen the righteous forsaken, nor His seed begging bread."*

And again, there is encouragement in Psalms 92:14: *"They shall still bear fruit in old age. They shall be fresh and flourishing."* I like this one.

As I am counting my blessings, I have a modest home with my son, Michael, and his wife, Karen. It was a two-family house with a deck between. We took the deck off and made what we call a Florida room between the two, so it is like one house. (If I burn the toast and my alarm goes off, they are right there.)

I still drive my own ten-year-old Pontiac station wagon, and my driver's license is good until I am 90. Incidentally, I have had a driver's license for over 70 years and, to the glory of God, I have never had a serious accident. **His guardian angels were with me. Praise the Lord!**

I love to do my own grocery shopping, because I take the cart and walk every aisle for exercise.

I quite often fly across the country on a mission by myself. It is my joy to preach whenever I am asked. I'm so grateful that I have finally written this book that I have been promising for so long.

Don't you think I have a right to be thankful?

The Secret

If there is a secret, I believe it is because I have tried to live Matthew 22:37-39: *"Jesus said to him, You shall love the Lord your God with all your heart, with all your soul and with all of your mind. This is the first and great commandment. And the second is like it. You shall love your neighbor as yourself."*

Others
"Lord, help me live from day to day
In such a self-forgetful way
That even when I kneel to pray
My prayer shall be for others.

Help me in all the work I do,
To ever be sincere and true,
And know that all I'd do for You
Must need be done for others.

Let 'self' be crucified and slain
And buried deep; and all in vain
May efforts be to rise again
Unless to live for others.

And when my work on earth is done,
And my new work in Heaven begun,
May I forget the crown I've won
While thinking still of others."

Chapter 46

Now In Closing

Doesn't that sound ministerial?

As I review the words of this book, I would like to feel it has not been written in pride of accomplishments, or arrogance on a controversial subject. But what is the answer from my heart to the question, "Should a woman preach the gospel?" Or to the question asked in the subtitle of the book, "Can a submissive wife and mother be an ordained minister of the gospel?" I trust that my life has been a living proof that the answer is, **"YES!"**

Thank God for His wonderful grace. Let us all repeat the words of Paul the Apostle in Ephesians 2:8-9: *"For by grace are you saved and that not of yourselves: it is the gift of God: not of works lest any man should boast."*

"Nothing in my hand I bring; simply to Thy cross I cling."

Or the words from Galatians 6:14 - *"God forbid that I should glory, save in the cross of our Lord Jesus Christ."*

I would like to bear record that, for almost three quarters of a century, my dear husband, Sidney North Correll and I, Helen Elliott Correll, have not been disobedient unto the heavenly vision. **I didn't say we were perfect nor that we never made a mistake,** but we could say it like Paul did in Acts 26:19: *"Whereupon O King Agrippa, I was not disobedient unto the heavenly vision."*

Our entire life together, we were never out of the ministry.

May I leave you with the scripture that both Sidney and I loved to preach from, I Timothy 3:16:

> *"And without controversy,*
> *Great is the mystery of godliness:*
> *God was manifest in the flesh,*
> *Justified in the spirit,*
> *Seen of angels,*
> *Preached unto the Gentiles,*
> *Believed on in the world,*
> *Received up into glory."*

Hallelujah!

To God be the glory,

To God be the glory,

To God be the glory

for the things He hath done.

A Legacy To My Grandchildren
and Great Grandchildren

It is with a grateful heart that I wish to say that I am not only thankful for the **call of God on my life to be a lady minister of the gospel**, but I am also so very fortunate to have had **sons and daughters**. More than that, I am thankful to have had **grandchildren and great grandchildren**. Who would have thought I would live to see **my great great grandson**? I feel **rich indeed**.

The Psalmist said in chapter 127: 3-5: *"Lo, children are an heritage of the Lord; and the fruit of the womb is his reward. As arrows in the hand of a mighty man, so are children of the youth. Happy is the man that hath his quiver full of them."* Wow! Sidney and I were blessed beyond measure.

But now I would like to speak a few words from my heart to all of these children. And if you don't mind, I would like to share them with the **whole world**.

I love you all very much. From the youngest to the oldest, each one of you has a **special place** in my heart. Believe it or not, I can recall each of your names. (Sometimes I might have to think a minute.) I believe I could remember something **special** about each of you also. Let me share a few.

One little fellow used to **love** to fish, whether on our boat or sitting on the wharf nearby. Time just passed and he didn't notice, as long as he could fish. He grew up to be a golfer.

How many of you kids learned to swim in our swimming pool?

I recall some of us sitting by the pool one day. The two littlest cousins were enjoying splashing in the water. You wore a bubble life saver on your back. You took it off to go into the house. When you came back, you forgot to put it on. You jumped into the pool and went down. Your mother and aunt Rosie jumped in to get you.

I can remember giving several of you your first bath. I cherish the memory. The other day, I was going through a file and found some letters from one granddaughter. One read, "Dear Loveable Grandmother". That called for a tear and I thought, "Could she know that it was only possible because of my lovely, loveable Jesus who lives in my heart?" She is now a mother herself.

I remember a little guy, 3 or 4 years old, who loved to walk the beach with his loveable grandfather. Each had a bag with a handle, and was picking up the trash that people had carelessly thrown there. That "little" guy is way over six feet tall today. He remembers.

My son, his wife, their eldest little blond-headed son and I were in a lovely Spanish restaurant in Tampa. I believe their son was still in a highchair. We had ordered our food and, though their were other guests seated in the room, it was **so** quiet. Out of the blue, our little guy threw his head back and shouted, "Abba dabba doo!" Everyone burst out laughing. Our towhead put his head down on the table, so embarrassed. That was years ago, but we laughed together as I told **his** children about it.

How could I forget my very youngest granddaughter? How many times she slept with me overnight. We would always pray together before we went to sleep. She insisted that we have the big panda bear sleep with us.

But you, dear Kent, have a **very special** place in our heart. For you were born with **spina bifida** (open spine). You knew surgery right from your birth. There were many trips to the doctor and hospital fifty miles away. You watched the billboards by the side of the road, and could almost read them all when you were age three. You learned to walk with braces, and even went to school. **Then** you had to go back to the hospital, where you stayed for eighteen months. Something happened, and you went into a coma that lasted for six months. Your mother never left your side. When you came out of it, you were paralyzed. You could not move or talk. You had to have constant ventilation into the trachea. But you had a loving family, and you were finally able to be cared for at home. Your brothers adored you. The doctor said you would never live past ten, but Kent, you are now twenty-eight years old. You cannot talk, but you can **smile, and it's a smile which radiates through the whole room. When you smile it brightens every day.** You are loved and cared for. You watch TV and listen to tapes. You were tested and found to have a high I.Q. Though you cannot talk, you have made it known that you have had an "out of body experience" which was **great**. In fact, you are ready any time the Lord says, "Come on home." And Kent, when you get there, you will have a brand new body. Isn't that **great**! I just had to share it.

Oh dear, I just must stop. **Please forgive me** if I didn't mention every one of you. But I can assure you, I remember something of each of you. I have cherished your letters and cards. I want to thank all the grandchildren who made a special effort to come to Grandpa's funeral. You were precious.

I have called this a **legacy**. The dictionary says that is money or property or **anything that is handed down to someone**. If I **could** leave **money**, alas, it would be so swiftly gone, and there would be nothing to show for it. But let me remind you of the **best** and **greatest treasure** you have already had:

1. You grew up in a home that believed in God, and the Bible was not a forbidden book.

2. You had parents that loved you and believed in you.

3. You have all had a home to live in. Not one of you was homeless, nor went hungry.

4. You all went to school, and can read and write. If my memory serves me right, you all had an opportunity to participate in sports or music.

5. Actually, these are the things you received from your parents. So what did your Grandfather and I give you? I guess you could say we gave you one of your parents. But mainly, we gave you **unconditional love and a lifetime of prayers for you.**

I have felt very deeply, as I have written my life story, that **I wanted your name in my book**. But what I want most of all is to have the assurance that **your name is written in God's book of life!**

There were so many of you, and you lived so far apart, we never could have a **complete get-together**. But let me leave you with this **reminder. We will have a great reunion in that place Christ went to prepare for us**. (John 14:3) The best part is, we will never have to go back home **because we are home**. **Some** of our loved ones are already there. I know Grandpa is waiting with open arms. **How beautiful heaven will be; don't miss it!**

Let Me Be Your Grandmother

Someone reading this might say, "I wish I had had a praying grandmother." So let me say, if that is your desire, let **me be your grandmother**. Though I may not know you, I will say a prayer for **you right now**. Then, if you will just give your heart to **Christ**, that prayer will already be answered. God bless you. You see, I am **so grateful I had a praying grandmother who prayed for me.**

323

Grandchildren
Ralph Stephen Correll
John Richard Correll
Cornelia Sara Mitchell
Janet Coughlin Baas
Pamela June Cauble
Robert Patrick Cauble
Kevin Dale Cauble
Gary Neil Cauble
Kathleen Elizabeth McDermott
Rebecca (Kitty) Gail Ponder
Trish Caldwell Rupert
William David Barnhart
Ann Marie Long
Karen Sue Phillis
Mark Allen Barnhart
Roger Scott Correll
Terry Lynn Correll
Kent Andrew Correll
Adam Mark Smith
Erica North Smith
Christine Brigitte Correll
Melissa Jean Correll

Great Grandchildren
Stephen Robert Correll
Michael James Correll
Jonathon Robert Correll
Laura Elizabeth Correll
Aubrey Helen Correll
Laura Ruth Mitchell
Joel David Mitchell
John Charles Baas IV
Janet Elizabeth Baas
Lillian Hollander Cauble
Correll Hollander Cauble
Ariel Lackey Cauble
Adrienne Lackey Cauble
Robert Gary Cauble
Kimberly Hoja Cauble

Erin Elizabeth McDermott
Johnathan Miles McDermott
Kelly Colleen McDermott
Danielle Marie Barnhart
Heather Ann Barnhart
Daniel Robert Long
Nichole Elizabeth Long
Joseph Michael Long
Michelle Lynn Correll
Jason Andrew Correll
Brian Kent Correll
Kayleen Elizabeth Correll
John Morgan Francis Correll
Donna Nichole Kennedy

Great Great Grandchild
Tyler Stephen Correll

Grandchildren attend Sidney's funeral

The first eight grandchildren, in 1958

The first eight grandchildren, in 1991

Helen and her great great grandson, Tyler Stephen Correll

The Drama of John's Gospel

Speak For Yourself, John

I love the gospel of John! I've read it, memorized it, researched it, and received the inspiration of John telling the story in person as a great drama. I saw in it action, pathos, romance, tragedy and thrill.

This is not another translation of John's gospel. It is not a paraphrase. It is not a verse by verse Bible study. **It is** a dramatic story surrounding the gospel of John.

As I wrote, I felt as though I was walking where Jesus walked. The disciples became personal friends. I felt I knew them all. Some of the stories are enlarged for a fuller picture.

Years ago, I presented this drama on my radio program. Now, with the help and encouragement of my son, Michael, and his musical expertise, we have prepared a six cassette book, produced for your listening enjoyment and edification.

My greatest desire is that God's Word will become as real to you as it is to me. So, when you listen to these chapters and you become curious and say, "Does the Bible really say that?", take the gospel of John and read it for yourself. **God's Word is true.** If this drama has enhanced God's Word, I will feel it has been worthwhile.

*If you would like to own **Speak For Yourself, John**, just send $22.00 today. Make checks payable to Correll Missionary Ministries, P. O. Box 12182, Roanoke, VA, 24023. Price includes shipping and handling. If you have any questions, please don't hesitate to call us at (703) 362-5196. God bless you!*